"Jenny Brown compellingly explains th[...]
primarily responsible for the labor of be[...]
(women) are responding as one should to lousy working conditions—
by going on strike! Brown's bold and brilliant book ventures into
terrain that left and feminist thinkers have avoided for far too
long. A breathtakingly accessible analysis, supported by riveting
and intimate testimonials, it's also an inspiring call to action."
—Liza Featherstone, *The Nation*

"*Birth Strike* is a well-researched and wide-ranging analysis of
how the public responsibilities of pregnancy and parenting
have been privatized to benefit a capitalist for-profit system
designed to minimize labor costs to produce wealth for the
few. Offers fresh insight into how women's biological power
may be harnessed to resist reproductive oppression."
—Loretta J. Ross, coauthor of *Reproductive Justice*

"An audacious analysis of the falling U.S. birth rate, of the exploitive
and often untenable conditions for raising children here and
now, and of what might be done to change things. Feminist
insight illuminates every chapter of this thoughtful book."
—Alix Kates Shulman, author of *Memoirs of an Ex-Prom Queen* and *A
Marriage Agreement and Other Essays: Four Decades of Feminist Writing*

"An astute analysis of power relations not only in the sphere
of reproduction but also in the worlds of work, immigration,
and government policy as they bear on women's ability to
control their bodies. . . . Brown lays bare why U.S. women who
want to be mothers, and those who don't, have it far worse
here than in Europe. Then she tells us how to change that."
—Jane Slaughter, *Labor Notes*

"A few years ago, statisticians discovered that the birth rate . . . in
the U.S. had hit an all-time low. . . . In her provocative book *Birth
Strike* . . . Brown jumps off from this evidence to discuss the history
of birth control and right to secure a legal abortion in the face of
the ruling class of men who traditionally have dictated the rules
of women's reproductive labor. This book is worth reading."
—Susan Brownmiller, author of *In Our Time: Memoir of a Revolution*

"This book lays bare how U.S. politics around race and immigration are closely connected to the struggle for reproductive freedom, both in the past and today. You will never think about reproductive rights in the same way again."
—Ibram X. Kendi, author of *Stamped from the Beginning*

"Jenny Brown reveals to us how and why reactionary ruling interests in the United States support heavy birth rates and oppose both abortion and birth control. Also given is a good report of various other countries and their prevailing interests. In all, an excellent read!"
—Michael Parenti, author of *Democracy for the Few*

"Why are we still struggling for childcare and paid leave in the U.S.? Basic rights to birth control and abortion? In *Birth Strike*, Jenny Brown exposes the economic interests at play and shows the mighty power of women to change the game."
—Lise Vogel, author of *Marxism and the Oppression of Women*

"*Birth Strike* is an important contribution to the subject of women and our reproductive rights. Unlike much of the literature on contraception and abortion, Jenny Brown situates her analysis within the larger economic context of both labor and human rights."
—Ti-Grace Atkinson, author of *Amazon Odyssey* and founder of The Feminists

"Jenny Brown's book *Birth Strike* is a game-changer and is equal in significance to Betty's Friedan's *Feminine Mystique* in the 1960s, which sparked a movement."
—Carol Downer, Feminist Women's Health Centers cofounder

"Jenny Brown provides a compelling case that the battle over abortion and birth control is not just a religious or cultural difference of opinion. Rather, within these battles are deeper debates over the control of human labor. . . . Filled with fascinating history and contemporary analysis, this book illuminates how women's liberation is in fundamental conflict with capitalism. Read this book to learn how women must take their political struggle beyond what are often narrowly misunderstood as 'women's issues.'"
—Stephanie Luce, professor of labor studies, City University of New York, author of *Labor Movements: Global Perspectives*

Birth Strike
The Hidden Fight over Women's Work

Jenny Brown

Birth Strike: The Hidden Fight over Women's Work
Jenny Brown
© 2019 PM Press.

ISBN: 978-1-62963-638-2
Library of Congress Control Number: 2018948918

Cover by John Yates / www.stealworks.com
Interior design by briandesign

10 9 8 7 6 5 4 3 2 1

PM Press
PO Box 23912
Oakland, CA 94623
www.pmpress.org

Printed in the USA by the Employee Owners of Thomson-Shore in Dexter, Michigan.
www.thomsonshore.com

To the next generation:
Alex, Amelia, Andre, Eli, Eliza, Ella, Enzo, Isaac, Kieran,
Malcolm, Max, Milo, Reina, Robin, Rory, Sadie, Sarah,
Simone, and Zoey

CONTENTS

INTRODUCTION

This book argues that the effort to block birth control and abortion in the United States is neither fundamentally about religion nor about politicians pandering to a right-wing base, nor is it a result of prudery, nor is it to punish women for having sex. It is about the labor of bearing and rearing children: who will do it and who will pay for it.

In the 1960s feminist movement, women's childbearing role was primarily seen as a vulnerability, an unfair burden, and an excuse to discriminate against women.[1] This is all true. But the "baby bust" we're now experiencing throughout the developed world has revealed the other side of women's procreative work, its necessity and power. Elites are foretelling economic doom if women don't step up reproduction. Just as workers have found that bargaining power comes from uniting and refusing to work—striking—women's bargaining power has increased when we have refused to produce children at desired rates.

In the United States, women have not yet realized the potential of our bargaining position. In comparable countries, panic over low birth rates has led governments to underwrite childbearing and childrearing, providing paid maternal or parental leave, free or subsidized childcare, universal health care, cash payments to parents, plentiful sick leave, shorter workweeks, free schooling through college, and subsidies for housing. But here in the United States, the labor of bearing and rearing children is done cheaply, with the costs pushed onto the family, to be paid out of our strained wages or added to women's unpaid workload. When it comes to compensating the labor of having kids, the United States is truly at the bottom.

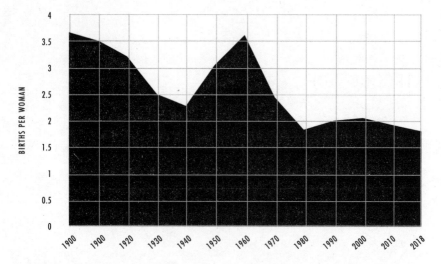

BIRTHS PER WOMAN

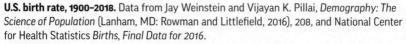

U.S. birth rate, 1900–2018. Data from Jay Weinstein and Vijayan K. Pillai, *Demography: The Science of Population* (Lanham, MD: Rowman and Littlefield, 2016), 208, and National Center for Health Statistics *Births, Final Data for 2016.*

For a time after World War II, people expected the wages of one full-time male breadwinner to pay his expenses and those of his spouse and their children. Women were kept out of higher-paying "men's" jobs by a mix of law and individual discrimination. Over several decades, women have broken down barriers to more rewarding jobs and careers, gaining a measure of economic independence and satisfaction. But wages have stagnated and work hours have lengthened. Now, two breadwinners are necessary to support a family. The job that the non-wage-earning spouse used to do—child rearing, housework, and caring for sick or frail family members—is squeezed into the few hours left in the day after paid work.

As a result, women are deciding to have fewer children. The U.S. birth rate declined precipitously after the postwar boom and has decreased 16 percent since 1990. "Fertility rates among all women and each major racial group hit series lows," one scholar observed in 2018.[2]

At the same time, U.S. women have faced a sustained assault on our ability to control whether and when we have children. Starting in the 1960s, the feminist movement was able to force the power structure to rewrite laws, making abortion legal and contraception more widely available. But since the peak of the movement's power, our access to abortion and contraception has been constricted. This started almost immediately after the 1973 *Roe v. Wade* abortion decision when the Hyde Amendment took away abortion funding for women covered by Medicaid or other federal programs.

Now women who seek abortions are faced with waiting periods, state-mandated ultrasound examinations, parental consent laws, doctors forced to read anti-abortion scripts, Crisis Pregnancy Centers that pose as abortion clinics but in reality are anti-abortion fronts, terrorism against clinic staff and doctors, and the biggest barrier: cost. The Supreme Court has approved a thicket of restrictions and has even allowed Congress to outlaw one abortion procedure.[3] There are 141 fewer abortion providers than there were in 2011.[4] In the face of these obstacles, women have turned to do-it-yourself abortions: a 2015 survey found that between 100,000 and 240,000 Texas women aged eighteen to forty-nine had attempted to give themselves abortions at some point in their lives.[5] Abortion clinics report calls from women asking about ingesting bleach, vinegar, or pills bought through the internet, or getting punched in the stomach, as abortion methods.[6] Prosecutors are arresting women for fetal homicide if they try to conduct abortions themselves, in an attempt to scare women away from the practice.[7]

Not just abortion, but birth control is under attack: Pharmacists refuse to dispense birth control pills, backed up by state "conscience" laws; federal drug regulators blocked over-the-counter access to the "morning-after pill" for a decade; government funding for family planning is attacked based on fraudulent videos of Planned Parenthood staff members; birth control is denounced or ignored in school sex education classes; employers claim religious exemptions to exclude some contraceptive coverage from health insurance—and get backing from the Supreme Court. In Texas, where restrictions and regulations closed eighty-two family planning clinics after 2011, birth control use went down and childbearing rose 27 percent for women in affected areas, compared to areas that still had birth control access.[8]

The costs and obstacles mean that our unintended birth rate is roughly double that in countries where birth control and abortion are free and readily available through national health systems. One in three births in the United States is unintended.[9]

At this juncture, it is appropriate to ask why this is happening. Why, when it is so hard to afford children and arrange for their care, is our government making it harder for us to control whether we have them? Is it irrational or rational? And whose interests does it serve?

Morning-After Pill Struggle

I am one among a group of women who spent a decade campaigning to make after-sex contraception, the morning-after pill, available without a prescription in the United States.[10] Dozens of other countries already had this when we started in 2002.[11]

In 2003, the Food and Drug Administration's medical experts agreed that the extra time and expense demanded by the prescription requirement was unnecessary and a public health hazard. They voted twenty-three to four that the drug should go over-the-counter, and twenty-seven to zero that the drug was safe.[12] But to read the controversy surrounding it, one would think this was the most dangerous pill in America. Congress members sent inflammatory letters urging the FDA to reject it. Powerful players in the George W. Bush White House pressured the agency, violating FDA rules. When the FDA finally recommended making the pill over-the-counter for all ages, the administration of newly elected Democratic president Barack Obama overruled it. Obama said he didn't want his young daughters to be able to buy it.[13] Why was this pill such a threat?

We debated this among ourselves as we testified about our experiences with contraception before the FDA's advisory panel, faxed thousands of signatures to the FDA pledging to (illegally) distribute the pill to friends, threw packages of the pill into crowds at rallies, and even linked arms and sat down to block the doors of the FDA's headquarters in Bethesda, Maryland, one cold January day right before the application was denied once again. Nine of us brought a lawsuit to force the pill over-the-counter for all ages.[14] After a ten-year struggle, overcoming opposition from both Republican and Democratic administrations, women and girls won unrestricted access when, in response to our lawsuit, a federal judge ordered the Obama administration to make the pill available over-the-counter to anyone.[15]

We were surprised that the Obama administration joined the attack on the morning-after pill. Although we had grumbled about the Democratic Party, it still seemed to largely support reproductive rights. This experience showed us how unreliable that support is and led us to ask why.

Contradiction?
The standard explanation for anti-abortion politics in the United States is that politicians are appealing to conservative "values voters."[16] It's easier to argue that when abortion is at issue, but as birth control has come under increasing fire, the explanation that politicians are buckling to grassroots pressure has become less credible. The U.S may be a religious country, but 99 percent of sexually active U.S women have used birth control.[17] According to surveys, even among men and women who

oppose abortion, 80 percent support access to contraception.[18] Far from pandering to a religious base, in attacking birth control, politicians are taking a stand that is wildly unpopular.

Planned Parenthood, long under attack for providing abortions, calls this "the glaring contradiction at the heart of the anti-choice movement. . . . The same forces who oppose abortion also vigorously oppose expanding access to the information and services that prevent unintended pregnancy and reduce the need for abortion."[19]

But it's only a contradiction if the goal is to reduce abortions. If the goal is to increase childbearing, both abortion and contraception would be targets, along with accurate sex education.

A stable population in the developed world requires a birth rate of 2.1 children per woman, enough to replace the woman and her male counterpart. The current birth rate in the United States is estimated at 1.76, considerably below this replacement level.[20] "The country has been living through one of the longest declines in fertility in decades," reported the *New York Times* in May 2018. "The fertility rate in the United States fell to a record low . . . extending a deep decline that began in 2008 with the Great Recession."[21]

In Europe, the birth rate is generally lower than in the United States, an average of 1.58 among the twenty-eight countries in the European Union in 2014. But there the birth rate is openly discussed as a problem by politicians, in newspapers, and on the street. Efforts to raise the birth rate in Europe have mostly focused on making it easier to have children, by fully funding childcare and creating child allowances and paid parental leave.

Here, the discussion is not so open, but as in other countries with modest birth rates, there are government and corporate planners who would like the U.S. birth rate to be higher. They discuss it in technical language: "age structure," "dependency ratio," "entitlement crisis," and "economic stagnation." But over the last decade their desire for a higher birth rate has become more evident as they argue over birth control, Social Security, immigration, military recruitment, child tax credits, and parental leave.

"Declining birth rates constitute a problem for the survival and security of nations . . . in the broadest existential sense of national security," writes Steven Philip Kramer of the National Defense University in his 2014 book, *The Other Population Crisis: What Governments Can Do about Falling Birth Rates.* "For several hundred years, economic growth has been tied to prosperity. . . . Growth in population has increased the size

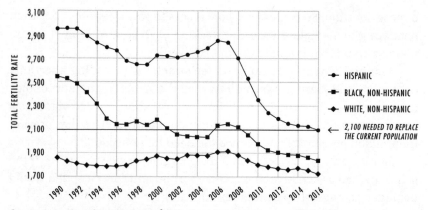

Comparison of total fertility rates (births for 1,000 women over a lifetime) by race and ethnicity, U.S. 1990–2016. Source: *Births: Final Data for 2016* and prior reports, National Center for Health Statistics. Compiled by David Drozd, UNO Center for Public Affairs Research.

of the domestic market and labor force," he writes. But now, he warns, "a small number of working-age people will need to care for a mushrooming population of seniors."[22]

In 2004, two books declared the establishment's unease, one from a conservative and one from a liberal. Ben J. Wattenberg of the American Enterprise Institute produced *Fewer: How the New Demography of Depopulation Will Shape Our Future*, and Phillip Longman of the New America Foundation wrote *The Empty Cradle: How Falling Birthrates Threaten World Prosperity and What to Do about It*. "Capitalism has never flourished except when accompanied by population growth," writes Longman, "and it is now languishing in those parts of the world (such as Japan, Europe, and the Great Plains of the United States) where population has become stagnant."[23] "When birth rates sink low enough," Wattenberg writes, "countries eventually lose population . . . [which] can cause economic turmoil of the first magnitude in the developed world." He particularly worries about fewer consumers and aging populations, and quotes a Center for Strategic and International Studies report: "The rapid aging of developed countries will pose a major challenge for global prosperity and stability during the first half of the twenty-first century."[24]

The media periodically churn out think pieces warning that low birth rates will destroy the economy. "The nation's falling fertility rate is the root cause of many of our problems. And it's only getting worse," conservative Jonathan Last cautioned in a *Wall Street Journal* article promoting his 2013 book *What to Expect When No One's Expecting*. The *Journal* followed that with "The World's New Population Time Bomb: Too Few People," which warned that the "developed world's working-age population [is] to start declining next year, threatening global growth in the decades ahead."[25]

The *New York Times* rues "a steep decline in the nation's production of young people—a birth dearth. . . . There just may not be enough young workers to go around in the not-too-distant future."[26]

"More Babies Please," pleaded *Times* columnist Ross Douthat in 2012, alarmed by the fertility plunge that followed the economic crisis. He suggested that American dominance in this century requires U.S. women to produce more offspring. "Today's babies are tomorrow's taxpayers and workers and entrepreneurs, and relatively youthful populations speed economic growth and keep spending commitments affordable," he writes hopefully.[27]

These writers and others fret about flagging consumer demand; immigration and its attendant political problems; an aging workforce causing rises in "entitlement spending" (Social Security and Medicare); and how to keep the U.S. military strong when both the working-age tax base and the supply of young people to enlist are shrinking. And they worry that the nation's women are not supplying a large enough workforce for employers.

Feminist Explanations

U.S. feminists of various stripes have tried to explain elite attacks on abortion *and* contraception, but the birth rate is largely avoided. I will argue that this is because second-wave feminism arose during a period when government planners were panicking about overpopulation.[28] Although establishment fears soon subsided, many feminists have continued to suspect that the power structure is preoccupied with too much population. This misunderstanding has caused us to tune out, even as establishment think tanks agonize about low birth rates, warn of worker shortages, and decry aging populations, which, they claim, will wreak fiscal havoc and precipitate economic decline.

Many sharp feminists discount birth rates as a factor in the struggle over reproductive rights. *Nation* columnist Katha Pollitt makes an energetic argument for abortion in her book *Pro: Reclaiming Abortion Rights*. But when it comes to the underlying reasons we've had to fight for so long, she talks generally about anti-abortion forces wanting to control women. They oppose contraception, too, she argues, because "what they really object to is sex without significant threat of pregnancy and the social changes connected to that."[29] One significant social change has been women bearing fewer children, but she doesn't address it.

Pollitt does say that anti-abortion forces use "demography" as one of their arguments, but she dismisses it because she doesn't think the problem is real. And it's true that lower birth rates are not, in general, a problem for the 99%. But that doesn't mean they're not worrisome to the power structure, as we'll see.

Many suggest the motive is to punish women for having sex. Pollitt writes that Texas refuses to apply for federal teen pregnancy prevention funds because they include birth control. She asks: "Does this sound like a state that cares more about preventing abortions caused by unwanted pregnancy or one that uses fear of pregnancy in a vain attempt to keep girls and women from having sex and wants to punish them with childbirth if they do?"[30] But this "punishment" happens to involve the extraction of women's valuable childbearing and childrearing labor. Which is the more important product of the policy, less sex or more population?

Feminist historian Linda Gordon, in her birth control history *The Moral Property of Women*, writes that early U.S. feminists did think the goal of anti-contraceptive laws was to raise the birth rate, specifically to supply armies for the incipient U.S. empire. Gordon gives the example of Theodore Roosevelt promoting a higher birth rate while justifying the takeover of the Philippines. "In Roosevelt's authoritarian image of society, it was clear where women belonged, and heightened militarism and imperialist passion required tightening their bonds."[31]

But for the current period, Gordon thinks the underlying reason has changed. She attributes current efforts against abortion and birth control to a religious revival in the late twentieth century, and to Republican politicians' desire to secure the religious vote. And they're anti-sex: "The more extreme, or forthright, antiabortion leaders extend their opposition to contraception because of their hostility toward sexual activity," she writes.[32] Gordon is asking us to believe that powerful anti-abortion forces care about sex among the 99%, but no longer care about reproducing the country's population.

Feminist journalist Michelle Goldberg tracks reproductive rights fights around the world in *The Means of Reproduction* and finds many governments dismayed by low birth rates. She argues that among developed countries, which all now have below-replacement birth rates, those with more rights and equality for women have raised their birth rates, as governments have made it easier for women to combine work and family. "Feminism is the new natalism," she says, quoting a British Conservative Party politician.[33] She relates attempts by various countries to raise their low birth rates through public spending and, in some cases, abortion restrictions.

But when it comes to the United States, she's baffled. We're supposedly an advanced nation, but we have the "highest fertility rates in the developed world." The United States has virtually no social supports for parenting, so it is hard to argue that women in the United States are being encouraged to have children through pronatalist programs. She concedes that lack of sex education and poor access to contraceptives might contribute to the excessively high U.S. *teen* pregnancy rate but finally attributes the phenomenon to a combination of religiosity and other factors. After all, she writes, abortion laws in the United States "remain among the world's most liberal."[34] She's probably thinking of the more restrictive abortion time limits in comparable countries, usually twelve or sixteen weeks, and it's true that the letter of U.S. law is less restrictive on that dimension. But it's peculiar to claim that U.S. women have relatively easier access to abortion given that abortion is free through national health care systems in the countries to which she compares us. Here we have to scrape together five hundred dollars. The Federal Reserve found in 2015 that nearly half of people in the United States can't come up with such an emergency sum without borrowing or selling their belongings.[35]

"There's a real danger," Goldberg warns, "that as countries become increasingly desperate for babies, women will find their life options curtailed in the face of a desperate, coercive pronatalism."[36] But, remarkably, she doesn't recognize the coercive pronatalism happening across her own country, as legislatures erect increasingly complicated and expensive obstacles to abortion.

Like many others, Goldberg is convinced that Republicans are just playing to a conservative base to get votes—they don't really want to outlaw abortion. Describing the Texas legislature's effort to keep Medicaid from paying for services at Planned Parenthood, she writes, "None of this, needless to say, has anything to do with abortion, late-term or otherwise. It's a way for Republicans to make an anti–Planned Parenthood gesture, no matter who gets hurt."[37] A more straightforward explanation is that they're attacking Planned Parenthood to block women from getting abortions and birth control.

"The war on contraception has moved from the political fringe to the mainstream of the Republican Party," wrote journalist Amanda Marcotte in 2017, noting various Donald Trump administration initiatives including flat-lining funds for Title X family planning, appointing contraception foe Teresa Manning to oversee the program, and banning women on Medicaid from accessing care at Planned Parenthood. Her explanation for the campaign against birth control is that "it makes squinty-eyed misogynist Republicans angry to contemplate women having all this sex without being punished for it." But they must be blinded by anti-woman ideology because contraception is good for the economy, she says, citing a study showing that in U.S. states where contraception was legalized in the 1960s, fertility dropped and women's wages rose. "Birth control is a reliable investment in our long-term prosperity. Why do Republicans keep attacking it?" Marcotte asks. But she neglects to specify whose prosperity we're discussing. Prosperity for wage-earning women is a cost for employers.[38]

Do powerful corporate owners really care about abortion and contraception? *RH Reality Check* correspondent Adele Stan followed the money that billionaires such as the Koch brothers have poured into anti-abortion and anti-contraception groups. "There is little doubt that the rash of anti-choice measures that flooded the legislative dockets in state capitols in 2013 was a coordinated effort by anti-choice groups and major right-wing donors lurking anonymously behind the facades of . . . non-profit 'social welfare' organizations," she writes. But she's mystified by the Kochs' involvement.[39]

Charles and David Koch own the second-largest privately held corporation in the United States, according to *Forbes*. But they call themselves libertarians, so why would they pour money into stopping abortion and contraception? Libertarians are supposedly for individual freedom in such matters. Stan turns to Sue Sturgis of the venerable Institute for Southern Studies for an explanation: "If you want to promote a pro-corporate agenda, you're only going to get so far [among the general public]. . . . But when you start weaving in these social issues like abortion and other reproductive rights issues, then you're gonna appeal to a broader range of people, and a very motivated voting bloc. They will turn out. So it serves your larger cause."

And, explains Stan, these blocs "share an interest with anti-choice groups in depleting the power of Democrats, who are more inclined to support reproductive rights." According to this standard explanation, corporate America has no interest in abortion and contraception as such, they're just mouthing opposition to promote their other political interests.

Certainly voter manipulation is a part of the story, but this explanation has come to overshadow a deeper saga: The age-old battle over control of women's valuable reproductive labor. Characterizing the current assaults as electoral trickery misses the submerged iceberg of uncompensated reproductive labor from which the rich and powerful have always derived their wealth.[40]

Stan is so steeped in the electoral explanation that she chastises the Kochs for wading into the fight over reproduction, "So much for that singular economic policy mission," she writes when a Koch fund urges abortion restrictions. But what if restricting abortion and contraception sit squarely in the middle of their economic policy mission? "Population growth is still the prime driver of economic growth," Longman observes.

As long as we think of the battle over abortion and birth control as primarily a cultural conflict, in which the two sides simply hold different worldviews, it's not clear why corporate owners and establishment planners would have much interest one way or the other. But if we look at the battle as a fight over the production of humans—how many, how fast, and at what cost—then it seems likely that employers, as a class, would have an intense interest. They would especially care when they are called upon to put in resources, as they are whenever we demand paid family leave or publicly funded childcare.

A higher birth rate does serve an economic goal: An ever-expanding workforce raised with a minimum of public spending and a maximum of women's unpaid work. Why would employers pay for parental leave if they can push us into maternity for free? Why would corporations pay taxes for a national childcare system if families can be induced to take that burden upon themselves? But women are refusing—by some measures our birth rate is the lowest it has ever been—so they can only achieve that goal if they further deprive us of reproductive control.

It may seem absurd that we still have to fight this old tyranny in a new century, but we do because it is not fundamentally about outdated religious doctrine, it is a struggle over our labor.

•

A Note on the Power Structure

We're used to political pundits and newspaper editorialists assuming that everyone wants what's good for all, or what's good for "the economy." Any disagreements that arise are about *how* to achieve common goals of freedom, prosperity, security, and democracy.

That won't be the assumption here. Look at history: Every advance we've made was hard fought against an opposition that wanted it stopped. Whether it was independence from the British empire, the end of slavery, two days off on the weekend, a minimum wage, a shorter work week, birth control, voting rights for blacks and women, the right

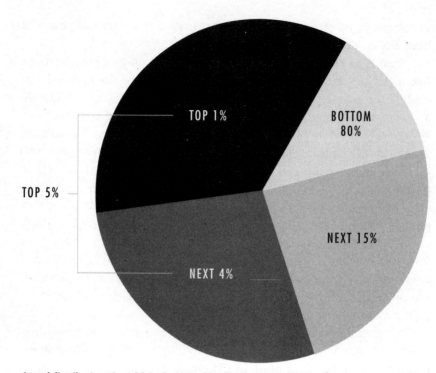

Actual distribution of wealth in the United States. Source: Economic Policy Institute, analysis of Broom and Shay (2000) and Forbes (2010).

to form a union, women having their own bank accounts, the right to divorce—there were people dead set against it, not because they were misinformed about how great life would be if the change occurred, but because they were actually going to lose something: power, money, prestige, or control. It's true that some in the oppressed group also opposed the changes, but when the changes came, they discovered they didn't want to go back, whereas many in the ruling group still yearn for the good old days.

In this book I'm assuming that these same conflicts, which seem clearer with historical distance, are also occurring now. There's a ruling group that has lots of power, money, prestige, and control, and it wants more.

Who are they? Nineteenth-century populists called them the "money power." In the 1960s civil rights movement, the Student Nonviolent Coordinating Committee called them the power structure. Left-wing student groups and some women's liberationists called them the establishment. Socialists and communists call them the capitalist class or the owning class. Unions call them the bosses, employers, corporations, or

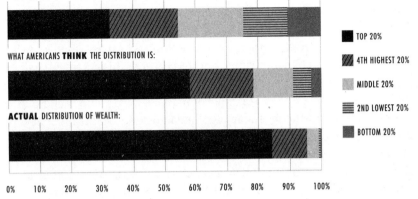

DISTRIBUTION THAT 92% CHOOSE AS **IDEAL**:

WHAT AMERICANS **THINK** THE DISTRIBUTION IS:

ACTUAL DISTRIBUTION OF WEALTH:

■ TOP 20%

▨ 4TH HIGHEST 20%

▨ MIDDLE 20%

≡ 2ND LOWEST 20%

▨ BOTTOM 20%

0%   10%   20%   30%   40%   50%   60%   70%   80%   90%   100%

U.S. wealth distribution: perception vs. reality. Source: Survey of 5,000 Americans at all income levels by Michael Norton, Harvard Business School & Dan Ariely, Duke University. Graph info appeared in "It's the Inequality, Stupid," *Mother Jones*, March/April 2011 (www.motherjones.com).

the corporate class. In 2011, Occupy Wall Street called them the 1%. In the 2016 presidential campaign, Vermont Senator Bernie Sanders called them the billionaire class. These concepts help beat back the incessant talk of a middle-class society, which has left most people in the United States with no idea that the top 5 percent own 67 percent of the wealth of the country, or that the 1% have an average net worth of $26.4 million. When the public is asked what distribution would be ideal, they'd like it to be much more egalitarian.

Whatever we call this powerful group of people, there's a general understanding that politicians answer to them more than they answer to us. Politicians in the United States, both Democrats and Republicans, worry all the time about keeping this powerful group happy, otherwise they may lose their financial backing and their jobs.

Among this ruling group there are conflicts of interest and disagreements about strategy, of course, and they are terribly vulnerable because we, the people, severely outnumber them. In fact, they are so scarce in numbers it's amazing they ever get what they want, but clever divide-and-conquer tactics and a lot of lying and manipulation do allow this small group a shaky control over many aspects of our lives.

The reason the elite spend so much money on think tanks and foundations is that they have to figure out how to get around people's natural demands for liberty, equality, and a fair share of the good things in life. When we unmask the lies they have carefully constructed and expensively maintained, that weakens them.

Women did that in the Women's Liberation Movement in 1968 when they launched "A Program for Feminist Consciousness Raising."[41] They thought the first job of the fledgling movement was for women to tell each other the truth about their lives. One thing they discovered was that many of them had had abortions, but told no one. This discovery gained power when women spoke out publicly about their illegal abortions, first disrupting an abortion reform panel of male "experts," and then holding their own hearing, the legendary 1969 Redstockings Abortion Speakout. Based on these experiences, they wrote in *The Redstockings Manifesto*: "Our chief task at present is to develop female class consciousness through sharing experience and publicly exposing the sexist foundation of all our institutions. Consciousness-raising is . . . the only method by which we can ensure that our program for liberation is based on the concrete realities of our lives."[42]

Collectively examining our experiences on abortion and birth control was necessary to get us the reforms we have now, and it will be at the heart of any advances we make in the future, especially combined with an analysis of our experiences with having children. (See chapter 3 for some of that.) But winning more freedom around reproduction additionally requires that we break through lies and misunderstandings about what the power structure is up to. We can't do that without first acknowledging that there is a power structure composed of people defending their own interests at our expense.

CHAPTER 1

INTERNATIONAL COMPARISONS

T alk in the 1960s of a demographic time bomb has now turned to fears of a worldwide baby bust. "Global fertility rates are in general decline and this trend is most pronounced in industrialized countries, especially Western Europe, where populations are projected to decline dramatically over the next fifty years," reports the U.S. Central Intelligence Agency.[1]

The *Wall Street Journal* claims stagnant economies will be the result. "Simply put, companies are running out of workers, customers or both. In either case, economic growth suffers."[2]

In an article called "Breaking the Baby Strike," the *Economist* reports: "As birth rates decline, more countries are turning pro-natalist (not long ago, Iran and Turkey worried that their populations were growing too fast, and handed out free contraceptives). And the baby-boosting is becoming fervent, even desperate."[3]

All the largest economies, as defined by the value of their economic output, have seen below-replacement birth rates: the United States, China, Japan, Germany, and the UK. (To be clear, I'm not saying this is a crisis for ordinary people. My point is that employers and governments are alarmed.)

Here in the United States, it's regarded as a fringe idea that the ruling class concerns itself with the birth rate. But political leaders in dozens of other countries openly discuss their low birth rates and promote policies to raise them, publicly deliberating about birth control, abortion, and family policies such as childcare and paid parental leave.

Perhaps those countries have a problem we don't have in the United States. Isn't our birth rate higher than theirs? Among developed countries,

INDONESIA	2.45
MEXICO	2.29
TURKEY	2.12
FRANCE	1.98
SWEDEN	1.90
AUSTRALIA	1.88
UNITED KINGDOM	1.87
UNITED STATES	**1.87**
CHILE	1.82
NORWAY	1.81
BRAZIL	1.78
IRAN	1.74
DENMARK	1.73
CUBA	1.70
RUSSIA	1.69
CANADA	1.61
CHINA	1.60
ITALY	1.42
GERMANY	1.42
JAPAN	1.40
GREECE	1.34
POLAND	1.33
SPAIN	1.32
PORTUGAL	1.28
SINGAPORE	1.23

Total fertility rates in selected countries 2010–2015.
Source: United Nations Population Division, *World Population Prospects, 2017 Revision*, www.un.org.

we do have a high birth rate, but it's not substantially higher, and lately it has become lower than some countries where politicians are publicly agonizing about low birth rates (see chart).[4] Since these United Nations estimates, the U.S. total fertility rate has dropped to 1.76.

Perhaps, then, the nation's secret is that we have a high immigration rate—working-age adults who are alleviating any demographic crisis. Still, Australia, Canada, Germany, New Zealand, and Sweden have more immigrants as a percentage of population. And our immigration rate is much too low to compensate for the deficit in births. (I take up immigration in chapter 7.)

In some places, like Turkey and Poland, leaders attack reproductive rights with the open goal of raising the birth rate. In others, with stronger feminist movements and institutions, governments promote policies that support parents to encourage more childbearing. Some countries, like Russia, are doing both, increasing maternity leave and monthly government payments to parents while they gnaw away at access to abortion and contraception. In all cases, the reasons for the policy are in the open—how can we get women to make more babies?

That question has led some to an answer that echoes feminists: equality at work. Steffen Kroehnert, a researcher for the Institute for Population and Development in Berlin, explains: "For a long time, politicians said that the high participation of women in the labor market is responsible for the low birth rate, because when women go into the labor market, they don't have children anymore. But interestingly, when you look at . . . western European countries, the fertility rate is higher in countries with a higher labor market participation of women."[5]

As an example, French demographer Laurent Toulemon listed the obstacles Japanese women face. "A [Japanese] woman entering into a relationship must also accept marriage, obey her husband, have a child, stop working after it is born and make room for her ageing in-laws. It's a case of all or nothing. In France the package is more flexible."[6]

"Ask Turkish women about work and motherhood, and the response is a torrent of grievances. Husbands do little housework. . . . Employers are unsympathetic," reports the *Economist*, explaining the falling birth rate in Turkey. "In short, mothers are generally still expected to stay at home. . . . Until that changes, Turkish women will perceive a sharp choice between work and parenthood, and often [go] for the first."[7]

U.S. journalist Stephanie Mencimer puts it more bluntly: "Conservatives thought that if they only made it harder for mothers to work, women would stay home. Instead, women stopped having kids."[8]

"The question today is not if women will work," says Kroehnert. "The question is if they will have children."[9]

Japan

The *Washington Post* frets that the entire global economy is being put at risk by the low birth rate in Japan, which has the world's third-largest economy after the United States and China. "The Japanese economy is in serious enough trouble that it could set the rest of us back," the *Post* warns, citing Japan's stagnant growth and large debts. "And the biggest source of that trouble is demographic: Japanese people aren't having enough kids to sustain a healthy economy."[10] By healthy, the author means healthy for employers and businesses.

Japanese women face overwhelming pressure from their employers to quit their jobs when they get married. As a result, many refuse to get married, further driving down the birth rate. Sexists label women who continue to work after they get married *oniyome*, "wife from hell." Japanese women have set up Angry Women Clubs to strategize against rampant job discrimination, and women are suing employers for firing them rather than accommodating their pregnancies.[11]

Female resistance to lousy child-rearing conditions has put the ruling conservative government in a tight spot. Because of the falling working-age population, the government is trying to press more women into the workforce, to ease a tight labor market that threatens to drive wages up. The ruling party "used to be the defender of the housewife," noted Haruko Arimura, the government's minister for women's empowerment. "Now it is sticking up for working women."

But at the same time, they want women producing more children. So the government has slowly taken measures to increase the availability of childcare. The Japanese childcare system is plagued with long waiting lists and a shortage of teachers willing to fill the low-wage positions.[12]

Some Japanese politicians have proposed more coercive methods. In 2013, Seiko Noda, a member of Japan's House of Representatives, proposed banning abortion and increasing adoptions. In the country's biggest newspaper, she wrote: "With 200,000 pregnancies being terminated per year, if we are to counteract the falling birthrate, then we must begin there. I intend to have this reviewed in the party's Special Committee on Population Decline in Society following the upper house elections. We will not only prohibit abortion, but . . . we must also create laws [to mediate] child adoption."[13]

In the face of labor shortages, Japanese politicians, long wary of immigration, have even started to crack open doors to foreign workers. Central Bank governor Haruhiko Kuroda warned in 2016 that to sustain growth, foreign labor would be essential.[14] A "training program" for unskilled foreigners has grown to 200,000 workers, becoming in effect a guest worker program, while new policies announced by Prime Minister Shinzo Abe encourage skilled immigration with a fast path to citizenship.

China

In China, uprisings of workers against factory owners have been the main factor in recent changes in population policy.

China's famous one-child policy, implemented in 1979 after revolutionary leader Mao Zedong's death, was introduced to slow the birth rate so that "the fruits of economic growth are not devoured by population growth."[15] It was connected to the "Four Modernizations" program led by Deng Xiaoping, which opened China to capitalist trade and markets.

The government's announcement of the policy in 1980 said: "As far as the country as a whole is concerned, as long as the rate of labor productivity in industry and agriculture is still rather low ... the rate of population growth will directly affect the accumulation of the capital funds necessary for the construction of modernization. A much too rapid growth of population will mean a reduction in the accumulation of capital funds, while a slowdown in population growth could mean an increase in the accumulation of capital funds."[16]

The government generally allowed urban couples to have one child, rural couples to have two (spaced five years apart), and ethnic minorities to have three.[17] Abortions, birth control—mostly IUDs—and sterilization were provided free. The limits were enforced with fines (called "social compensation fees") and, although it was against official policy, instances of coerced or forced abortions or sterilizations.[18]

As China developed a capitalist sector and became the largest manufacturer in the world, employers took advantage of China's giant labor force. Workers resisted this exploitation, resulting in a massive strike wave starting in 2008. One organization counted 1,171 strikes and protests from June 2011 to the end of 2013, mostly in manufacturing but also among bus drivers and teachers.[19] The strikes have resulted in higher wages, the scourge of employers everywhere.

Desiring an increase in the labor supply, China loosened its one-child policy in 2013, allowing two children if one of the parents had been an only child—and many had, since they were born during the one-child policy. Then in 2015 the government scrapped one-child limits in favor of a two-child policy. China's National Health and Family Planning Commission reasoned that more children would "increase labor supply and ease pressures from an aging population" and "benefit sustained and healthy economic development."[20]

Western media, too, say the low birth rate could hamper China's economic growth, warning that as a result of the one-child policy "a plentiful supply of workers will suddenly be in short supply and a population that has grown used to improving living standards might fall on hard times." They warn of the expenses of a "granny state."[21]

The media are calling China a granny state when 10 percent of the population is sixty-five or over, and 15 percent will be by 2027.[22] Meanwhile the U.S. proportions are 15 percent now, and 20 percent by 2027, so we are at least as much of a granny state as China.[23] Corporate media are happy to link flagging economic growth to aging populations in China, especially if they can blame a communist policy. But you won't often hear them discussing U.S. population policy in that way or even admitting that we have a population policy.

Russia

The Soviet Union became the first modern country to legalize abortion after its 1917 socialist revolution, giving the explanation that illegal abortions were widespread and dangerous, and should be replaced with safe, legal ones.[24] The law went into effect in 1920, and most abortions were free. With Adolf Hitler in Germany threatening to make parts of Russia a colony, the government outlawed abortion again in 1936.[25] Official documents cited a need for repopulation after several years of war and emphasized a doubling of the budget for childcare and maternity hospitals to ease the burden on women of increased births.[26] "We need men," wrote Joseph Stalin at the time. "The Soviet woman has the same rights as the man, but that does not free her from a great and honorable duty which nature has given her: She is a mother, she gives life. And this is certainly not a private affair but one of great social importance."[27] Nonetheless, women complained, and abortion was still widely practiced.[28] After 1955, abortion was again made available free or cheap to all women on request. (Meanwhile, abortion was illegal in the United States and much of Western Europe into the 1970s.)

After the USSR was dismantled in 1991, a rampaging capitalism resulted in economic collapse and abrupt drops in life expectancy, with unemployment and poverty hitting a population that had previously enjoyed secure jobs and decent retirements. Between 1992 and 1994, average life expectancy dropped four years, unprecedented outside of war, famine, or epidemic. As people faced poverty and insecurity, the birth rate also plunged. The fertility rate in the USSR had hovered around 2.0 for most of the post–World War II period, reaching 2.2 under Gorbachev. By 1999 it had plunged to 1.17.[29]

In 2006, Russian president Vladimir Putin declared the demographic crisis the main problem facing the country and announced incentives for parents in the form of increased monthly allowances for each child and bonuses on the birth or adoption of a second child of $12,500. Mothers can deposit the money in their pension account, pay for education, or use the money for living expenses. Paid maternity leaves would be extended to eighteen months and childcare would be subsidized. After the 2007 incentives were introduced, the birth rate rose to 1.7 children per woman, just above the European average of 1.59.[30] Some states have pitched in with their own incentive programs. The government of Ulyanovsk instituted a half day off for "conception day." Women who applied for the day off and gave birth nine months later could win refrigerators and cars.

In 2011, Putin again focused on demography, pledging, "First, we expect the average life expectancy to reach seventy-one years," and "we expect to increase the birth rate by 25–30 percent in comparison to the 2006 birth rate."[31] In his 2012 state of the nation address he said, "Demographers affirm that choosing to have a second child is already a potential choice in favor of a third . . . it's important that families make that step. . . . I am convinced that the norm in Russia should become a family with three children."[32]

That year the government also enacted restrictions on abortion with the explicit reasoning that more population is needed. Russia banned abortion after twelve weeks, with some exceptions, and required a waiting period of two to seven days. Ads for abortion were also restricted.

Patriarch Kirill, the head of the Russian Orthodox church, addressed the Russian parliament in January 2015, saying that abortion was "infanticide," but he also discussed demography. "If we manage to cut the number of abortions by 50 percent we would have stable and powerful population growth," he said. It was the first time a religious leader had ever addressed the body, according to Moscow-based medical journalist Fiona Clark.[33]

Abortion is currently legal and free up to twelve weeks. But further legislative attacks in 2015 sought to stop public funding as well as institute compulsory ultrasounds before abortions. They also seek to make the morning-after pill a prescription drug (it's currently over-the-counter). Sound familiar?

Turkey
Turkey is another country where leaders explicitly link the birth rate to birth control policy. Government officials began to worry aloud about Turkey's flagging birth rate in 2008. Turkish prime minister and later president Recep Tayyip Erdoğan has repeatedly called on women to have at least three children and charged that "birth control advocates sought to weaken Turkey."[34] He lectured a couple at their wedding, saying, "For years they committed a treason of birth control in this country, seeking to dry up our bloodline. Lineage is very important both economically and spiritually." (Turkey's fertility rate, at 2.05, is higher than that of the United States.) Erdoğan has also denounced the morning-after pill. In

2015, Health Minister Mehmet Muezzinoglu "caused uproar by saying women should prioritize the 'career' of motherhood."[35]

Abortion is legal on request up to ten weeks in Turkey; married women must get their husband's permission. In 2012 Erdoğan attacked abortion "as a secret plot to stall Turkey's economic growth," and his health minister proposed banning abortion after four weeks, effectively banning it altogether.[36] Outrage from feminists stopped the change, alongside a medical establishment worried about deaths from illegal abortions. The Istanbul Feminist Collective sat-in at Erdoğan's office and thousands of feminists protested in the streets—one woman's sign said "State, take your hands off my body"—until the proposal was withdrawn.[37]

Turkey has also started instituting incentives. "The government fears that an ageing population could eventually lead Turkey down the same path as more developed economies in Europe, towards a shrinking workforce and rising welfare spending," writes Jonathon Burch in a Reuters article.[38] Among the incentives considered are free fertility treatments, payments upon the birth of children, and increasing maternity leaves (unpaid) from four months to six months. They're also considering special commemorative gold coins for first-time mothers—apparently they think women's work can be bought with bling.

Prime Minister Ahmet Davutoglu called for these measures because Turkey's future economy would be "at risk." He said Turkey should aim for a fertility rate of 2.1 so the population can "replace itself naturally," reported Agence France-Presse. "The economy can be restored after a crisis but if the fabric of the family is damaged, we cannot restore it," the prime minister said.[39]

Some analysts think the government is also concerned about the Kurdish minority population having a higher birth rate than Turks. During the abortion debate, Deniz Ülke Aribogan, an Istanbul international relations professor wrote, "The problem is the rapid rise of population in eastern [Kurdish] regions, while it has almost come to a standstill in western regions." She ascribed the attempted abortion ban to these demographic concerns rather than to religious opposition to the procedure.[40]

Germany, France, and Sweden

Women's decisions to have fewer children have been the primary impetus for generous family policies in these three countries, with Sweden the leader and a reunified post-socialist Germany the laggard.

In Europe, the phrase "social wage" denotes a social supplement to the individual wage, universal programs that all citizens have access to no matter their income or employment status, such as health care, public school (childcare through college), paid family leave and sick leave, paid vacations, public pensions, and other universal programs. The social wage is paid for by employers through taxes and it supplements the individual wage one receives from an employer. Many things that are part of the social wage in Europe, like health care and paid vacations, are provided in the United States only at the discretion of employers—as "fringe benefits."[41]

Germany

The social wage was highest in socialist East Germany. "Day care and all-day schools were long synonymous with communism," said former West German Family Minister Ursula von der Leyen in 2010.[42] East German women more easily combined work and family life than West German women because health care and childcare were provided free, and they could take a year of paid maternity leave. As a result, at reunification, 90 percent of East German women worked, compared to 55 percent in the West.[43] East German women gained some access to abortion starting in 1950 and full access to abortion in the first trimester starting in 1972. West Germany began to allow abortions in some extreme cases in 1976 but still had lots of restrictions until reunification, when parliament had to reconcile the restrictive Western law with the permissive Eastern one in 1992. Now Germany requires a counseling session and a three-day waiting period for first trimester abortions, but abortion is free like other health care.

With the overthrow of socialism, East Germans faced sudden instability and insecurity in jobs, housing, pensions, and childcare. The fertility rate in the east plunged from 1.52 in 1990 to 0.77 in 1993, a phenomenon the East German women's magazine *Esprit* called a "birth strike."[44] West Germany's rates were stable during that period—but lower than East Germany's—an ongoing birth strike that bedevils German officials to this day.[45] (There is more on the early twentieth-century birth strike debate in Germany in chapter 9, Cheap Labor.)

Although some demographers are puzzled by Germany's low birth rate—they blame everything from the Protestant Reformation to an individualistic society—the answer seems clear. It's nearly impossible for German parents to combine work and child rearing, especially because the school day ends at lunchtime. "Childcare is scarce and expensive, employers do not provide flexible working hours, and the restriction of school hours to mornings only means that childcare problems stretch into school-going ages," write demographers John Caldwell and Thomas Schindlmayr.[46]

"Women who decide they want a modern life, with financial independence and their own professional career are very often deciding to have no children at all," says Kroehnert, the German demographer. "The lack of child care makes women dependent on their husbands. And most women don't like this."[47]

The state has made some concessions in an effort to raise the birth rate. Child allowances at first only went to married families with three children, then gradually expanded to cover all families, married or not.

In 2004, the German government made childcare a priority, panicked by a fertility rate that had plunged to 1.3. "When it comes to childcare, compared with the rest of the European Union, Germany is a third-world country," said the country's family minister, Renate Schmidt. Germany put $1.5 billion over five years into ramping up its childcare system, with "full-day kindergartens which would include children under the age of three."[48]

Germany has also been coping with its low birth rate through immigration. In the 1960s and 1970s many Turks and Yugoslavians settled in Germany. Now many refugees are coming from war-ravaged Iraq and Syria. "We need people. We need young people. We need immigrants," said Interior Minister Thomas de Maiziere in 2015 as waves of Syrians fleeing war made their way to Germany. "All of you know that, because we have too few children."[49]

There is a backlash against immigration, however. German Chancellor Angela Merkel has faced domestic opposition and punishment at the ballot box for welcoming refugees, and neo-Nazi attacks against immigrants and refugees are an ongoing menace.[50]

France
France was a prolific source of emigrants, to Italy, Spain, and the New World, until the latter part of the eighteenth century—that's when demographers noticed that French peasants had instituted a "two-child system." In order to not have to split up farms or other property into smaller and smaller pieces for their offspring, they avoided unwanted pregnancies, mostly using coitus interruptus (withdrawal). "The husbands themselves take care in their raptures to keep from adding a child to the household," as dramatist Louis-Sébastien Mercier put it in 1771.[51] With the revolution in 1789, more contraceptive information and recipes became available. The trend of small French families alarmed civilian and military leaders,

and population growth has been a worry for leaders in France ever since, expressed by organizations like the National Alliance for the Growth of the French Population (founded in 1896). Popular novelist Émile Zola in his 1899 book *Fécondité* (Fruitfulness) depicted personal catastrophe for those who have few children while celebrating the immense family of his fecund hero. Some private companies gave incentives for their employees to have large families, and then in the 1930s the government took over, providing child allowances to encourage births while outlawing birth control.

France had a baby boom after World War II, but when women started to slack off, French politicians still wanted more, with President Charles de Gaulle and Defense Minister Michel Debre calling for a doubling of the French population to 100 million by the year 2000. "A satisfactory rhythm of births to aim for is at least three children in every family. It is in the national interest," said Debre in 1963.[52]

In 1969 U.S. newspapers reported that the French government was launching a "Make More Babies" campaign with TV and radio advertising aimed at young married couples "showing the joys of more—and earlier—children."[53] Despite the ad campaign, the bluster of leaders, and the illegality of abortion, the birth rate continued to decline.

In 1971 a group of French feminists signed a declaration that they had had illegal abortions. They rewrote the Ten Commandments to parody the coercive pronatalist policies of their government. Among the new commandments:

> Thou shalt not allow any abortions as long as Debre is calling for 100 million French people. Thou shalt have 100 million French people, as long as it costs you nothing. Thus shalt thou have a reserve army of unemployed to please thy capitalists. Thou shalt preserve the fetus, for it's much better to kill them at eighteen, the age of conscription. Thou shalt create a great need for these young men by pursuing a policy of imperialism. Thou shalt utilize contraception thyself, so as to send thy few children to the Polytechnic or the ENA, because thine apartment is only ten rooms. As for other people, thou shall disparage the pill, because that would be the worst possible thing for them.[54]

With rising feminist protest and illegal abortions common, the government legalized birth control in 1967 and abortion in 1975. Fertility continued to decline, hitting a low in 1994. But then it started to climb, reaching a Europe-beating 2.01 in 2010 and hovering nearby ever since.

Nowadays, France proudly touts its birth rate, with delegations from low-birth-rate countries visiting France's National Institute for Demographic Studies to find out how they do it. "In the past four or five years we've had over ten Korean delegations," demographer Olivier Thévenon told a reporter in 2015.[55] While birth rates dropped in most places after the 2008 economic crisis, in France they stayed up.

What changed? The government poured resources into child allowances, childcare facilities, nurse visitors, and paid parental leaves. Each parent can take up to 156 weeks (three years).[56] Anne Chemin, writing in the *Guardian*, sums up the experience of France and other countries: "In the 1960s–70s advocates of traditional family values claimed that the birthrate would be the first thing to suffer from [the trend of gender equality]. Fifty years on it seems they were mistaken: fertility in Europe is higher in countries where women go out to work, lower in those where they generally stay at home."[57]

Sweden

Sweden's social wage makes people in the United States envious, and with good reason. The country seems to have comfortably combined work life with parenting through lengthy family leave, excellent childcare and preschool, and generous wage supplements for parents. Where did all this come from?

It started with a panic about low birth rates. In 1900, Swedish women were having four children, on average. A growing industrial sector led to rapid urbanization, with cramped housing and harsh conditions for workers. By 1930 that figure had dropped below two, causing conservatives to call for a crackdown on contraceptives and a stop to women working outside the home. On the other side of the debate, the union-linked Social Democratic Workers' Party—the dominant party in the Swedish parliament starting in 1932—was focused on improving working conditions and schools. They favored more birth control freedom and "on the whole they did not worry about the risk of depopulation but believed, rather, that it might even help cut back unemployment."[58]

Into the debate stepped a young Social Democratic couple, Gunnar and Alva Myrdal, an economist and social psychologist, respectively. They cowrote a controversial blockbuster, *Crisis in the Population Question* (1934), which forged a third path between conservatives and the Social Democrats. What they did with the two opposing positions "seemed to the public almost like magic," writes Sissela Bok, Alva Myrdal's daughter. "They wholly accepted the conservative view regarding the great danger that depopulation posed to the country, but managed to draw the opposite conclusion, that this danger presented 'the most forceful argument for the profound and radical reshaping of society.'"[59]

Under the new economic circumstances, Swedish women resisted their traditional roles. A government commission found that women didn't want to get married, "locking them in a cycle of child rearing and housekeeping" that "prevented them from participating in paid labor and higher education."[60]

The Myrdals prescribed free health care, free school lunches, housing subsidies for families with children, and laws protecting women from getting fired when they got pregnant. They also favored sex education in schools and complete access to contraception. Their book launched a furious debate, and resulted in discussion groups all over the country.

While conservatives had only threats and punishment as their population program, the Myrdals suggested reforms that would benefit everyone, but especially women, who were engaging in what Alva Myrdal thought of, disapprovingly, as a "birth strike."[61] While she disliked the strike, it created the pressure that made possible her ideas for changing the condition of women.

The government took up many of the Myrdals' suggestions, protecting pregnant women from firing and subsidizing hospital births. Universal child allowances were introduced in 1948, along with a system of health care for all which ramped up after World War II.

The birth rate has continued to be a worry for Swedish industrialists and politicians, but the government's answer over the last fifty years has not been to attack birth control, but to adjust programs making it easier for women (and men) to work and raise children at the same time.

Prenatal care and childbirth are basically free. "Many Swedish hospitals have adjoining 'hotels' where new mothers and their partners may stay for two or three days (with all meals included) after a birth so nurses can monitor the mothers and provide postnatal care for newborns."[62]

Swedish parents are entitled to 480 days of paid leave upon birth or adoption of a child—most of them at 80 percent of their pay. Employers pay a tax on salaries, and parents are paid from the fund. Those unemployed at the time are also eligible for a parental stipend. Parents can split the leave between them however they like, and men take nearly a quarter of parental leave in Sweden, according to the government. The parents' jobs are protected.

Swedish policy pushes fathers to do more child-rearing work through a "daddy quota." Three months of the paid leave can't be transferred to the mother, which means that the father has to use it or lose it. (Mothers have the same amount of untransferrable leave.) There's also a "gender equality" bonus payment if the parents split the leave evenly between them. Parents also have the legal right to cut their work hours 25 percent until their child is eight.

In addition there's a monthly check—currently around $125—for each child until they're sixteen years old, and an extra family allowance if you have more than one child. Childcare and preschool are heavily subsidized and on a sliding scale, and all schooling through college is free.

Health care is free through age twenty, at which point some copays kick in. Sick leave pays 80 percent of your wages. Leave to take care of a sick child also pays 80 percent, up to 120 days a year for each child under twelve years old. And all workers get five weeks a year of paid vacation.

The workday is eight hours in Sweden, but some employers have been experimenting with six-hour days in the last decade. This may become national policy.[63]

•

The birth rate is a topic in lots of other countries. So why don't U.S. policymakers more openly discuss our birth rate? It's one thing for a government to say, as Sweden and France have, we think the birth rate is too low, so we're going to extend paid parental leave and institute free public childcare. It's another to say, our birth rate is too low so we're going to make abortions harder to get, make birth control expensive, keep sex education out of the schools, and in case you get any ideas, we're going to prosecute women suspected of aborting their pregnancies themselves. The first sounds like a country you'd want to live in, the second sounds like one you'd want to flee.

CHAPTER 2

SMALL GOVERNMENT, BIG FAMILIES

O ne obstacle to understanding the value of our childbearing and rearing work is the utter individualization of it in our country. While the whole society gains the benefits—and especially employers— the costs are privatized onto parents, especially women. Until public school starts at age five or six, the main government support for child rearing or parenting takes the form of a tax credit. This has led women to have fewer children, resulting in debates among the powerful over what can be done to get U.S. women to fire up the ovens again, preferably with a minimum of public spending.[1]

As it stands now, the costs fall on the parents. The parenting website The Bump advises new mothers not to stay in the hospital too long as costs can mount surprisingly fast, and to remember that as soon as your child is born, she will have her own insurance deductible.[2] Unpaid leave— assuming you can afford to take it—is limited to three months, and four out of ten workers don't even qualify for that.[3] A quarter of employed moms return to work within two weeks of giving birth—only 13 percent have access to paid leave.[4] Women have turned to crowd-funding sites so they can afford to take leave. "I've found myself in a position where I will now be unable to stay home with my newborn nor have time to heal after the whole intensive labor that we as women have to endure," wrote Megan, who said she works as a security guard. "This is both heartbreaking and stressful knowing I can't come up with the money to stay home any other way than asking for help."[5]

We have no nurse visitors, as are dispatched to help families with newborns in Denmark and France. Here, exhausted mothers just home from the hospital bundle tiny newborns into cars or busses in all weather for their checkups. There is no income assistance or health care unless you can prove you're very poor, and then there are humiliating restrictions and arbitrary rules. If you break a rule, you can be cut off, judged no longer worthy of public support.

When you have a baby, there are some government forms to fill out, but there is no acknowledgment from the government or the larger community that you are making any contribution to the greater good by bearing and raising a child. In fact, unless you are quite affluent, you may be looked upon as creating a burden on society. Contrast this to the generous programs that surround young families in dozens of countries. In Finland, a few weeks before the baby's due date, the government sends each family a box stuffed with well-designed baby clothes, a snowsuit, and other essential gear, all free. The mattress-lined box can even be used as a crib. "This felt to me like evidence that someone cared," said one new father who received the box after moving to Finland from Britain. "Someone wanted our baby to have a good start in life. . . . And now when I visit friends, it's nice to see we share common things. It strengthens the feeling that we are all in this together."[6]

U.S. parents are more likely to feel that they're utterly alone, especially when their children are small.

Children as a Personal Indulgence

Our perilous conditions are supported by a pernicious ideology. Children are regarded as an indulgence for those who have the resources, but certainly not a project you should take on unless you are well-prepared with housing, money, time, and probably one stay-at-home parent. Feminist economist Nancy Folbre notes that our society "treats parental expenditures on children as a form of personal consumption no different than expenditures on hot tubs or golden retrievers."[7]

The U.S. Department of Agriculture, which periodically calculates the average cost of raising a child, encourages parents to "think of the act of reproduction as above all a personal economic choice" writes public school defender Megan Erickson.

Erickson describes a flier produced by the USDA that "depicts an imaginary online shopping website modeled on Amazon.com, with the image of a baby priced at 'US $245,340' and a mouse arrow hovering ominously over the phrase 'Add to family?' Under a 'Details' section, the breakdown of costs shows percentages allocated to housing, food, transportation, clothing, health care, child care and education, and miscellaneous. College is 'Not included.'"[8]

Hardly anyone thinks of the work and care required to raise a child as a community responsibility, a community benefit, or a common good. Raising children is primarily portrayed as a lifestyle choice, like an expensive hobby or an exotic pet, instead of a needed job that parents take on at great individual expense and which the larger community, because it benefits, should support and assist.

This fiction that children are only an individual concern serves the employing class well. Budget cutters attack funding for parks and libraries, for after-school programs, for schools themselves. How do they get away with it? Blame the parents: Why should the rest of us pay for your expensive hobby? And U.S. parents tell themselves: Well, we should have known what we were getting into. After all, we "chose" to have children.

To make up for the cuts, parents try to make things better for their kids by putting in *more* work and resources. School lunches made with cheap, unhealthy ingredients? Make the lunches yourself before work. No after school programs? "Flex" your work time and resume work after the kids go to bed. Parks closed and library hours cut? Enlist grandparents and other family members to do childcare. New costs for kids to participate in sports or school extras? Get a weekend job. Schools cut staff? "Volunteer" in the classroom. Meanwhile little is asked of the employing class, and they give even less.

"CAN'T FEED 'EM? DON'T BREED 'EM," states a surly bumper sticker, while liberal commentators give the genteel version of the same sentiment, insisting that birth control must be the solution to poverty because parents tend to be poorer than nonparents.[9] Well, yes, if you have no paid leave and have to pay market prices for childcare, you would tend to be poorer from having children. The average childcare bill in the U.S. is $9,589 a year, slightly more than in-state college tuition.[10] That U.S. parents are made to bear these costs is a political choice. In other countries, childcare is free like public schools.

Here, reliance on the community at large is classed as parental neglect, and mothers get most of the blame. The police are called in to enforce this individualist ideology. Debra Harrell of South Carolina was arrested and jailed because she allowed her nine-year-old daughter to play in a park near her job at a McDonald's.[11] The parents of a ten-year-old and a six-year-old in Maryland were found responsible for "unsubstantiated child neglect" when police, responding to a complaint, picked up the children walking home from a nearby park. "I was kind of horrified," said the mother, Danielle Meitiv, reacting to the judgment. "You try as a parent to do what's right. Parents try so hard. Even though I know [Child Protective Services] are wrong, it's a painful judgment."[12]

For unemployed and low-waged parents, the situation is truly dire. Instead of universal assistance, we have targeted enforcement. Parents may have their children taken away by Child Protective Services if they are not deemed to have provided a wholesome environment—which is difficult to do when you have little money. Black feminist scholar Dorothy Roberts describes the devastating effect on families in her book *Shattered Bonds*. She writes: "The child protection approach is inextricably tied to our society's refusal to see a collective responsibility for children's welfare. . . . Thousands of poor families in this country lack the income to meet their children's basic needs of food, clothing, and shelter and live in a deprived environment that is dangerous for children. The child welfare system hides the systemic reasons for families' hardships by laying the blame on individual parents' failings."[13]

As a result, thousands of children are taken from their parents and put into the foster system—around four hundred thousand are in foster care at any given time—but unlike birth parents, foster parents are provided a stipend for the children in their care. (Roberts also charges that since child removal hits black families disproportionately, it undermines community and family ties, weakening low-income working-class black communities as a cohesive political force.)

Child support enforcement is tasked with solving the problems created by low wages, unemployment, and miserly government programs. So the police track down "deadbeat dads," even when it is impossible for these dads (or less often non-custodial moms) to pay child support because their income is too low. Of the money owed by "deadbeat" parents, 70 percent was owed by those who made less than $10,000 a year, an Urban Institute study found, and they were obliged to pay 83 percent of their income for child support, on average.[14]

Some states jail those who fail to pay, or take away their driver's or occupational licenses, making it even harder to earn a living. Often when money is obtained from low-waged parents, rather than going to the caretaking parent, it goes to the state to offset the costs of welfare the family already received. In fact, many child support claims are not initiated by the custodial parent but by the states, to fund welfare.[15]

The enforcement model can make life hell for low-waged parents. One of the unarmed black men shot dead by the police in 2015, Walter Scott of South Carolina, had been relentlessly pursued for child support despite his low income. The first time he was arrested for failure to pay child support (he had paid, but there was a clerical error) his time in jail caused him to lose "the best job he ever had," his brother Rodney Scott recalled. "Every job he has had, he has gotten fired from because . . . he was locked up for child support." When Walter Scott was again stopped by the police in 2015, his brother speculated that he was afraid he'd be sent to jail again and lose his job as a forklift operator. A video recorded by a bystander shows the police officer shooting him in the back as he fled.[16]

Because child rearing appears to be an individual concern, people complain if they are asked to help. "Why should I have to pay for property taxes for schools when I don't have any kids?" is the refrain of many an anti-tax commentator. Well, because those kids are going to pick up your garbage, install your internet, and zap your tumor, not just when you're old but in ten to fifteen years.

This complaint is not just a conservative or libertarian one. There are plenty of aggrieved liberals who complain about "breeders," and even the occasional feminist who regards the meager assistance provided to U.S. parents as a rip-off of the childless.[17]

At the same time, we endure lots of sentimental rhetoric. "Children are our future," we're told. But this cliché obscures the point. Children aren't just the future; they are the present. In a complex society, everyone depends on everyone else, and many of those someones are younger than you.

As wages stagnate and time pressures mount, families are compensating by having fewer children. As they discovered in Europe, if women are forced to choose between work and children, they'll choose work. This has led to a debate among opinion makers and power brokers about how to get women to take on more reproductive work. On the Democratic side, there have been moves to create twelve weeks of paid family leave. Right now, the United States is virtually the only country in the world not to provide some form of paid parental leave—fifty countries provide more than six months of paid maternity leave by law, and forty-three countries provide fourteen weeks or more of paid *paternity* leave.[18] Obama's Department of Labor even employed international comparisons to show how behind the United States is. On the Republican side "Reformocons," or reform conservatives, have been pushing tax incentives and even a small cash "baby bonus." Neither Democratic nor Republican proposals approach anything like the kind of programs we need and deserve, but it is especially revealing to listen in on the Republican discussion, because in the course of trying to make the case to skeptical fellow conservatives, they speak more frankly than liberals do about the effect of a lower birth rate and about how they would like to solve the problem.

Pro-family

Most politicians portray themselves as "pro-family," but none do it more vigorously than conservative Republicans. This might seem ironic, as it is the most loudly pro-family who try to block increases to the minimum wage, cut Head Start childcare and school lunch programs, slash welfare payments for parents and health care for children, oppose any kind of family leave (even unpaid), and generally make life less livable for children and families.

But it is not just hypocrisy, and it's worth decoding. What "pro-family" really means is families *instead of* government: Cut government, and put the work on families. And by "families" they mean women, and women's unpaid labor.

Listen to conservative reformers Ross Douthat and Reihan Salam's vision of a small-government, big-family America: "Crafting pro-family policies . . . is not a question of turning back the clock to some lost Ozzie-and-Harriet golden age. . . . Quite the opposite: Precisely because the world has changed, with the demise of lifetime employment and increasing returns to education, strong families are growing ever more important and policies that encourage people to form them and keep them together are ever more necessary."[19]

When unemployment and the necessity to retrain hit, in other words, people should be made to rely on their families for solace and support, the better to allow for cuts in unemployment insurance, welfare, and education funding.

Douthat, now a *New York Times* columnist, explained in an interview that not just "strong" families but *large* families are important to his vision:

> Conservatism has always been based around the principle that people need to be independent, they shouldn't be dependent on government largesse and so on. One of the things we've seen over the last thirty years is that in the absence of government programs people aren't able to function usually as atomized individuals, you need some intermediary institutions if you're going to have small government. So you need strong families, you need people who are willing to have large families, for instance, which can then help provide for them in their old age. . . . So if Republicans are serious about reforming Social Security, or finding a way to increase the

number of young workers paying into the program, then having a country with higher population growth, larger families, is an obvious and conservative way to do it.[20]

But Douthat and Salam are troubled by parental leave and childcare tax breaks because these encourage women to "follow the male career track, which assumes a seamless transition from school to full-time employment, and a career path that begins in the early twenties and continues an unbroken ascent until retirement." They write, "For many women, this is an appealing model—but many more find themselves losing their best childbearing years to the workplace, and then scrambling to squeeze in a child or two before middle age arrives."

Women, it seems, must be dislodged from career tracks and tracked into prolific motherhood by a "generous baby bonus, a pro-natalist child benefit designed to defray the costs of children and to encourage larger families." Douthat and Salam acknowledge that the costs of raising a child, in women's foregone wages and direct costs, "can top $1 million for a family of modest means." What is a "generous baby bonus"? They are not specific but refer readers to Quebec's Allowance for Newborn Children, at the time $500 for the first child, $1,000 for the second, and $8,000 for third and subsequent children.[21]

Conservatives favor cash incentives rather than universal programs. Cash is easier to whittle away than, say, a universal childcare system would be. Often policymakers just wait for inflation to eat up the benefit, as they do with the federal minimum wage.

Tax credits are another conservative favorite. Reformocon Robert Stein suggests a new child tax credit to parents of $2,500, a proposal taken up by Republican Senators Marco Rubio and Mike Lee in 2016.[22] These plans, as Elizabeth Bruenig writes in the *New Republic*, reduce taxes among those who are doing well, and help the bottom 20 percent not at all. She challenges Democrats and Republicans alike to provide a universal child allowance as many other countries do.[23]

The gap between the estimated million dollars a family will put in to raise a child and the tiny amounts proposed by Reformocons quantifies the enormous contribution parents are making while highlighting the problem facing cash bonus pronatalists. Children require a lot of resources to raise. Big programs, costly to employers and the rich, will be required to move the needle even slightly. Sweden and France were able to increase their birth rates, but only after instituting universal childcare and long paid parental leaves, involving both parents. If we did that here, the money would have to come from employers and the 1%, or possibly from cutting the part of government they cherish the most, the military.

This may explain why there's a split in the Republican Party. Douthat, Salam, Rubio, Lee, Stein, and the late Ben Wattenberg represent the more liberal faction, the tax break and cash-bonus pronatalists, the velvet glove over the iron fist.

The iron-fist faction doesn't think the government should spend a penny more on kids. They prefer to recreate the conditions that Betty Friedan denounced in *The Feminine Mystique*, and feminist sociologist Leta Hollingworth denounced two generations earlier, in which women are tracked into childbearing by closing off "the avenues . . . of escape therefrom," as Hollingworth put it.[24] Consider Pat Buchanan and Rick Santorum, both of whom think abortion should be outlawed and oppose what they call the "culture of contraception."

Buchanan, the former Nixon and Reagan aide, presidential candidate, and Fox News commentator, blames the drop in the birth rate on the inclusion of "sex" in the Civil Rights Act of 1964, outlawing job discrimination against women. He laments that women could finally earn a living, independent of men. "America's young women found they could achieve independence on their own. They need not get married, certainly not yet. . . . The young family with a batch of kids is now an endangered species. . . . The call of the gods of the marketplace for more women workers prevails over the command of the God of Genesis: 'Be fruitful and multiply, and replenish the Earth.'"[25]

Buchanan reflects back on the "golden age of marriage," 1945–1965, "when the average age of first marriages fell to record lows for both men and women [twenty-two and twenty, respectively], and the proportion of adults who were married reached an astronomical 95 percent."[26]

Buchanan's subtext—and it's not very sub—is that women need to be discriminated against more vigorously so they'll be dependent on marriage for their livelihood. Then they'll get married earlier and have more kids. Abortion needs to be illegal and contraception, if not illegal, at least frowned upon.

Buchanan is not just a commentator—he was a key player in destroying a plan for comprehensive childcare we almost won in 1971. The U.S. House and Senate passed a bill with bipartisan support and the encouragement of the Nixon administration. It would have provided "childcare at a sliding scale to every child that needed it."[27] But in a surprise reversal, Nixon vetoed it, saying the law would "commit the vast moral authority of the National Government to the side of communal approaches to child rearing over against the family centered approach." Buchanan wrote the statement and takes credit for pushing Nixon to veto. "I think when we ran the sword through [childcare] in '71, it may have killed it for more than half a century," he reflected in 2014.[28]

But Buchanan's current obsession is his fear that people of European descent will be overrun by the out-of-control breeding of people of color. He blames feminists: "If the preservation of peoples of European ancestry, and of the Western civilization they have created, were up to the feminists, Western Man would have no future."[29] Buchanan is sensitive not only to the undermining of the male supremacist order but to the undermining of the racial order. (There is more on the power structure's conflicted thinking on race in chapters 8 and 9.)

Get Married!

Rick Santorum, former Republican senator from Pennsylvania and a perennial "family values" presidential candidate, wrote a book called It Takes a Family as a rebuke to Hillary Clinton's book It Takes a Village.[30] (Her title adopted the proverb "It takes a village to raise a child," although Clinton supported the crippling 1996 welfare reform that pushed women with small children into sub-minimum-wage workfare jobs.[31])

In Santorum's world, the problem is that women are working outside the home instead of taking care of children in it, and too many people are not getting married or are getting divorced. This is partly due to premarital sex, abetted by contraceptives. He thinks that stigma and shame should be revived for out-of-wedlock births, an idea also beloved of Florida's ex-governor Jeb Bush, who recommended public shaming to discourage the unmarried from having children. In 1995 Bush wrote: "Society needs to relearn the art of public and private disapproval and how to make those who engage in some undesirable behavior feel some sense of shame." Perhaps the red 'A' should be brought back? "Infamous shotgun weddings and Nathaniel Hawthorne's Scarlet Letter are reminders that public condemnation of irresponsible sexual behavior has strong historical roots," Bush writes, perhaps missing the point of the novel.[32]

Why are these public figures so worried? Are they horrified at single motherhood and extramarital sex? Are they pandering to a prudish electoral base? I submit that their overarching goal is more cost-effective—from their standpoint—child production. Shaming single mothers and proscribing premarital sex are time-honored ways to create pressure to marry, and a married couple is not only more likely to have children, it is also a more efficient baby-raising unit.

Employers and the government would like working-class families to be frugal and require the minimum in wages and subsidies, so marrying off welfare recipients has become an objective for policy tinkerers. "One of the main points of the 1996 welfare reform was to end the scourge of single motherhood and promote marriage, 'the foundation of a successful society,'" writes Matt Bruenig, an expert on, and critic of, coercive welfare policies. It did this by creating various marriage promotion programs with unimpeachable names: "Building Strong Families," "Supporting Healthy Marriage Project," and the "Healthy Marriage Initiative." Despite the utter failure of these programs to foster marriages among their targets, Bruenig writes, "States still redirect . . . funds meant to provide cash assistance to poor families to these dead-end ideology projects."[33]

For U.S. welfare administrators, a cheap way to decrease poverty—at least on paper—is to make one-parent households into two-parent households. If two people making $12,000 and $15,000 a year are put into the same household with a couple of kids, Bruenig points out, suddenly you've lifted that household above the official poverty line, and can cut their benefits. This creates an incentive for pressing marriage upon women receiving public assistance, but of course it does nothing to solve the problems of that still-struggling family, and completely ignores the underlying problems of unemployment, low wages, exploitative landlords, and lack of childcare.

Is it really true that single parenthood is a cause of poverty? Bruenig helpfully compares U.S. child poverty to that in Finland, Norway, and Sweden, where there are just as many or more single-parent families, but very low rates of poverty among them. Although establishment think tanks "tout the wonders of married-parent families in the United States, the reality is that they too have mind-bogglingly high levels of poverty, compared to low-poverty countries." Child poverty in U.S. *two-parent* families is six times that of Sweden and seven times that of Finland, Bruenig notes.[34]

But U.S. policymakers aren't interested in providing the kind of higher wage floors and universal benefits that make child poverty so rare in Scandinavia. A floor like that would raise wages across the board, while universal benefits would decrease what economists delicately call "incentives to work." In fact, employer organizations attack any program that might decrease the incentive to work. Even the wholly inadequate Affordable Care Act was attacked on this basis because it provides subsidies to buy health insurance otherwise only accessible through a job.[35]

While those who want to cut welfare claim to be against "dependency," what they're really against is public resources going to support families. While they claim to champion liberty, they are in fact pushing people toward a more onerous dependency: on employers.

Mommy Tracking Women

To Santorum, marriage is not about a loving commitment between two people or a partnership to face the struggles of life. No, marriage is about having children. In an attack on gay marriage, Santorum writes: "What happens to a society that disconnects marriage from babies in this way? . . . Once same-sex marriage becomes firmly entrenched as the law of the land, we can expect to get even more children being raised outside of marriage. And we will also have fewer children, period."[36]

Santorum supports his view that there will be fewer children by pointing to Europe's lower birth rates. "The nations of Europe are slowly dying off—sometimes not so slowly. Today, European governments are struggling with an increasingly aging population, [and] large-scale immigration challenges." He links these low fertility rates to "the movement away from marriage," by which he means women should become housewives and stay-at-home mothers.[37]

In a review of his book, Ruth Conniff of the *Progressive* writes that "Santorum scolds working mothers. Helping support the family, he writes, 'provides a convenient rationalization for pursuing a gratifying career outside the home.'"[38]

Women in Pennsylvania objected vigorously to their former senator's views. After a Santorum article attacking childcare ran in the *Pittsburgh Post-Gazette*, women objected that it was all very well for Karen Ann, his wife, to homeschool the couple's seven children, but "For the last thirty years women have had no choice but to enter the workforce, and more now than ever. When good paying jobs are gone and more couples are trying to make ends meet on two salaries or more, it is just inconceivable that a senator could even question women working to help put food on the table and a roof over their families' heads."[39]

Self-described "conservative Republican" Eileen R. Sisca wrote in response to Santorum's attacks on women who work outside the home: "Both men and women have studied for years and are working very hard. . . . To suggest, as Sen. Santorum has done, that women with young children don't have a place in, or aren't needed, as a part of this vital process is insulting."[40]

Death of the Family Wage System

All this fussing and fuming is about how to extract women's unpaid labor, not just of bearing, raising, and educating children, but caring for the sick, injured, disabled, and frail, and comforting, nurturing, and sending back out to work those family members who are assaulted daily by an economic system that creates few winners and many losers. The trick is how to extract that work when those women have other jobs, for pay, outside the home.

Each of these conservative writers seeks to solve the problem in a different way. Douthat and Salam think that a little cash incentive will fix it. Buchanan thinks reducing women's pay and increasing their dependence on men will fix it. Santorum and Bush think pushing women into marriage, shaming single mothers, and making divorce harder will fix it. Buchanan and Santorum oppose birth control and abortion, in part to fix it.

Part of the problem, as explained by Pittsburgh letter writer Linda Bear, is that the "family wage" is dead. This refers to a wage sufficient to support two adults, one full-time breadwinner and one full-time care-giver, and their children.

Feminists opposed the discriminatory higher male pay of the family wage, but nothing has replaced it. Kathie Sarachild of Redstockings writes:

> The [family wage] system, when it actually does pay a family-sup-porting wage . . . means that the woman, as an unpaid family car-egiver, is in a condition of dependency on the breadwinner who earns and owns the wage on which all live. . . . But the family wage has one progressive element to it. . . . It recognizes the employers' obligation to pay something for the labor of family care, includ-ing the labor of replenishing and maintaining generations of the workforce.[41]

With the demise of the family wage system, Sarachild explains, a couple is now doing three jobs where they used to do two. In a family wage there was (at least in theory) enough money in the wage-earning job to also support the person doing the family-care-and-maintenance job. Now each couple is working two wage-earning jobs, plus the family-care-and-maintenance job done largely by the woman in her "spare time," leading to the crunch of the double day.[42] We see the zombie remnants of the family wage system in job- and marriage-based fringe benefits like health insurance, and in a school day that presumes there is a parent at home at 3:00 p.m.

Now, there is no longer any recognition that the employer should contribute for family care—not paid family leave, and certainly not taxes for schools or libraries or parks or playgrounds or, heaven forbid, child-care or college.

We don't want to return to the sexist family wage system suggested by Santorum and Buchanan, and the tiny cash bonuses and tax breaks suggested by the Reformocons are an insult. We should instead fight to replace the remnants of the family wage system with a social wage system.

So far, the powerful have been resolving the conflict by pushing the unpaid work onto women. Women are resisting by having fewer children—but we have not been demanding the supports we need, in part because we have not understood the full value of our labor raising the successive overlapping generations that make up our society. The idea that children are our individual concern is protecting employers and the rich from our wrath. Seeing the value of our work more clearly will give us a basis to demand a bigger contribution from those who are benefitting the most.

CHAPTER 3

IS IT A BIRTH STRIKE? WOMEN TESTIFY

B lack and white, immigrant and native-born, women are having fewer children—by some measures, the U.S. birth rate is the lowest it has ever been. But can we really say women are striking?

One indication is the blast of passionate responses to a comment by U.S. House Speaker Paul Ryan that women should have more children: "Baby Boomers are retiring and we have fewer people following them into the workforce. . . . We need to have higher birth rates in this country," he said at a 2017 press conference, teeing up an attack on Social Security.[1] Angry testimonies appeared wherever the news was reported. "I'll tell Paul Ryan the same thing I tell my parents and all their noisy friends: you want me to have babies, create an environment where having and raising a child doesn't cost an entire adult person's salary and I'll think about it," wrote MazzieD on the *Jezebel* blog. Another wrote, "I don't get my health insurance through my workplace and Republicans are trying to take away my affordable ObamaCare insurance so how the hell do they think I am going to afford to have a kid and then raise one?" Another described working in a low-paid industry: "Basically, my income won't cover daycare, but also if you take away my income (and I become 'stay at home') I have no idea how we continue to make our rent."

Parents weighed in: "I have one child. Daycare for one child where I live cost[s] $2,200 a month. Two thousand two hundred f...ing dollars. If we have another one, I have to quit my job, because it would cost us money for me to go back to work." Another responded: "Even with [health] insurance our little bundle of joy cost twenty thousand dollars and daycare costs seven hundred a month. A second one, no matter how lovely, is completely f...ing out of the question."[2]

These testimonies matched what we found when we investigated our reasons for having children, or not, in the group National Women's Liberation. This chapter is composed of our testimonies.[3]

We found that many of us had postponed children because we were trying to get to a point in our lives where we were secure in a job and a relationship, and financially ready. For some of us the puzzle seemed impossible to assemble, with missing pieces: we faced unpaid leave, unaffordable childcare, financial insecurity, unstable jobs, unreliable male partners, or high health care costs. And some of us felt that if we had children we would be falling into a sexist trap that would squash the other parts of our lives. Others had children despite the obstacles, and then, as one said, "We feel like we're chumps for having our kids anyway."

Many of us faced social pressure to have children—from our parents, our partners, our friends who had kids, coworkers, the drumbeat from the culture, and even anti-abortion zealots. At least in the case of partners, this sometimes tipped the balance toward having kids.

After having one child, many women found that their circumstances were a deterrent to having more, even though some deeply wanted another. We mentioned overly long work hours for us and our partners, the exhaustion of pregnancy and the trauma of childbirth, the difficulty of baby care and the time crunch of child rearing, the expense of childcare, male mates who didn't share the load or even made the work harder, and additional fears and strains due to the bad health of a mate. When we thought about having another child, we found that we wanted to put our limited money or time into other aspects of our lives: housing, jobs or careers, education, health, friendships, relationships, making art or playing music, and feminist or other movement work. So we didn't have a second child, or if we had two, we avoided having a third.

It was hard for us to tell whether, if our conditions were like those in Sweden or France, with guarantees of paid leave, health care, and childcare, we would have more children or not. A few of us said we definitely would, others weren't so sure, but we all agreed that current conditions in the United States were appalling enough to make us hesitate—even those of us who wanted children very badly.

We agreed that this should be described as a slowdown or a strike, because we were responding to bad conditions. True, it wasn't coordinated like a workplace strike and didn't yet have a clear set of demands, but it's still a slowdown in resistance to intolerable working conditions. We joked that we were on an unfair labor practice strike.

Seventeen women testified. Among us were six women of color: three African American and three first-generation immigrants (or 1.5 generation, as those who arrived as children are sometimes called). The rest were European American, second-generation immigrants or more. There were two lesbians, and two women who had been in long-term relationships with women but are now with men. Our ages ranged from twenty-three to seventy, but clustered in the thirties and forties. Our jobs included high school teacher, clerical worker, administrative worker, nurse, pharmacist, lawyer, childcare teacher, union staffer, and librarian, and we were mostly from the South or Northeast, with a few from the Northwest or West.[4] The testimonies have been edited for clarity and length, and reviewed for accuracy by the testifiers. Names and identifying details have been changed.

What are your reasons for wanting children? Reasons for not wanting them? Has your thinking changed?

Mia

In my mid-twenties to early thirties I didn't want children. I'd hear from my sisters, they would cry on the phone to me, about exhaustion and always struggling, one was trying to go to school with a child, it was very hard. I remember I thought, "Oh my god, I do not want to do this." An unplanned pregnancy when I was thirty-two or thirty-three made me change my mind. The thought that this would be my last chance to have a child made me pause about having an abortion, but ultimately I did decide to have the abortion since I had only been with the person, who is now my husband, for four months. So I made a plan to wait for one year to see how the relationship went and to start trying after that.

After I had my daughter Tessa, I *really* didn't want another. I thought there is no way in hell I want to go through this again. But as the trauma of the experience has faded away. [Another testifier: You mean childbirth?] Yes, and being pregnant, and probably the whole year or two after it just all seems like a *very* traumatic experience. And I am turning forty-two this month . . . so I painfully think about whether or not to have another child on a daily basis. I want another child in a deep way that is hard to talk about. Why do I want another one? Why would I introduce more of what seems to be such an exhausting existence with one? I want Tessa to experience being a big sister and the love and camaraderie that comes along with that. I want a family and it just feels like we're not whole with one, and I want to expand the love that is just unexplainable that I have for her. I worry about who will take care of me when I'm old. I worry that it will be a lot to do by herself with two aging parents. I have two sisters that will be part of the difficult aging process that is already happening to my parents.

So why, if I get so emotional, don't I have another child? We finally have reached a point where Tessa will start public school in the fall, and even with after-school care the monthly cost will go down. Maybe we won't have to live so close to paycheck to paycheck and I could maybe buy a massage or even have a vacation. Having another child would mean Carl would have to quit his job to stay home, since that is more cost-effective than paying for infant childcare. . . . I wanted many times to stay home instead of him and this created much resentment and guilt during the first four years until voluntary pre-K which lowered the cost of preschool and made it possible for him to go back to work. There's also summer camp—you don't realize how expensive that is. I can't imagine what I would do if I had two kids, and then one is in diapers. We just couldn't do it. I don't have family support in town. I also don't have maternity leave at my job, so I'd have to eat into my annual leave that I have been holding onto, just in case. I do have flexibility at my job but I know I would pay for it in other ways at work, things would be rough. The toll on my body, exhaustion, sleep deprivation, which I already deal with every night—having a second kid you don't get to go to bed at seven o'clock like I did during my first pregnancy. I can't imagine managing two kids, the way I feel. I feel really tired.

Danielle

I think I always wanted children, no matter hearing my sister's experiences that were very tough or hearing from my feminist sisters. I think I was still very idealistic about kids. I've always loved kids and they've loved me, I've had fun with my nephews, worked in childcare . . .

When I first tried to answer this I was extremely sad and negative about my experience as a parent. A couple of days later I was certainly not overjoyed, but more balanced. Well, having a child—up until recently I didn't think my child liked me very much, like I'd get home from a work trip and he'd say "Go away, Mom." He was mad at me for leaving or maybe mad at me for something else or maybe just being cranky, but it hurt, and I felt like walking on eggshells a lot of the time. . . . I'd think, god, every other kid in the world loves me, except mine.

We've now realized my child has some issues and we're working on them and now I have strategies—something's bothering him and you can fix that something and it's not as bad. . . . I feel less and less like a bomb might explode at any moment and I start to plan things that I want again and not have everything revolve around our child. But a lot of it still revolves around our child: my marriage, how I structure my life, how I structure my time. It feels very individual: my husband's and my project. And now therapy, having access to that, which if you have a problem in your family, working on it is honestly four hours a week [of therapy], so if we didn't have good insurance through my union job we'd be screwed.

And I'm in one of the privileged parts of the working class—got a house, got a good income, got a mate who's trying to do 50 percent and sometimes more, because he's staying home now because he's unemployed. But as far as the overwork and I think the isolation, I would *still* say conditions suck. Your work takes so much out of you and so much is on the parents.

If we had a shorter work week, if we had more support, maybe I'd have more children but I really don't think so because of my experience. It's too much work. It is hard enough to take care of the one that I have right now.

Bernadette

My mother was a stay-at-home mother, my dad worked as a lawyer, and it just seemed shitty. The housework wasn't ever done, it seemed upsetting to her, she didn't seem that happy. When she was young she really wanted to go to medical school and she was very smart and good at science, but her father had blocked her from going because he said she'd be an "old maid." My dad kind of did the same thing to her. He said, you need to stay home and raise the children. By the time I turned eleven or twelve, I think my mother had won the argument. The kids were old enough, she shouldn't have to stay home anymore. At that point she faced age discrimination and sexism. She got several med school interviews and they kept asking, well what about your kids? When she lied and said she didn't have kids, they asked if she was a lesbian. This is in the 1980s, basically the stereotype of the woman trying to get back into the workforce but in this highly aspirational way. Finally, although she didn't want to be in a nurturing profession, she became a nurse practitioner.

Sexism blocked her, and I could feel that from her, she just seemed really angry and resentful, even resentful toward me. I interpreted having kids and being married as limiting my mother's potential, so I was not going to do either. Around twelve I announced I was never getting married. When I did finally get married at thirty-seven, my parents were really happy. My mother never pressured me. It's a wonderful feminist thing she did for me, probably because of what happened to her.

I didn't have kids. I did have an abortion. . . . I wanted to go out and be in the world, have a really interesting life, I saw marriage and children as blocks to that, it just didn't seem possible, there were too many material obstacles. So it's hard to tell, but if I had all those social supports, maybe I would want children.

When I helped my father take care of my mother when she was passing away from cancer, it was really good that I could go in and help, and thinking regretfully I won't have that, I did feel wistfulness. But even that felt like a horrible individual responsibility and it shouldn't be that way. It's like we were trapped, drowning, trying to take care of her, I was grabbing, trying to get social supports, and it was so hard.

Grace

The one time I didn't want to have a kid was when I first got pregnant and I had an abortion. I was nineteen and just wasn't ready to be a parent. I was in a relationship that I thought would continue but I wasn't ready at that moment. I wanted to time having children when I felt more established in my life. But I knew I always wanted to be a mom. I love children, and having been a teacher, I like the child development, seeing children grow. I wanted to be a part of that. So I had in my mind that I wanted to be married, I wanted to have a house, and I wanted to have two kids—a boy and girl, five years apart, so I wouldn't have both kids in diapers and two childcare payments—and it worked out that way, with Flora now fourteen and Jonah nine.

And having prepared the perfect plan to have children, all the reasons that I wanted to be a mom have been fulfilled, and the thing that has been most difficult about being a mom is being a wife. That continues now that I'm divorced.

Did my thinking change? No, that's been the same, even post-divorce. In fact I would say the parenting has been better in terms of the shared parenting post-divorce. Granted, because my kids are older, I will admit you have parenting amnesia, things seem rosier now than they probably did when you have these little kids and you're a little sleep-deprived. But even in my worst parenting moments, screaming at Jonah, "Damn it, why don't you have your socks on? And you're still in your underwear on the stairs—we have to leave for school in five minutes!" That's bad mothering, but even that I could live with, I mean, it's fine.

Divorce is hard. If there's any way to avoid divorce, you should probably do that, but if you're going to do it, the upside is that if you get a good parenting plan, it's awesome. I have a legally mandated 50–50 split. The week they're not there, I'm able to overwork without guilt, I'm able to clean my house and keep it clean for at least a week. Then when I have my kids, I'm able to fully enjoy them. I don't care if the house is dirty 'cause I know in a week I'll have time to clean it again. I don't feel resentful that I'm missing out on something.

While I was in the hospital having Jonah I got fixed [sterilized], 'cause I wanted to just have two. I was in this horrible marriage—Todd was lucky to have even been allowed in the hospital. He asked, "Why do you want to get fixed?" I said, "I don't want to have another child with you, I don't want to have a child with anybody." So just for anybody who thinks I'm too rosy about it, I was conscious of the level of work that it takes to rear children and knew that with two, that's what I, on my own muscle, could do.

Rana

I always wanted a child, always wanted to be a mom. I was a preschool teacher after college, dreamed of adopting a houseful of children. I pursued a difficult professional path that required a lot of hours, so I didn't date. I didn't meet my husband until four or five years ago, after I was established in a career, and in my late thirties I had my daughter. I felt a sense of urgency, I knew I was getting older, and I got pregnant almost right away, so we didn't get to be a couple much without a child. I regret that because I think it's an important part of a relationship. One thing I love, my baby makes it all worthwhile. I come home completely emotionally drained, and she says, "Ta-da, mommy, supwise!" It's work, but I can't put it into words how completely amazing and precious it is.

I always thought I wanted more than one child, but I will be forty-two in June. Now, Aisha's three, and my husband has had health problems. At work, going on maternity leave would be supported, but I'm really, really tired. Working, taking care of a child, dealing with my husband's recent illness, and there's just so much to do all the time that I don't know how I would do it with another baby, materially, logistically, how that would work. When my husband Kabir was really sick recently, one week when he was in the ICU, I had clinic, my daughter was in daycare, and he was going into surgery. I didn't even have time to call my friends to tell them I needed help. It shouldn't be like this!

I need to work fewer hours; I would like to have health benefits whether I work or not; I wish I'd had more maternity leave, at least a year, then I wanted to go back to half time. I want there to be places where people bring their children and their families and there's food—healthy free food—and the kids can play together and you can eat supper. I want that much societal help. I want free daycare, after-school care, health care. The hardest part of my day isn't taking care of a terminally ill patient; it's coming home and deciding what to make for supper.

Bernice

I do want kids. Why don't I have them yet? The incredible amount of work I hear and see, tiredness—it's hard to turn back. What if it's more tasks and not enough joy, task after task? And what if the partnership doesn't work and it becomes a single project and not a joint project?

Growing up with a black parent and a white parent, I really felt like it was an ongoing struggle that for many years couldn't be articulated, of identity: who are you, where are you? I really desire to raise a black child that is part of a black movement or, even if they're not, someone who's very clear about who they are, what family they're part of, who they are in the world.

I don't want to feel like it's just me. I feel like I do everything by myself, even at work. I don't desire it enough to do it without a clear and strong attachment [to a partner]. I have been fighting with this ex-partner—the only reason we are not together is the question of having children. Do I want to have kids? I already feel so overwhelmed, maybe I shouldn't.

Beatrice

I grew up with my mom and grandma and grandpa. My father was by artificial insemination. Mom was thirty and wanted to have a kid and decided she was not going to wait for someone to do this project with.

The only time I wanted kids was when my grandma died last summer and we were able to keep her out of a nursing home and be with her the whole time. It would be great if I could do that for my mom and have that for myself. Other than that, the rest of my life has been completely shadowed—I've been trying *not* to have kids forever.

I'm from South Dakota, and the anti-abortion people are so ruthless it's not a joke. They had this big van with a giant picture of blood and a dead baby parked at my public high school for two and a half years—these totally terrorizing tactics against young women. I had no idea about abortion, and I was not subjected to abstinence-only sex education, I had real sex ed, but I thought abortion entailed this big bloody fetus that I would see.

The idea of having kids is so far removed from anything that I want. I work at a preschool, and I just see the minutes fall out of people's lives. You don't get that back. I have no time for myself as it is, I work three jobs. I want to have time to work on these paintings that I have half-finished and read all these things that I want to read. There's no way I'd be able to do that with a kid. And the people that I know who have children, don't have, well, interests. "My kid, work." "You don't want to read? Go on a trip?" "Oh yeah, vacation, I wish." It sounds terrible, it sounds really bad.

Maybe it wouldn't be so bad if we had all these social support systems but I don't even know how to conceptualize that because it seems so bleak. I see these parents that have a great kid and a great relationship, it seems, and they still say, "Oh, I'm exhausted," "Oh, we don't spend any time together." Plus I don't think I ever want to sleep with men ever again. I've found much more fulfilling partners with women.

I notice that the gay agenda, when it was shoved into this monogamous-marriage-you-can-adopt-a-child framework, then it became OK. When homosexuality became part of having kids and raising kids, then it became acceptable. One of the things I like about being in a lesbian relationship is I can't accidentally get pregnant.

Nona

I didn't have children, though I expected to. When I was very young, my mother's friend got me a job in a newborn nursery, trying to interest me in nursing, and I observed a couple of births. In the 1960s there was the episiotomy,[5] it horrified me. Basically I wasn't interested until about age thirty-six, but then I didn't have a partner. By the time I did have a partner, we still lived kind of low-[rent] but I guess there have been choices that I made, not just that I couldn't afford it. When I got together with Nadine—this would have been at the very end of the possibility of getting pregnant—we could either afford to buy a house or we could afford to have a child, and I picked the house.

Also, my best friend from college—she's heterosexual, same age as me—had saved money, went for those fertility treatments, and when it didn't work, she decided to adopt. Her children, while lovable, are so difficult that this woman, who I have tried to figure out life with since age eighteen, stopped reading. I was horrified by that and still am. . . . I'm sorry that I didn't have a child, but a child under supportive circumstances, which at present do not exist in this country . . . when I think of what work would be required and what I would have had to give up. I am sorry that I didn't give my parents grandchildren. I was an only child, and they were very disappointed.

Elena

Mom was one of seven, dad was one of nine, I grew up in a community of changing my aunt's baby when I was little, and our grandparents lived above us in [a South American country]. . . . It was a huge family. It felt like raising me was a collective effort—though from mostly women—but collective nonetheless. I had a really great childhood experience with that, and it has shaped my perception of child rearing. My mom was always a working mom, so she was not necessarily always present; my dad was more involved. My sister has two sons—she actually gave birth two weeks ago. I witnessed the horrific [births]—it was really scary.

Part of the reason I want children is expectations from my family. I think it's hard to accept that, but it's true. I'd like to give them grandchildren, and the pressure is on me to not wait too long, I want them to be young enough to enjoy them.

Also, I definitely love children. I think my partner would be a great dad. We have a good group of friends, and we have this ongoing joke that we're all going to have children at the same time. I feel like that would be so awesome.

But there's a lot of reasons for me not to want children. I mean, the struggles that I hear from my own sister but also my feminist sisters on parenting. It scares the shit out of me to have a child and not be in control of how their life is going to turn out. I'm also fearful that our future is pretty bleak, and that I'm going to have a kid that's going to inherit a crappy world with no clean water and a destroyed environment.

And there are the selfish reasons of not being able to fulfill my goals and my life and my potential because if I have a child, that's all going to have to stop. So I'm afraid of that. I'm the only person [in my family] that's going to go to graduate school. In a superficial way, I'm the successful kid that's doing things, and I want to keep doing those things to fulfill that promise for my parents, who are immigrants. I want to get the trophy to show it to them, and I feel like maybe a kid will stop that.

There's also no social support in this country. I always feel like as an immigrant I was lied to, because I felt like moving to the U.S. was going to be so great, but especially for motherhood, for parenting, it's so awful, and honestly—no paid parental leave, no daycare that's mandated—there's just no social support structure at all. And my family's not here, either, so my kids would not have the beautiful collective child-rearing experience that I did.

Kathleen

I did not ever want to have children. I've been a preschool teacher since age twenty. That's my passion and the work that I am driven to do, and do best, but I didn't want to have my own children. I had an accidental pregnancy with someone that I loved who did not know his biological family. . . . He was adopted and does not like, or feel close to, his parents or his sister. And in that moment of loving him and knowing that he was going to be such a good father—and he is—I made the decision to keep the pregnancy.

Motherhood makes me feel like I have a split personality. I have a fabulous son. I was so fortunate to have someone that I enjoy being with and who is so like me in so many ways, but his attachment to me is overwhelming and stifling. I feel claustrophobic, and it makes me feel so guilty, because he's giving me so much love, but at times it feels like: fourteen-year-old boyfriend. His existence has stolen everything in terms of me having the time to pursue my creative self, and it made my relationship [with my partner] into a thing where I don't feel a connection to that man anymore besides loving him as a father. It's so hard because I can so deeply regret my choice but never want to not have made it in the same breath.

Miriam

I'm thirty, in a long-term relationship, but do not have children. At various times I have wanted and not wanted children but regardless of what I want, I think that I will have children. Having children feels like an inevitability, like a truck with no brakes going downhill and headed toward a boulder.

I grew up with the idea that that's what you do, you grow up, get a job, have kids. I just wanted to be normal, even though it's really not that normal in my family, I have three aunts and an uncle and none of them have children. Still I grew up with the idea that that's what you do.

I can't remember wanting them for sentimental reasons or maternal instinct kicking in. I don't see kids on the street and feel any pull like I think others do. And I don't really think it's worth it without that urge to have children because when I try to envision what my life would be like, I think I would always be exhausted: waking up early to get the kids ready for school, dropping them off, going straight to work, working all day, coming home late and not getting to see them because I work late and they're already asleep, and figuring out how the kids will get from 3:00 p.m. school dismissal to 8:00 p.m. bedtime when I have to work the whole time. How much it will cost to do all that . . . and then not being able to go to the gym, or out with friends, or a date night with Nick. You only really give these things up if you want to spend time with a kid, and I don't really. Life is stressful enough.

But I think I will end up having kids anyway. Nick wants kids, and I love him, so I want him to have that opportunity. Our families want grandkids, and I just don't feel like I have the courage to go against the grain on that. It sounds crazy, but it almost feels easier to have a kid. I don't like rebutting the presumption all the time, explaining it to every- one, why you don't want kids. I feel like it makes me sound like I am a selfish, unloving person.

Then there's exclusion from things later on, your friends having kids, and organizing their lives that way and I wouldn't be a part of it, being left out, the whole way your life is supposed to go. It would feel like con- stant resistance and it just doesn't really feel worth it.

If motherhood were easier, if I wouldn't be so pressed for time, if I had a shorter workday, inexpensive and good options for childcare and school, maybe the pressures I feel from other people and the world in general wouldn't weigh on me so heavily. Maybe the theoretical promise of fulfillment or meaning or purpose of having kids would outweigh the burdens and then maybe I would actually look forward to having kids even though I don't have a strong desire for them.

Fiona

I want to create a family. I had a really crazy, insane, unstable childhood, with multiple divorces, terrible stepfather, losing my mom, and never feeling like I fit into a family, so a lot of it is wanting to create my own family, these little kids that are going to love me and my husband, and that this is our core unit. It feels secure to me in a way, even though I know it's not secure—I should know that from my [situation] growing up. It's creating the family I didn't have.

Now my friends in New York are all starting to get pregnant. We had a dinner party Thursday, so different from what it was three to four years ago when we were all talking about guys and hooking up. Now it's morning sickness and can you believe my husband said this, and I left early and cried in my car the whole way home. . . . I'm totally being left behind. I can love their kids, but I'm not part of the group anymore, all of their lives are centered on kids. And I want that too, so I do feel really sad.

There's so much individual responsibility . . . the hustle that I have to think about if I have them. I just had to move out of my apartment because it was a total crisis and it was rent stabilized, and my rent is $500 more a month now. How am I going to pay for daycare?

I have to think about having them on my own. . . . I've had all these different affairs but no guy has wanted to work on things enough to make it be a good relationship. I could go on about how I feel like I'm probably pretty demanding and guys back out because of that. Maybe I should just move back to [a midwestern state] and have my parents help. I've been offered jobs there, but then I think of all the things I'm giving up to have a kid—should I have to give all that much up? And why do I want them so bad that I'm willing to leave so much to do it? One of my biggest demands on this is if men were better. So I'm in this limbo . . . there are all these things I have to factor in, whereas if we had universal daycare, I could probably have a kid right now, to be honest.

Bettina

When I was younger, I didn't like children. I worked at an education center for five years, and dealt with babies and children every day. I had no interest in them. I wanted independence, and children just seemed like a drag. Then when got older I did start to want to have a kid, but I put it off, because I worried about money, not being able to afford health care, not having paid leave, and the cost of childcare. I also worried about whether my husband was really going to put in the work. And I was at a point in my life where my younger brother was having a lot of problems . . . and seeing the difficulty that my parents were going through with that. Probably if there were more social supports I would have had a kid one to two years earlier.

I had Luca, despite the worries, about two and a half years ago. I would say I have zero desire for a second kid right now. I thought I wanted to have two kids in the abstract, but . . . I'm kind of doing OK, and Nathan and I are kind of doing OK, but it's like the water is up to your neck. The thought of another kid is just being swallowed up and going under, like a vortex. I just think it would be too hard, even the thought of it makes me feel nauseous. If there were no abortions available, I can imagine myself looking into getting a back-alley abortion if I got pregnant right now.

I feel bad saying that because it sounds like Luca, or having a kid, is such a burden, but I just feel if I had more resources and time, even if our conditions were better, I would want to put those resources and time and energy into my own quality of life, my own mental health, and being able to put that into my [relationship with my] husband and the child that I have and not another one.

Loretta

I have always wanted children. I can't remember a time when I questioned this. . . . But, even with this intense want that I have for children, I don't just want a child, I want a family. Most of my life I thought that even if I didn't have a partner (which has always seemed the most likely outcome) that I would still have children. At this point, this isn't what I want. I have chosen not to have a child without a partner, not because I think that would make everything perfect or easy, but I think most of the time it does make it easier—even when the man doesn't do much—because there is another brain, someone with whom to share the emotions, another set of hands, and it would be difficult for me to raise a child without another paycheck too. I make enough money to take care of myself comfortably, but when I think about how much kids cost, it would be a struggle. Most of my fear around choosing to be a single parent is around time and money—what would maternity leave look like, how will I figure out and pay for childcare, how will I manage my time working and still be an available, present parent? And all of that makes me worry about being emotionally available, that all my time would be spent figuring out the logistics and the finances, so I would basically be working much harder to have a child with whom I then couldn't even spend time. I know that lots of women raise children on their own . . . but I do want to *try* to have what I want—a family—without creating more hardships or obstacles than what children and partnership already produce. I just don't see children as an option in my current situation.

What's changed for me is that I definitely thought I would already have kids by this age, and now I think that if I'm lucky I might be able to have one kid, when I always wanted two or three or even four. I think that my view of motherhood has become more realistic, because most of my friends now have children, so I've realized single parenting is not the right option for me. Now I work on accepting that I probably won't ever have a family, that it is just me.

I try to listen to reasons my friends give for not wanting children. One of the things that I hear is that kids will limit what they want to do in life, but when I think about raising a kid I think about all of the potential.

Kim

I didn't have children and I'm forty-nine. When I was younger I did think it would be fabulous to have someone who is a combination of me and my mate—sort of a concrete version of our relationship. But my husband and I were living a bit on the edge, about fifteen years with no health insurance at all, and when we did get it, it was bad. Ken was against having a kid because it would be financially hard and he'd have to work a lot more, and I would have to work more too, so then would we even have time to be with a child? And I think also that he knew he'd be required to do his share, so he didn't have any illusions, which may have made him less enthusiastic.

I thought having a kid might be great but did not feel an urge about it until my father died—and also my uncle and my mom's husband—all in three years. This happened when I was around thirty-five. I really had a sense of a generation passing away and no one to replace it, to carry on the family stories. So we stopped using birth control. But we had crappy insurance with high deductibles (around $6,000 per person) and we had to buy special insurance each year to cover a potential childbirth, plus they specifically wouldn't cover anything to do with my reproductive organs due to a preexisting condition. All that really deterred me from investigating why we weren't getting pregnant, and I was ambivalent because of the money and work problems.

I do worry that there will be no one who cares enough to watch out for me when I'm old. Now my aunt Kathleen at eighty-seven, my mother's older sister, is going through medical emergencies and my mother, who is seventy-eight, has been living in a motel in Alabama for many months next to the nursing home, battling inattentive doctors and penny-pinching administrators. Kathleen's sons who live far away have each visited for a couple of days, but only when they expected her to die imminently—one is in very bad health himself. So I guess having kids is no guarantee they'll help, or be able to help. It would be less of a worry if we had a better system of eldercare and health care, where the workers were paid well and there were enough staff and decent shifts, but as it is, it can really border on torture.

Cathy

Growing up I assumed I'd be a mom. After college I was a nanny, and for the first time I didn't want to be a mom. As a nanny I was responsible for three little boys for sixty hours a week. I always fed them breakfast, and sometimes I put them to bed. I loved seeing them, but I felt completely exhausted at the end of the day—and I had zero financial responsibility for them. It scared me. I thought that instead of parenting, I'd just be a good aunt. But that feeling changed when I stopped my job as a nanny and moved to another state to go to graduate school.

I missed the boys I'd nannied; I missed them so much that I cried on and off for weeks. I missed having them in my life. . . . That experience taught me how precious a relationship with a child can be, and I assume that I would love my own child more. So after I moved away, I decided that I wanted to be a parent.

We could be good stable parents. . . . The problem was, we couldn't afford it. Both my husband and I were in graduate school. We talked about having a child during school because my school offered reduced-price daycare, but it seemed too stressful to study and parent. And I was supposed to have internships in the summer, which would mean that we'd have to come up with childcare. We assumed we could afford to be parents when we graduated.

But when we graduated we couldn't find work, and we had student loans that were due. I worked temporary jobs and put my loans in defer-ment. My husband found part-time work. About eight months after grad-uating, my husband was offered a full-time job in our home state. We moved home. His job wound up being terrible. I found work, and he found another job. Meanwhile, we're getting older; he's thirty-eight, I'm thirty-two.

Now we both have full-time work, health insurance, and time off. My work doesn't have maternity leave, but I have stashed some leave time. We have a lot of debt, but we have come up with a budget where we think we could afford to have a kid. The problem now is that we don't seem to be physically able to make a kid. We're not sure what's wrong, but I know that we can't afford IVF, or hormone shots, or really anything extra. (I'm also afraid of the impact that something like that would have on my ability to work.) We're barely going to be able to afford to raise a child—we didn't set aside money in our budget to make one.

We still want to be parents, but I'm not willing to get a loan to do it. We're applying to adopt through the foster care system, which is free (unlike private adoptions, which can easily be $40,000 or more).

Ondine
My whole life I thought I'd have a kid, I'm the oldest of three girls, my mom is one of nine, and her mother, even though she was married, her husband kind of disappeared at some point. So she taught us from as

far back as I can remember that there was an order of things: you go to school, you get a job, you get married, you have a kid. When I was nineteen, I got pregnant. I was in school, and I was with a guy I didn't want to have a kid with, nor see myself with long term, so I decided I did not want to have his baby, and I had an abortion. Part of that, when you have a kid, like it or not, you're potentially connected to that person for the rest of your life.

Then I did meet someone who I fell in love with and married, and I wanted to have kids with him, for sentimental stuff: embodiment and reflection of our love, and I wanted my mom to be a grandma. This is her first, and possibly only, grandkid. So, I assumed I would have more than one kid, 'cause I'm one of three, and I can't imagine not having my sisters. I'm very close to them.

The pregnancy was uneventful (except I had to have a C-section) but my husband spent my whole pregnancy neurotic and worried. He thought I was going to die. Then when I had the C-section and he was in the room for that, he was so terrified. . . . And the first week I was home with Sarah, I remember saying to him, "Did we make a horrible mistake having this baby?" because it was like our whole world had been turned upside-down. Mind you, when we brought Sarah home, my sister was in between jobs, so she lived with us for three months. My mother was switching careers, so she was spending weekends [with us], and my mother in law is retired so she was over as much as possible. Those are all three women who I love dearly, who I love having in my home, and they were cooking . . . you want to talk about the perfect conditions to bring a child into—but it was emotionally hard and the hardest part was my relationship with Kevin.

Honestly, the mommy stuff has been—I have a kid that sleeps through the night, I have this wonderful creature who I love, I want to have another one. But Kevin is like, "Absolutely not." For me, the reasons for not having another child more have to do with sexism, and his reasons are more capitalism. For me, it's having time for myself. If we're both at home, part of it is, Sarah comes to me when she wants something, she doesn't go to her dad. The money stuff, we're lucky in the sense that I don't have to be home with my kid, she's home with my mother-in-law, who I know loves her as much as I do. There is something about, especially for me as a person of color, wanting my kid to be around people of color as opposed to—I live in [a small southern town] with a bunch of white people. There's something about having my kid raised by someone specifically from my community.

The main thing for me as far as why we're probably only having the one is—Kevin has his own neuroses, but my neurosis is that he doesn't take care of himself, and at some point the likelihood of me being a single parent is pretty high as far as him dying. And so I feel like I can do one by myself, but anything more than that would just be impossible.

CHAPTER 4

COMSTOCKERY TO THE BABY BOOM

Feminists have debated the motives for birth control and abortion laws ever since these laws were first instituted in the nineteenth century. Are governments trying to push us into marriage? Keep us pregnant to prevent us from competing with men for jobs? Control women's sexuality? Do they want us to produce more children? A look at our history indicates that while some things are new in our present situation, it is not new to argue that these laws are aimed at keeping up reproduction. Nor is it new for some feminists to insist that these laws are merely a mistake on the part of the powerful and that a leadership enlightened by our logic would abolish them.

The U.S. birth rate steadily declined throughout the 1800s, with white women having an average of seven children in 1800, declining to 3.56 in 1900. Black women's births also showed a decline, but started higher, at around eight children in 1800 (though figures from the era of slavery are unreliable), and declining to 5.6 by 1900. There was no baby boom after the Civil War, which killed at least 2 percent of the U.S. population.[1]

For most of the nineteenth century, abortion was unregulated or slightly regulated, but not illegal. Contraception mostly involved douches, pessaries, condoms, and withdrawal, and was subject to virtually no regulation. That changed in 1873 when Congress banned both contraception and abortion with the Comstock Law. Not only was manufacturing or advertising contraception made illegal, possession or even discussion of it was also made illegal.[2]

Why did Congress pass Comstock? Some historians say they were primarily worried about obscenity and driven by a puritanical urge to suppress anything to do with sex. The law was championed by Anthony

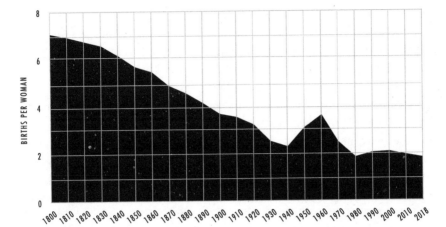

U.S. birth rate, 1800–2018. Data from Jay Weinstein and Vijayan K. Pillai, *Demography: The Science of Population* (Lanham, MD: Rowman and Littlefield, 2016), 208, and National Center for Health Statistics *Births, Final Data for 2016.*

Comstock, a founder of the New York Society for the Suppression of Vice. But, as we'll see, many feminists who lived under Comstock thought that raising the birth rate was an important goal of the law.

Discussions of abortion in the 1860s are peppered with references to declining birth rates. State laws against abortion were enacted by men worried that women were "avoiding the duties and responsibilities of married life" resulting in smaller families.[3] They feared that women were abandoning their child-rearing work at home to get jobs or take up careers. And they worried that Protestant, native-born women were using abortion to limit births, while Catholics and recent immigrants were having lots of children. "Shall we permit our broad and fertile prairies to be settled only by the children of aliens?" asked an Ohio Senate select committee convened in 1867. If not, the committee said, native-born women must be convinced not to have abortions by making the practice illegal.[4]

In 1800, the United States had no laws about abortion. But in the absence of pregnancy tests, the distinction between abortion and contraception was less clear than it is today. Medical books designed for home use recommended various "preventatives," alongside recipes and instructions to restore menstrual regularity, should a period become "blocked." Later, ads for "periodical pills" or "lunar pills" offered to restore regularity.[5] Starting in the 1830s some states and territories gradually enacted statutes forbidding abortion, but they were generally aimed at punishing practitioners who accidentally caused women's deaths. Following English common law, the new laws generally defined abortion as after "quickening," when a pregnant woman first feels the fetus move, around eighteen to twenty weeks. Before quickening, it wasn't regarded as abortion. And quickening relied on the woman's report, so later abortions were hard to prove, and rarely prosecuted unless the woman died.

Before 1840, abortion was widely considered to be an uncommon procedure used by unmarried women to conceal premarital affairs. As such, it was regarded with some sympathy by medical practitioners. But by the 1840s and '50s, ads for pills and services fed a growing demand, and doctors and legislators became worried that abortion was being used by married women who wanted smaller families, or, as a Michigan doctor put it, there was "widespread determination on the part of many who are married to avoid the labor of caring for and rearing children."[6]

"Almost every neighborhood or small village," fretted a Detroit physicians group, "has its old woman . . . who is known for her ability and willingness for a pecuniary consideration" to provide an abortion.[7]

Ads peddled pills or elixirs, and some purveyors guaranteed that if those didn't work to bring back your period the seller would provide a cure, presumably through physical intervention. The most famous abortionist, Madame Restell, made such a guarantee. She operated in New York starting in the 1830s, with only intermittent legal trouble, until she was arrested by Comstock in 1878. Drug companies made money selling abortifacient pills, and newspapers relied on advertising revenue from Restell and hundreds of others.

The first organized opposition to abortion came from the ranks of regular medical doctors, a profession then struggling to gain respect. These men wanted to stamp out their competition among the irregular doctors, "doctoresses," midwives, and herbalists who generally dealt with abortion. They sought to convince legislators that scientifically there was no bright line between an "unquick" fetus and a quick one. Still, most people were unconcerned. According to historian James Mohr, the doctors spent decades trying to get the clergy and the press to come out against abortion.

One argument that got traction was the concern that the married birth rate was going down, especially among U.S.-born Protestants. Horatio Storer, a regular doctor, led the charge in the late 1850s to get the newly formed American Medical Association to lobby for abortion laws. While he mostly wrote for a medical audience, his 1866 book *Why Not? A Book for Every Woman* tried to convince women not to get abortions. He made various moral and medical arguments, but a major argument was that families were becoming smaller: "Instances of an excess over three or four children are not nearly as common as we know was the case a generation or two back."[8]

"In so far as depends upon the American and native element," Storer wrote, "and in the absence of the existing immigration from abroad, the population of our older states . . . is stationary or decreasing." He also noted with alarm that abortions were "infinitely more frequent among Protestant women than among Catholic."[9] And he expressed the view—then general among doctors—that there were now many more abortions among the married than the unmarried.

Edwin Hale, a prominent homeopathic doctor, wrote a book against abortion in 1867 called *The Great Crime of the Nineteenth Century*. Hale gave the birth rate as his first reason for opposing abortion: "It is a crime against the State. It lessens the population of a State or country, in an appalling degree. . . . At this rate, if the ratio of total deaths over births goes on increasing, it will not be many years before the Americans left on American soil, will be few and far between . . . the national government ought to interpose some check to its alarming increase."[10]

Storer and the AMA's arguments finally gained adherents after the Civil War. The *New York Tribune* quoted Storer's nativist argument in 1868, and a grand jury, citing the *Tribune* editorial, demanded a public foundling hospital in New York, with the goal of saving "some of those native American babies by assuring the mothers who did not want them that they would be cared for if allowed to be born," writes Mohr.[11]

This reflected a hunger for laborers. Starting in the 1850s, destitute children, abundant in big cities like New York and Boston, were scooped up by religious do-gooders and sent "to the country" to be adopted by farm families who needed workers. "Orphan Trains" whisked children hundreds of miles west or south, even though many were not orphans—their parents just didn't make enough money to care for them.[12] Of the receiving families, one critical Illinois newspaper wrote in 1858 that they wouldn't *think* of having slaves, "Oh mercy, no! . . . and yet the whole truth be told, it is to fill the office of servants [that] they want [these children]." In 1882, a North Carolina orphanage superintendent, J.H. Mills, criticized the Children's Aid Society, the largest of the orphan train organizations, saying "Men needing labor, their slaves being set free, take these boys and treat them like slaves."[13]

The AMA eventually even won denunciations of abortion in the newspapers. After the end of the Civil War, the *New York Times* ran a series of grisly articles about women who died due to the malpractice of abortion quacks. Between 1860 and 1880, forty states and territories enacted anti-abortion laws, and they were much stricter than previous statutes. They erased the quickening doctrine, many outlawed advertising, and some held the woman criminally liable, which was unheard of in earlier legislation. By the time Anthony Comstock started lobbying for federal anti-obscenity legislation, abortion was illegal in most of the country. Contrary to the impression left by some accounts, the Comstock Law was not the accomplishment of one freakishly effective prude, but the triumph of a crackdown decades in the making against women who were curbing their reproduction.

Comstock himself was no lone nut. He had financial support from many wealthy citizens, among them Samuel Colgate, owner of the Colgate soap company.[14] With the federal law, Comstock maneuvered himself into the position of a special federal agent. With the whole country as his jurisdiction, he and his minions proceeded to conduct a reign of terror against abortion providers, purveyors of birth control advice, feminist and anarchist speakers, free-love advocates, novelists who mentioned sex, and booksellers, including those who sold medical texts with anatomy diagrams he deemed obscene. Pills, potions, devices, and information on birth control could no longer be sold or sent through the mail.

Twenty-four state legislatures went on to pass mini-Comstock laws and fourteen states, including New York and New Jersey, "went beyond the federal law to criminalize private conversations among individuals about contraceptive methods. . . . In seventeen states and the District of Columbia, no doctor might advise on birth control even in the course of treatment of a patient."[15] Abortion advertising ceased. Madame Restell committed suicide after Comstock arrested her in 1878.

Still, the birth rate fell.

In 1905, as president, Theodore Roosevelt launched an attack on women for using birth control, jump-starting the national debate about "race suicide."[16] In an address to the National Congress of Mothers, he charged that women were selfish to limit their births, and as worthy of contempt as military deserters: "The existence of women of this type forms one of the most unpleasant and unwholesome features of modern life . . . if the average family . . . contained but two children the nation as a whole would decrease in population so rapidly that in two or three generations it would very deservedly be on the point of extinction."[17]

Sanger and Comstock

Margaret Sanger is such a towering figure in the fight for birth control that even today she is attacked by anti–birth control forces. The up-to-date

attack is that she was a racist whose goal for birth control was the elimination of black people, and a eugenicist who advocated "more from the
fit, less from the unfit"—a statement she never made.[18]

Sanger's Irish immigrant mother died at age forty-nine after eighteen pregnancies. Sanger was sixth of the eleven children who survived.
In her thirties, Sanger worked as a visiting nurse in New York City, where
she was involved in the Socialist Party and the Industrial Workers of the
World, and wrote columns for the *New York Call*, the socialist daily newspaper. By day she scheduled obstetrical visits in New York's immigrant
communities. She was appalled by how little information women had
about their bodies and shaken by the deaths she witnessed from unrelieved childbearing and botched abortions.

Sanger first ran afoul of Comstock when the post office's anti-vice
department stopped an issue of *The Call* from going through the mail
because it contained a column she had written on how women could
avoid sexually transmitted diseases. The newspaper was forced to dis-
continue her column but printed a blank space under her title, "What
Every Girl Should Know," with the caption "NOTHING! By order of the
Post Office Department."[19]

Sanger's campaign to make birth control a birthright would result in
jailings and a year of exile in Europe, during which she took the opportunity to learn about new birth control techniques in Holland and England,
where the laws were no longer as strict. Her direct action and trials, and
the organizing of countless others, slowly broke down the Comstock
regime during the 1920s and '30s.

Sanger and her compatriots understood that their opponents were
motivated by, among other things, the desire for a larger population.
Introducing the first issue of the *Birth Control Review*, the editors wrote:

> This Review comes into being . . . to render articulate the aspiration
> of humanity toward conscious and voluntary motherhood. . . . But
> those to whose advantage it is that the people breed abundantly,
> well intrenched in our social and political order, are not going to
> surrender easily to the popular will. Already they are organizing
> their resistance and preparing their mighty engines of repression
> to stop the march of progress while it is yet time.[20]

While Sanger was in exile in 1915, her husband William was arrested
by Anthony Comstock himself after giving a birth control pamphlet to a
police agent who posed as an ally.[21] Mr. Sanger told the court, "I deny the
right of the State to compel the poor and disinherited to rear large families,

driving their offsprings into child labor when they should be at school and at play."[22] An abundant supply of children was useful to employers, not just because they were dexterous and inexpensive workers, but because they could drive down the wages of all workers. Children's lower wages undermined those of their parents, driving a cycle of desperation in families and leading them to send more children out to work. William Sanger served thirty days in jail rather than pay a fine.

Black Women and Comstock

Economic exploitation and repression against blacks in the South, including lynchings and massacres, meant that many African Americans relocated to urban areas in the North and Midwest. The steady flow became a flood during World War I. During this time of rapid urbanization, black women were having fewer children too, and feminist scholar Jesse M. Rodrique writes with irritation that "researchers who explain this phenomenon insist that contraception played a minimal role, believing that blacks had no interest in the control of their own fertility." Rodrique uncovers plenty of evidence that black women were practicing birth control, not just in their declining birth rates but in the many recipes passed around among women and, after Comstock was weakened, in ads for contraceptives in black newspapers.[23]

The Comstock Law was a topic of vigorous debate in black-run newspapers and lecture halls. The Women's Political Association of Harlem held a lecture series with birth control among the topics in 1918, and in 1923 the Harlem Community Forum invited Margaret Sanger to speak on the subject. Black newspapers carried editorials in favor of birth control, and abortion, though illegal, was prevalent. A 1938 survey estimated that 28 percent of black women had had abortions, remarkably similar to the rate for all U.S. women now.[24] Sanger's *Birth Control Review* published three issues for black audiences, and Sanger helped set up a black-run clinic in Harlem.

While black nationalist Marcus Garvey opposed birth control and the Universal Negro Improvement Association passed a resolution opposing it in 1934, most black activist intellectuals on the left like W.E.B. Du Bois, Hubert Harrison, and Mary McLeod Bethune supported birth control. Bethune and Du Bois, along with E. Franklin Frazier, Adam Clayton Powell, and Walter White served on an advisory board of Planned Parenthood. Du Bois supported birth control from a position of feminism. In 1920 he wrote: "The future woman must have a life work and economic independence. She must have knowledge. She must have the right of motherhood at her own discretion."[25]

African Americans fought to get equal access to the birth control information and devices that were becoming available to white women. As a result, by the 1930s, many black-led birth control clinics existed in both northern and southern cities. At the same time, black activists denounced efforts to legalize involuntary sterilization, which at the time was aimed at people in jails and mental institutions, the unemployed, and those receiving public relief. "It behooves us to watch the law and the courts and stop the spread of the habit," Du Bois wrote in 1936.[26] (Du Bois was prescient, as we'll see in chapter 8, Reproduction and Race).

While the depiction of Sanger as a white supremacist is wrong, she did, like many of her white and even black contemporaries, subscribe to eugenics, the elitist idea that "superior" humans breed more "superior" humans. This was not only, or even necessarily, a racist position. Its bigotry was broader, decrying childbearing among the destitute, the disabled (those with epilepsy, deafness), alcoholics, the mentally ill, and those regarded as "feebleminded," a category that included anyone stamped as socially undesirable. Adding confusion, Sanger and others applied the term "eugenics" to things we might think of today as common sense, like wider spacing of births and fewer births overall to protect women and their infants from the toll of unrelieved pregnancy, or permitting women with tuberculosis to use birth control to protect their health.

Black leaders of the time had their own eugenic views, although a movement "based on classist, nativist, and racist assumptions . . . had obvious ideological limitations for people of African descent," writes historian Michele Mitchell.[27] Du Bois worried that the "masses" were having more children than the "classes."[28] The poisonous fog of eugenics distorted thinking everywhere.

At the same time, black and white women, immigrant and native born, all were eager for information on how to control their fertility. Rich women had small families, what was their secret? Anarchist speaker Emma Goldman carried copies of Sanger's *The Woman Rebel* (a predecessor to the *Birth Control Review*) when she gave what she called her "Birth Strike" lecture. After a talk in Schenectady, New York, in May 1914 she wrote to Sanger, "Not one of my lectures brings out such a crowd as the one on the birth strike and it is the same with the W.R. [*Woman Rebel*]. It sells better than anything we have."[29] Goldman was arrested and given fifteen days in the workhouse for speaking on the topic, and her boy-friend, physician Ben Reitman, received sixty days on one occasion and on another was fined $1,000 and served six months in jail for distribut-ing birth control pamphlets.[30] While it is sometimes portrayed as silly prudishness, Comstock repression was no joke.

Feminists Debate Comstock

Even in the face of exhortations by the president to have more chil-dren, some feminists argued that birth control was not really a target of the Comstock laws. Contraception, they said, had gotten swept up in anti-obscenity campaigning designed to protect young people from pornography.

Feminist birth control advocate Mary Ware Dennett makes this case in her 1926 book *Birth Control Laws: Should We Keep Them, Change Them or Abolish Them?* She claims that the anti-contraceptive portions of the Comstock Law were a blunder by a Congress which took no time to debate the consequences: "For over half a century the people of the United States have been the victims of a great error which Anthony Comstock and Congress unwittingly committed in connection with their commendable effort to free the young people of the country from con-tamination by those who were then trafficking extensively in smutty literature and inducements to sex perversion."[31]

She argues that Comstock himself "had no intention of penalizing normal birth control information." Congress never intended to restrict the actions and words of respectable people like doctors, she writes.[32] Perhaps Dennett, like later feminists, is using this argument disingenu-ously to sway fence-sitters. Her argument certainly has echoes in Planned Parenthood arguments today that, because readily available contraception reduces abortions, it's a blunder for anti-abortion forces to oppose both.

But Dennett's assertions are contradicted by Comstock's sting opera-tions aimed at anyone who advertised or distributed popular birth control methods. And they don't explain how dozens of state legislatures made this same blunder, with most explicitly extending the ban to doctors, or how this "error" had managed to persist for what was then half a century against widespread criticism and organized challenge.

Other feminists had no doubt that the Comstock Law was designed to raise the birth rate. Feminist sociologist Leta Hollingworth argued in 1916 that both legal and social devices were being used to "compel women to keep up the birth rate" including forbidding "the communica-tion of the data of science in the matter of the means of birth control."[33]

Of Comstock specifically, she wrote: "The American laws are very drastic on this point. . . . They conscript women to bear children by legally prohibiting the publication and communication of the knowledge that would make childbearing voluntary."

In addition to suppressing birth control information, Hollingworth cites other "inexpensive" devices deployed to encourage maternity, including an educational system "drilling into the young and uninformed mind . . . such facts and notions as would give the girl a conception of herself only as future wife and mother," and art, poetry, and fiction "replete with happy and adoring mothers."

Maternal "instincts" needed a lot of shoring up with social pressure. "While affirming the essential nature of women to be satisfied with maternity and maternal duties only," Hollingworth writes, "society has always taken every precaution to close the avenues to ways of escape therefrom."[34]

Other feminists agreed with Hollingworth that the goal of the Comstock Law was increased population, although in some cases they underestimated the opposition. Suffragist and socialist lawyer Crystal Eastman wrote during World War I: "No genuine human interest will be against the repeal of [the Comstock Law]. Of course capitalism thrives on an over-supplied labor market, but with our usual enormous immigration to be counted on as soon as the war is over, it is not likely that an organized economic opposition to birth control will develop . . . and a suffrage state should make short work of repealing these old laws that stand in the way of birth control."[35]

Women's suffrage passed in 1920 but birth control took another forty-seven years. The federal ban on contraceptive advice and materials was ended—but only for doctors—in a 1936 appeals court decision with the beguiling name *United States v. One Package of Japanese Pessaries*. State laws persisted, however, and it was not until 1965 that *Griswold v. Connecticut* finally made contraceptive advice and practice legal for married people all over the United States. It took another seven years to extend that right to unmarried people, with *Eisenstadt v. Baird* in 1972. Abortion became largely legal again with *Roe* one year later.

CHAPTER 5

POPULATION PANIC TO THE BABY BUST

E arly twentieth-century debates about the birth rate were familiar to women at the beginning of feminism's second wave. Betty Friedan says of the generation before her that "their low pregnancy rate led to warnings that [women getting an] education was going to wipe out the human race."[1]

But in 1963 this was no longer a concern. Friedan, whose blockbuster *The Feminine Mystique* sold millions, was writing in the height of the postwar baby boom, a phenomenon that she noticed was lasting substantially longer in the United States than in other countries. The U.S. birth rate continued to rise from 1950 to 1959 while it was falling in France, Norway, Sweden, the Soviet Union, and Japan. She wrote that the U.S. birth rate was surpassing India's and described an epidemic of young marriages, with half of U.S. women married by age twenty.[2]

Echoing Hollingworth, she attributed the long baby boom to job discrimination backed up by the "feminine mystique"—all the heavy ideology that women should be fulfilled by marriage and kids.

While the U.S. baby boom was filling schools to bursting, U.S. planners became uneasy about oppressed nations in revolt, throwing out colonial powers, electing socialists and even achieving socialist revolutions. Many of these nations were also experiencing the demographic transition that had already occurred in Europe and the United States, a transition from high birth and death rates to low birth and death rates. As this transition occurs, due mostly to sanitation and vaccines, there is a period when the birth rate greatly exceeds the death rate, resulting in a sharp rise in population. A faction of the elite became panicked that population was growing too fast, globally and at home. Some argued that unless growth slowed it would lead to communism.

Their population panic lasted two decades, from the mid-1950s to the mid-1970s, coinciding with the period that the feminist movement built into a second wave. This coincidence affected the feminist movement's understanding of birth control and abortion laws, with ramifications that are still felt today.

Population Panic

In population alarmist Hugh Moore's 1954 pamphlet *The Population Bomb*, he wrote, "there will be 300 million more mouths to feed in the world four years from now—most of them hungry. Hunger brings turmoil—and turmoil, as we have learned, creates the atmosphere in which communists seek to conquer the earth." Moore, who made a fortune cofounding the Dixie Cup Company, recruited John D. Rockefeller III to the cause, writing to him, "We are not primarily interested in the social and humanitarian aspects of birth control. We are interested in the use which communists make of hungry people."[3]

Moore's Campaign to Check the Population Explosion specialized in placing alarmist and arguably racist newspaper ads, including one that described U.S. cities "packed with youngsters—thousands of them idle, victims of discontent and drug addiction. . . . You go out after dark at your peril. Birth control is an answer."[4]

Another ad read: "A world with mass starvation in underdeveloped countries will be a world of chaos, riots and war. And a perfect breeding ground for Communism. . . . We cannot afford a half dozen Vietnams or even one more. . . . Our own national interest demands that we go all out to help the underdeveloped countries control their population."[5]

In 1967, a book called *Famine 1975!* suggested that the United States should cut off food aid to countries whose population growth made them hopeless cases—Egypt and India were given as examples.[6] Paul and Anne Ehrlich further popularized the panic with their 1968 bestseller *The Population Bomb*. "Population Control or Race to Oblivion?" one cover asked. The authors suggested that the United States should lead on reducing its own birth rate and that acting domestically first would deflect charges of racism when the United States recommended population control in other countries.

Of course, population in itself isn't the cause of poverty and starvation. Under capitalism, the causes are the exploitation of people's work for low pay, the looting of natural resources, and the suppression of the production of necessities in favor of luxuries for those few who can afford them. As people in the United States came to understand during the Great Depression, "needed" population can become "surplus" overnight when the boom-and-bust cycle of capitalism turns to bust and throws millions out of work. No sudden increase in population occasioned this. Even famines are the result of political decisions, not an absolute lack of food, as renowned economist Amartya Sen demonstrated in his study of the Bengal famine of 1943 among others.[7]

Still, starting in the 1950s, the United States and various private foundations set up population control measures aimed at developing countries, hoping to forestall revolutions. Worried that India might have a revolution like China, the United States funded programs there to sterilize young men.[8] Black feminist pioneer Frances Beal wrote about this in 1969 in *Double Jeopardy: To Be Black and Female*. In the United States, she wrote, "perhaps the most outlandish act of oppression in modern times is the current campaign to promote sterilization of nonwhite women in an attempt to maintain the population and power imbalance between the white haves and the nonwhite have-nots."[9] (There is more on this history in chapter 8, Reproduction and Race.)

The case of Puerto Rico gives us a window into the operations of these top-down population controllers. In 1917 Congress thrust U.S. citizenship upon Puerto Ricans, just a month before the United States would enter World War I. This allowed the U.S. military to draft twenty thousand Puerto Rican men for the war.[10] Citizenship did not quell the unrest caused by low wages and mistreatment by colonial overlords. It did, however, create fears among the U.S. elite that these newly minted citizens would flood the U.S. mainland. An economic envoy sent by Washington to report on the situation in Puerto Rico in 1932 wrote:

> I rather dislike to think that our falling fertility must be supplemented by these people, but that will probably happen. Our control of the tropics seems to me certain to increase immigration from here and the next wave of the lowly . . . succeeding the Irish, Italians, and Slavs . . . will be these mulattos Indians, Spanish people from the south of us. They make poor material for social organization, but you are going to have to reckon with them.[11]

Behind the racist fears was a land grab. By 1930, less than 2 percent of the island's population owned 80 percent of the land and 40 percent of farmable land had been transformed into U.S. sugar plantations.[12] As farmers were squeezed off the land and into cities, the liberal Brookings Institution released an influential 1930 study that blamed the bad economic conditions on rapid population growth.[13]

In response to the dire economic conditions and U.S. domination, Puerto Ricans protested, at first peaceably, but security forces responded with a massacre in 1937. When the anti-colonial movement engaged in armed uprisings all over the island, notably in 1950, they were answered by the U.S. Army, National Guard, and aerial bombing. In response, two nationalists attempted to kill U.S. President Harry Truman in Washington. In 1954, four *independentistas* unfurled a Puerto Rican flag and opened fire in the U.S. House of Representatives, wounding five members of Congress. All this must have been worrisome to the U.S. government.

Moore, Rockefeller, and other population controllers applied to Puerto Rico their idea that "hunger brings turmoil"—by which they meant organizing and protest. But rather than redistribute land or wealth, they instituted forty years of programs aimed at Puerto Rican women's reproductive capacity.[14] These ranged from pushing sterilization operations (in some cases women were not told it was permanent) to experimentation with every birth control method imaginable, including early trials of the pill (the safety of which had not been established), diaphragms, IUDs, Depo-Provera, and even spermicidal foam. Even with these experiments pocking the island, sterilization was the only way most women had to control their fertility. And no wonder, it was favored by population controllers whose goal was fewer children, not giving women full control of their reproductive lives. Certainly Puerto Rican women were not to be given the right to abortion—it was illegal there until *Roe v. Wade*. Or at least it was illegal for most women: During the 1960s, women from the U.S. mainland who could afford a "San Juan weekend" could fly there and pay $300 to get an abortion at a private clinic (over $2,000 in today's dollars).[15] Because sterilization was the only birth control available, and because it was pushed relentlessly by the authorities, by 1968, one third of Puerto Rican women had undergone sterilization operations, the highest percentage in the world.[16] Sterilization was so widespread it was simply referred to as *la operación* (the operation). Filmmaker Ana María García used this term as the title of her 1982 film exposing sterilization and birth control testing programs in Puerto Rico.[17] Yet, as García pointed out, the resulting lower birth rate did not lead to prosperity.

Women Workers Wanted

There was an additional motivation for U.S. corporations to encourage sterilization of Puerto Rican women. When U.S. companies started locating factories in Puerto Rico in the 1940s, employers wanted women to be available for work. Some provided birth control "counseling" on site and on work time, and there were rumors that women who had been sterilized would be hired more readily because they wouldn't need to take maternity leave.[18]

U.S. employers on the mainland, too, had an interest in looser birth control laws. The long postwar economic boom meant employers wanted to hire women—as a cheaper pair of hands and a lever to ratchet down men's wages—but they couldn't do it when women were having so many children.

The U.S. birth rate finally began dropping in the early 1960s, coincident with a sharp increase in women joining the paid workforce. Feminist journalist Caroline Bird wrote, "We do not like to admit it, but in 1968 our prosperity depends on the labor and earnings of women."[19] The invention of the birth control pill made this easier. It was officially available only to married women, and initially marketed in 1957 to "regulate periods," but in 1960 it was approved as a contraceptive, and widely available by 1965.[20]

End of the Panic

The decline in U.S. birth rates, already visible by 1970, signaled the end of the baby boom. In other countries, too, steep inclines started to level off. This new demographic data led to splits between persistent alarmists like Moore and Ehrlich on one side, and John D. Rockefeller III on the other.

By 1974, U.S. population controllers had lost a good deal of their momentum. U.S policy was roundly attacked by developing world representatives at the United Nations World Population Conference in Bucharest, and "Rockefeller stunned delegates [with] a speech criticizing the use of family planning programs to address social and economic problems."[21] His reversal coincided with the news that births were slowing at home and abroad.

Population controllers continued in their efforts abroad with U.S. funds into the 1980s, but they were more circumspect, targeting countries they worried might be politically unstable. With the threat of socialist revolution thought to be vanquished, overseas family planning funding peaked in 1995 and then stagnated, though it increased 25 percent during the Obama years.[22] It is possible the fear of communism has been replaced to some degree by the fear of terrorism. Among twenty-four countries the U.S. Agency for International Development (USAID) makes a priority for family planning funds, fifteen are in sub-Saharan Africa—the only continent showing large population gains—along with several countries across Asia which the U.S. State Department worries may be "unstable": Yemen, Pakistan, Nepal, Bangladesh, and the Philippines. But campaigners for USAID funding complain that public spending is stalled, and private funders have turned to other issues besides family planning, believing the population problem—or perhaps the revolution problem—to be essentially solved.[23]

Half of the world's population now lives in countries where the birth rate is below replacement levels. In ten years, the UN projects, 67 percent will.[24] The reversal in elite scaremongering is remarkable. China, which the authors of *Famine 1975!* described as "on the brink of famine," has been in the last decade roundly criticized for controlling its birth rate through its one-child policy, with the financial press complaining that the policy has restricted the supply of Chinese labor.[25]

The change in elite opinion tracks the graph from baby boom to baby bust. A look at the Bush family trajectory is instructive: Prescott Bush, father of George H.W. Bush, was the treasurer of the Birth Control Federation of America, soon to be renamed Planned Parenthood, in 1947. George H.W. Bush supported birth control as a member of Congress from Texas 1966–1970; he was such an advocate that fellow House members nicknamed him "Rubbers."[26] In 1973 he advocated that "in the United States family planning services be available for every woman, not just the private patient with her own gynecologist."[27] As UN ambassador, in 1974, he supported the *Roe v. Wade* decision.[28] The standard explanation for Bush's switch to an anti-abortion position when he joined Ronald Reagan's ticket as vice president in 1980 was that he had to curry favor with a religious base that had made abortion a litmus test for Republican politicians. But it's also possible that the drop in the domestic birth rate, apparent by the mid-1970s, was a factor in their newly minted anti-abortion politics.

By 1984 the Reagan administration had instituted the Global Gag Rule, which was maintained by George H.W. Bush and later reinstated by George W. Bush. That rule bans foreign aid to any family planning agency that so much as mentions abortion. The rule broadened the Helms Amendment, which in 1973 had already dictated that no foreign aid could go toward abortions.

Effect on the Feminist Movement

At the very moment that the Women's Liberation Movement was gathering strength in the late 1960s, there was conflict among the ruling class on what to do about birth rates. It wasn't just raw numbers that caused the conflict—the power structure was under pressure from many sides to loosen up on abortion and birth control. Employers wanted women available to work now, unencumbered by children, and they certainly weren't going to pay for childcare. Cold warriors were under pressure to look democratic compared to socialist countries where birth control and abortion were readily provided. Anti-colonial and anti-imperialist struggles of colonized people made them look threatening and possibly over-numerous, and urban revolts made the U.S. power structure jumpy. Even though this period turned out to be quite brief, it affected the way the feminist movement understood the issue, with repercussions for how we think about it today.

Judith Brown, who coauthored the foundational 1968 paper *Towards a Female Liberation Movement*, recalled the confusion generated by the power structure's U-turn: "In the mid-70s, the backlash against abortion baffled me. Before we won the abortion victory, the conservatives and men had focused on how we had too many children, were having sex just for fun, were overpopulating the world."[29]

How could power structure resistance to birth control and abortion be related to a desire for more babies? Brown, like many second-wave feminists, had the impression they wanted us to have fewer, based on evidence from the 1960s. But although the power structure generally reunited around a "make more babies" position by the late 1970s, the feminist movement, by and large, still assumes that the establishment wants fewer or is neutral on the subject.

Women's Liberation Movement organizing spread across the United States starting in 1968, and by 1970 its agitation had won a liberalized abortion law in New York State. It was introduced by a Republican state senator, Constance Cook, passed with bipartisan support, and signed by a Republican governor, Nelson Rockefeller.

Roxanne Dunbar (now Dunbar-Ortiz), a leader of the radical feminist group Cell 16 in Boston and later the Southern Female Rights Union in New Orleans, said at the time that she thought the government was secretly *for* abortion law repeal because of the baby boom. A 1970 interview reports her saying: "We are no longer needed as reproducers. This contributes to the possibility of our liberation, but it has also devalued our existence a very great deal. . . . I'm convinced the government . . .

wants abortion repeal and could put it through any time it wants. . . . Clearly, the center of life in the future is not going to be reproducing great numbers of people. . . . Certainly in the last fifty years or so, women have become ridiculed and useless people."

Dunbar identifies women's reproductive capacity as a source of power for women, a striking claim that we will return to. But she says we've lost our leverage because of overpopulation. She also calls overpopulation fears "nonsense" and "a smokescreen for much deeper problems in the world."[30]

By contrast, abortion movement pioneer Lucinda Cisler and radical feminist theoretician Shulamith Firestone thought that overpopulation was a real problem, although not one that the establishment was interested in addressing. They thought women were acting responsibly by taking matters into their own hands with birth control and risky (and sometimes deadly) illegal abortions. Cisler estimated in 1969 that one in four U.S. women had had an illegal abortion. Undeterred by the dangers, women were seizing control of their reproduction.

In the earliest edition of the trailblazing feminist health book *Our Bodies, Ourselves*, the authors did give the birth rate as a reason for abortion laws, but only in the old days:

> As biologists in the 19th Century began to understand conception, women began to practice more effective contraception. Catholic countries like France began "losing" the population race, and the Church wanted to keep its mothers running. So the Church itself turned to biology and used the idea that "life" and therefore soul-infused human life begins at fertilization. This reasoning also spread to England and the USA. It so happened that English and American industries needed workers, the huge farmable territories of the new world needed farmers, and the Civil War had depleted America's labor crop. Abortion laws saw to it that woman took her place beside the other machines of a developing economy.[31]

But the up-to-date reason for opposition to birth control, wrote the editors in 1970, is "the idea that sex for pleasure is bad, that pregnancy is a punishment for pleasure, and that fear of pregnancy will reinforce 'degenerating' modern morals."[32] In 1970, the power structure seemed to be alarmed by overpopulation, so feminists attributed anti-abortion policy to a different source.

But there were hints even then that the overpopulation scare might be limited and transitory. The young radicals of the Women's Liberation Movement took as their guide Simone de Beauvoir, the French woman whose 1949 book *The Second Sex* became available in translation in the United States in 1953. Beauvoir wrote that women's reproductive work is needed, at some times more than others: "Woman cannot in good faith be regarded only as a worker; her reproductive function is as important as her productive capacity. . . . There are periods in history when it is more useful to have children than till the soil. Everyone knows how radically the USSR has had to change its family policy to balance out production needs of the moment with the needs of repopulation."[33]

She believed French abortion and birth control laws were designed to increase population, but said that they weren't working, as everyone ignored them. The laws are "totally powerless to ensure an increase in births. A point of agreement for both partisans and enemies of legal abortion is the total failure of repression."[34]

Beauvoir said there were as many abortions each year in France as births. "There is no way to directly oblige a woman to give birth; all that can be done is to enclose her in situations where motherhood is her only option: laws or customs impose marriage on her, anticonception measures and abortion are banned, divorce is forbidden."[35]

On Beauvoir's side of the 1960s debate were Ti-Grace Atkinson and Kathie Sarachild. Both these feminist thinkers suspected that despite a population panic on the part of some, the bulk of the power structure still wanted women to have more children than we desired. Atkinson, who led the New York chapter of the National Organization for Women and later founded The Feminists, believed that keeping the birth rate up was a goal of the Catholic Church and the governments with which it allied ("the more fascist the government, the stronger the Church," she noted). In notes for a 1971 speech at Catholic University, she wrote that control of women "is essential for population control and manipulation": "Population rate, overpopulation, must be maintained and manipulated for guaranteed unemployment, which maintains a rigid economic class hierarchy, since wages can be controlled through fear of unemployment. Obviously, either birth control or abortion, at the discretion of the individual, would jeopardize one of the Church's most powerful political levers." She also noted that greater population is needed "in the event of ground wars," and that it is desirable for the Catholic Church, "especially when the conversion rate is going down."[36]

Kathie Sarachild of Redstockings, an originator of consciousness-raising, argued that the struggle for abortion was another episode in the continuing struggle of woman "to determine the use (and non-use) of her valuable sexual and reproductive organs."

In a 1971 article in the feminist movement newspaper *Woman's World*, Sarachild analyzed the experience of the movement with abortion reform in New York. She wrote:

> All the Establishment talk about population control means just what the term says . . . controlling the population, whether in the form of increasing it or decreasing it. . . . Despite what the Establishment says, the present policy of the men at the top . . . is still to push motherhood, not to curb it. . . . The laws of this country still force the masses of women to have children. . . . This is what all the Establishment talk about "overpopulation" does. It confuses people, makes them think that the government is supporting abortion law repeal and even maybe trying to ram it down their throats. It also serves to shift the blame for the problems of this nation from the few rich who run it to the millions of poor.[37]

She also noted that Republicans were the ones who complained the most about "rising welfare loads due to women having so many 'illegitimate' children." Yet they were the ones who tried to cut Medicaid funding for abortions at every opportunity.

Several years of militant feminist organizing pushed the Supreme Court to reverse burdensome anti-abortion laws with the *Roe v. Wade* decision in 1973. But just three years later, restrictions on public funds for abortion would become national policy with the Hyde Amendment. From 1973 to 1976, before Hyde went into effect, the federal government paid for a third of the abortions in the country through Medicaid, around three hundred thousand a year. After Hyde, the program covered only a few.[38] According to recent studies, "Approximately one-fourth of women who would have Medicaid-funded abortions instead give birth when this funding is unavailable."[39]

The Hyde Amendment wasn't a Republican-only effort, either. Republican president Gerald Ford was unwilling to sign it, and it became an issue in the 1976 presidential campaign, with Democratic candidate Jimmy Carter staking out a position for Hyde. He signed it in 1977, saying, "Well, as you know, there are many things in life that are not fair, that wealthy people can afford and poor people can't."[40]

Carter pointed to three Supreme Court rulings that found the government was not obligated to pay for abortions for women whose health care—including childbirths—it was already providing. The cases mention the birth rate as a legitimate state interest. In *Maher v. Roe*, the court's majority found that the state can encourage childbirth over abortion by refusing to fund abortions. Justice Lewis Powell wrote, "The State unquestionably has a 'strong and legitimate interest in encouraging normal childbirth,' . . . an interest honored over the centuries." In a footnote, the court wrote that birth rate concerns could override women's abortion rights: "In addition to the direct interest in protecting the fetus, a State may have legitimate demographic concerns about its rate of population growth. Such concerns are basic to the future of the State and in some circumstances could constitute a substantial reason for departure from a position of neutrality between abortion and childbirth."[41]

For 150 years, feminists have been digging down to the roots of anti-birth control ideology and arguing that the goal of these laws and strictures is to keep us producing children. And for 150 years, there have been those who argue that the laws are about sex or religion or just a mistake on the part of the powerful. Mary Ware Dennett's Comstock-era arguments that the law's ban on contraception was an unwitting error, and the 1970s arguments that the establishment doesn't care about the birth rate anymore, echo in our era when we are again told that nearly every other motive prevails, other than the obvious one: "Make more babies!"

CHAPTER 6

LONGEVITY: CRISIS OR BLESSING?

The Social Security debate illustrates just how valuable our reproductive work is to employers and the elite, as well as how important it is for the rest of us. A healthy ratio of working-age people to children and elders makes a society sustainable. But what constitutes a healthy ratio? The interests of the 99% and the 1% diverge on this point. Is it really true that there are "too many" retired people compared to the working-age population, as establishment think tanks insist? In a highly productive society, how much reproduction is needed?

"Social Security is going broke," says Republican House Speaker Paul Ryan. "A central factor in the looming financial crunch is the fact that our society is aging."[1] What Ryan and others conceal with their talk of "too many old people" is that our society is fantastically productive, with plenty of surplus to support those who are not working—young and old. But corporate owners, not workers, have benefitted from the productivity gains of the last fifty years, and that is reflected in our public retirement system.

Intergenerational Solidarity

Social Security is the public pension program hailed as one of the most successful and popular (or, from the corporate viewpoint, the most intractable and expensive) parts of the 1930s New Deal. It is also widely misunderstood due to a campaign of lies aimed at weakening public support.

"Today the distortions and lies about Social Security are so widely and so often repeated on television, in the newspapers, and in magazines that many younger Americans accept as uncontestable truth the dire predictions that they will be taxed all their working lives for benefits they will never collect," says investigative journalist David Cay Johnston.[2] Nearly every mainstream publication and even the Social Security trustees use what economic analyst Doug Henwood calls "dodgy projections, innuendo, and the occasional lie."[3]

How does Social Security work? Workers and employers each dedicate 6.2 percent of every paycheck to Social Security. It is universally said that workers are "saving for retirement" through these payroll taxes, but that is wrong. In fact, the system uses those funds to pay currently retired workers. Social Security is, in effect, paying my mother's retirement check this month with money it deducted from my check last month. This is called a "pay-as-you-go" system, and it is the same in every national pension system in the world. It reflects life itself: the economic production of the currently working generation feeds and houses those not working. This is the structure of any society, whether it has a pension system or not. Working-age people support themselves with their economic activity, while also supporting the young, old, sick, and unemployed. The society as a whole cannot save up work done today in the form of money and expect to spend it thirty years later. There must also be enough working-age people thirty years later to harvest food, collect trash, dispense medicine, and string utility wires. This is why the age structure of society is an important concern for everyone.

But Social Security has made a significant change, one we are now so accustomed to that it is almost invisible. The unwaged old and the disabled are no longer dependent primarily on the members of their *own* families for economic survival. Whether your family is small or large, financially comfortable or struggling day to day, Social Security means you will have some income in your old age. This in turn means that having children is no longer each individual's chief strategy for securing their old age. In effect, Social Security spreads the risks and rewards of reproduction over the entire national family.

Longer Life Spans and Women's Equality

In the last hundred years, the United States has undergone a demographic transition common to countries that experienced industrialization, urbanization, and improved sanitation. We are living longer and having fewer children.

My paternal grandmother Violet Mary Cooke was born in 1898. She was one of five children born to an Irish immigrant seamstress in New York, but my grandmother was the only one who survived past the age of two. So my great-grandmother spent an accumulated four years pregnant (more if she had miscarriages), meanwhile feeding and caring for babies and toddlers, only to watch them fade and die one after another. In such a situation of high infant and child mortality, one had to have many children to be sure some would survive to adulthood. Life expectancy in the United States in 1900 was forty-seven, an average pulled down by infant and child deaths. But also, many adults didn't live as long as we do now. A third were carried off by contagious diseases, with tuberculosis and influenza at the top of the list, while death in childbirth killed many women. Now the average expected life span in the United States is around seventy-nine.

Better child survival rates mean women don't have to dedicate so much time and energy to bearing and rearing children to replace ourselves and our mates in the population. With vaccinations, sanitation, and antibiotics, women's specialized job of bearing children has become less dangerous and less onerous. We are having fewer, and spending a smaller portion of our lives in pregnancy and childcare. Rather than having five children and one surviving, or four children and three surviving (as happened in my maternal grandmother's family), we can have fewer with the reasonable expectation that they will live to adulthood and even old age. You could say these advances in medicine and infrastructure have increased the productivity of our childbearing and rearing work.

"With a life span lengthened to nearly 75 years it is no longer either necessary or possible for women to devote the greater part of their lives to child-rearing," wrote Betty Friedan in the founding document of the National Organization for Women.[4] Longer life spans give women more time outside of the demanding child-rearing years to pursue other interests, something men long had time for since their child-rearing years were not so demanding.

But even with these life span advances, there is still pressure on each woman to have children as security later in life. This is where public pensions solidify the gain: Women can now expect that Social Security will provide something for us upon retirement, whether we have children who will help us then or not.[5] Childbearing and rearing is no longer the only work available to women to secure our old age.

But this advance is under attack by those who want us to have more kids. "Social Security and Medicare have crowded out the traditional incentive to raise children as a protection against poverty in old age," writes Robert Stein in a report by conservative think-tankers who argue that lower birth rates are stunting the U.S. economy. "Even as the old-age pension system collectively depends on a population of young workers, it diminishes the economic need for adults to raise them, and so undermines its own sustainability," Stein writes.[6]

Looked at from women's standpoint, what Stein is saying is true, and liberating. Public pensions *have* allowed women to have fewer children. Care in old age is a common reason people give for having large families in countries where there is little pension provision.[7] But it was always a risky proposition. One hopes that one's children will grow up and become prosperous enough to help their parents. Some will, certainly. Some will live long lives, while others may die before their parents. Some will be caught in economic upheavals and may need support rather than provide it. It's a gamble.

Social Security has pooled the risk of raising the next generation. And by doing so, it has removed some of the unfair pressure on women to find an economically reliable man, get married, have kids, and stay married. This has been an important stride forward for women's freedom.

Social Security does this by providing a pension for women's paid work outside the home, something women otherwise rarely receive given that discrimination segregates us into jobs that mostly don't offer pensions. And unlike private pensions, which require us to stay in one job, Social Security tallies our work even when we have intermittent job histories from jumping in and out of paid labor to have children or care for sick or frail family members.

Social Security also recognizes women's work inside the home. Starting in 1939, the Social Security Administration recognized the contribution of women's work to the family unit by introducing benefits for divorced or widowed women. Women had to stay married for twenty years, but after divorce they could receive an amount equal to half of their husband's Social Security when they reached retirement age. Feminist movement agitation changed that from a wife-only benefit to a spousal benefit in 1975 and changed the required duration of marriage from twenty years to ten in 1977.[8] (It's not full recognition: If you only work inside the home and stay married, the man will still be the one legally controlling the Social Security check that accounts for both spouses' work, extending the sexist family wage system into retirement.)

So Social Security has taken some of the pressure off of women to reproduce, but without abortion and birth control, that freedom is hard to exercise. The long struggle for birth control—and then the fight that legalized abortion—made it easier for women to do something with their lives other than, or in addition to, raising children. Both control of our reproduction *and* Social Security have made it possible for women to gain more equality in the home and on the job.

But to some, things that gave feminism a major boost—accessible contraception, abortion, falling birth rates, and longer life spans—are a big problem. Indeed, they are the cause of a national crisis. Rick Santorum, in his abortive run for the Republican presidential nomination in 2011, said, "The reason Social Security is in big trouble is we don't have enough workers to support the retirees. Well, a third of all the young people in America are not in America today because of abortion, because one in three pregnancies end in abortion."[9]

Jill Stanek of the anti-feminist Concerned Women for America suggested that those who have had abortions should have their Social Security benefits cut. She writes: "As more and more baby boomers reach retirement age, they will continue to reap what they have sown. . . . [One] of their pitiful harvests will be the lack of young workers paying into the Social Security system. Approximately one-third of them have been aborted. And it's not just aborted children who will never pay Social Security. Some of their children would now be nearing entry-level work age, but they have been offed as well."[10]

It is not just anti-abortion activists who insist that lower birth rates will destroy Social Security. In a presidential speech arguing for the privatization of Social Security, George W. Bush said: "In 1950, there were 16 workers to support every one beneficiary of Social Security. Today, there are only 3.3 workers . . . by the time our youngest workers . . . turn 65, there will only be two workers supporting each beneficiary. . . . And, under the current system, today's thirty-year-old worker will face a 27 percent benefit cut when he or she reaches normal retirement age."[11] And conservative population alarmist Jonathan Last suggests that Social Security and Medicare "could be salvaged by drastically altering the tax and/or benefit structure. But they could also be saved if Americans started having more babies."[12]

Even feminists echo this rhetoric. Michelle Goldberg warns of the "grave threats" represented by increases in longevity and falling birth rates: "There will be fewer young workers to support this expanding elderly population. To maintain pension systems, taxes will have to be raised or benefits cut, or both. An older population will put an increasing strain on health systems, which, again, will have fewer workers supporting them through taxes."[13]

So what's going on? Are there really too many elderly and not enough young? Did women deciding to do something with our lives besides motherhood ruin it for the country? Is feminism to blame?

Social Security privatizers and even anti-abortion forces are right that for a society to function and thrive, we need to have a steady flow of children, but they are cooking the books when they say we are coming up short. This is where the interests of women and the 99% depart from the interests of the 1%. We'd be fine with a stable or slowly shrinking population—as the numbers will show—while they want a population that grows endlessly so that support of retirees doesn't squeeze their profits.

To make their case for an ever-growing population, establishment sources distort Social Security's current and future outlook.

First, they claim that there aren't enough workers to support the coming retirees. But the ratio of workers to Social Security beneficiaries has actually been remarkably stable since 1960 when there were fifteen people aged sixty-five or over for every hundred of working age. In 2017 there were twenty-two people aged sixty-five or over for every hundred of working age.

Second, productivity per worker has more than doubled in the last fifty years. That means that, if no one were siphoning off the gains in private profits, each worker could support twice as many people as they could in the 1950s. (We'll look at this more closely soon.)

Third, the Social Security trustees have for decades used absurdly grim projections of future economic growth, as Doug Henwood pointed out in 1998. "Were the economy to grow at a more normal pace, then the Social Security system could easily pay its projected benefits with no cuts or tax increases."[14] *New York Times* columnist and Nobel Prize–winning economist Paul Krugman picked up Henwood's critique in 2005, noting that privatizers who want to put Social Security money in the stock market exaggerate economic growth when projecting how the stock market will do, but they minimize growth when projecting how traditional Social Security will do. They can't have it both ways. "If the economy grows fast enough to generate a rate of return that makes privatization work, it will also yield a bonanza of payroll tax revenue that will keep the current system sound for generations to come."[15] Analyzing the 2016 Social Security Trustees report, economist Dean Baker observes that even using the trustees' gloomy figures, Social Security can be kept healthy with an increase in the Social Security tax of 2.66 percent over a forty-year period, a period during which wages should rise in real terms by 52.9 percent.[16] Such a modest payroll tax increase hardly constitutes a crisis.

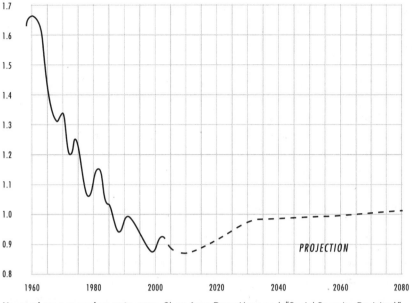

Nonworkers per worker, 1960–2080. Chart from Doug Henwood, "Social Security Revisited," *Left Business Observer* 110, March 2005.

Fourth, they predict a dire shortage of workers at the same time that the U.S. labor force participation rate is worryingly low. Of U.S. men aged twenty-five to fifty-four, 12 percent had no jobs and weren't even looking, and for women it was even worse.[17] While the official unemployment rate is around 4 percent at this writing, the number of people in the United States who would be in the workforce if there were decent jobs is much higher.

Europe is famously a few years ahead of us in the "elderly crisis," and as we have seen, planners there also worry about the ratio of workers to retirees. But unemployment is also a problem in Europe, especially among the young. "Both problems cannot exist at the same time," writes Baker. "If the aging of the population leads to shortages of workers, then the high levels of unemployment in countries like France, Italy, and Germany, indicate that the shortage can be alleviated . . . by drawing from the currently unemployed population."[18] As we've seen, Europeans have shorter workweeks, longer vacations, plenty of paid parental leave, and earlier retirements. The alleged crisis of a shrinking workforce hasn't led them to give up any of that, although in some cases these countries have forced through higher retirement ages, as the United States did in 1983.

Fifth, it's true that we're supporting more old people, as a society, but we're also supporting fewer young people. Nearly every politician and pundit trying to undermine Social Security pulls out the "dependency ratio" to scare us. For example, George W. Bush implied that the burden of one non-working person on two working ones—a two to one ratio—would be an impossible burden for a society to bear. But here's the trick: demographers usually express the "dependency ratio" as the number of people over sixty-four and under fifteen for every hundred working-age adults. The idea is an important one: non-waged workers in a society are supported by the economic activities of waged workers. But Bush and others leave out the under-fifteen population to make it look like our society has never faced a similar situation.

If you count those under age fifteen and over sixty-four as dependents, there were sixty-six dependents for every hundred working-age people in 1960, and fifty dependents for every hundred working-age people in 2013. The dependency ratio, in other words, is going the opposite direction of that claimed, because we're having fewer children. This misrepresentation betrays a bias for future workers (a source of future work and profits) and against past workers (retired and regarded as an unwarranted expense).

The combination of increased productivity per worker, a larger waged workforce due to more women getting jobs, the non-working population who could be working if available jobs weren't so onerous and stingy, and the fact we're supporting fewer young people, means that there is not a crisis in the number of workers available to support non-workers, which is the chief claim of Social Security privatizers and advocates of higher birth rates. But there is a problem of *distribution* which they would prefer we not examine.

Undermining Social Security

In the early 1980s, a congressional aide memorably described Social Security as the electrified "third rail" of U.S. politics—if you touch it, you die. But since then, both Republican and Democratic administrations have been risking political punishment to take whacks at the program. "Years ago, only right-wing ideologues wanted to privatize Social Security; now it's the entire American establishment," Henwood noted in 1998.[19] Yet the program has been saved again and again. Under Republicans, it has been saved mostly by the public and some Democratic lawmakers defending it. Attacks by Democratic administrations have been more dangerous because they threaten to swing both parties behind the changes, but we've twice squeaked by with lucky breaks.

A deal between the Republican Reagan administration and Democratic House Speaker Tip O'Neill in 1983 resulted in the biggest cut, a gradual increase in the full retirement age from sixty-five to sixty-seven. The change went largely unnoticed because the first people to be affected were then in their thirties and not yet paying attention to retirement. The deal also increased the payroll tax in anticipation of a wave of baby boomer retirements to start in 2008. As a result, the system started to take in a lot more than it was paying out each year, accumulating a surplus in the Social Security Trust Fund. Paradoxically, this surplus has made the system vulnerable because politicians have made it a political football, which they couldn't do when the money mostly just flowed through the treasury from workers to retirees.

The trust fund is a magnet for distortion. First politicians disingenuously claim that it's already been spent—which is superficially true. The government owes that money to future seniors as they retire, and the U.S. government (like all governments) maintains debt, of which this debt is a part. But the U.S. government is perhaps the most responsible payer of debts in the world, which is why anyone who wants a safe haven for their money buys U.S. Treasury bonds.[20] For politicians to suggest that the U.S. government would default (not pay its debts) is fantastically irresponsible.

When they're not claiming the fund is just a bunch of IOUs, they switch to claiming the trust fund is emptying out, that Social Security is, in Paul Ryan's words, "going broke." Again this conceals more than it reveals. The surplus in question is being collected to pay the Social Security of the large cohort of baby boomers as they go through the system. When they have mostly died, around 2045, the fund will have fulfilled its purpose and *should* be empty. Claiming it will be "broke" makes no more sense than spending your college fund on a college education and then, as you clutch your diploma, bemoaning that your college fund is broke. But because most people think Social Security is like a savings account the government keeps for you for when you retire, an empty fund sounds serious indeed. In reality, working people will still be paying their payroll taxes, and retirees will still be paid out of them, independent of any trust fund.

These politicians mostly know better, but they make these claims to convince younger people that all *their* money has been consumed by greedy seniors, in an attempt to pit generation against generation. As Simone de Beauvoir writes in her book about old age, "It is to the interest of the exploiting class to destroy the solidarity between the workers and the unproductive old."[21]

The attacks have been generally unsuccessful because most young people realize that it's not some grasping "other" under discussion but older members of their own families.

Bipartisan Attacks and Hair's Breadth Escapes

One illusion we need to shed is that Democratic administrations have been defending Social Security. The establishment is united in destroying Social Security as we know it, Democratic administrations as well as Republican ones. Bill Clinton, leading the first Democratic administration after twelve years of Republicans, worked out a deal with Republican House Speaker Newt Gingrich to raise the retirement age further, reduce cost of living increases, and create private accounts within Social Security, a proposal that would undermine the pay-as-you-go model and divert retirement funds to fees for banks and brokers.[22] Clinton and Gingrich met secretly in October 1997, according to Steven Gillon's book about the two men, to "create a new center/right political coalition of moderate Republicans and conservative Democrats to push their ambitious overhaul of Social Security and Medicare through Congress." But then Clinton's affair with Monica Lewinsky was exposed, and he needed every vote he could get from the liberal wing of Democrats he had been planning to shaft. "If we cut a deal with the Republicans on Social Security there was every possibility that the Democrats, who were the only people defending [Clinton] in the Congress against these charges, could easily get angry and abandon him," explained a White House official. And so, by a dose of luck, the bargain was shelved.[23]

George W. Bush, declaring he had "political capital" to spend after returning to office in January 2005, announced a program to privatize Social Security. He proposed diverting the money currently going to pay retirees into private savings accounts. The plan collapsed due to public outrage, helped by the plan's unworkability.

Barack Obama then took up the effort to "reform" Social Security. He appointed a bipartisan commission to cut the deficit, named Bowles-Simpson after its co-chairs. The panel suggested raising the retirement age gradually—including the early retirement age, currently sixty-two. "Index normal retirement age . . . and earliest eligibility age [now sixty-two] to longevity so that [retirement age increases by] about one month every two years," said a report summary. Retirement ages would creep upward. Then, because some workers couldn't work at the advanced ages that would result, it would create a "hardship exemption" so some people could still retire at sixty-two, but only if they could *prove* they couldn't work.[24] Obama was ready to cut a deal with Republicans, but an incoming cohort of Tea Party–identified congress members refused to support anything he proposed. This lucky combination sank the plan.

Obama's next whack came in the form of a proposed recalculation of cost of living increases, called the "Chained CPI," which would have cut benefits. An outraged public beat back the plan.

Why are both parties going after Social Security? Employers want to stop paying for retirement entirely—they've been shedding pension obligations in the private sector as fast as they can. Now they're turning on the public retirement system—what some derisively call a twenty-year paid vacation.[25] The employer contribution to Social Security, 6.2 percent of every paycheck, is a big bill that corporations would like to avoid. Workers' longer lives—for us a blessing—are for the employing class an expense they'd like to dodge.

Social Security also gives workers a little bargaining power. Employers would like to see experienced workers stay on the job—and lay us off when *they* decide we're all used up. And they want a maximum number of people of all ages competing for jobs, so they can lower wages and cut benefits. Social Security, when it's enough, frees us up to quit, and to quit looking.

Some enemies of Social Security are very explicit about increasing the pool of available (not to say desperate) workers by raising retirement ages. They want to cut the program so people will keep working longer. "The designs of federal entitlement programs [Social Security and Medicare] are problematic because they undermine economic growth in at least three ways," write Social Security Trustee Charles Blahous and coauthor Jason Fichtner. "They encourage us to save less, have fewer children (the productive taxpayers of the future), and stop working earlier."[26] Like Bowles-Simpson, Blahous and Fichtner want to push us to work longer into our retirement years by eliminating Social Security's early retirement at age sixty-two. Currently, if you draw Social Security before your full retirement age (sixty-seven for those born after 1959), you'll receive a lifetime of lower benefits. Even in the face of discounted benefits, only about 15 percent of workers wait until their full retirement age to start collecting Social Security.[27] Around 35 percent retire at the earliest possible moment, age sixty-two, despite suffering a permanent 25 percent cut to their benefit. But Blahous and Fichtner want to get rid of this option entirely and keep us working: "The current design discourages work in paid employment, especially for younger seniors and for secondary earners. . . . Our potential for future growth . . . involve[s] close attention to influences upon work participation, particularly at the margins when those in late middle age are weighing whether to continue their working careers or to begin their transition to retirement."[28] Under

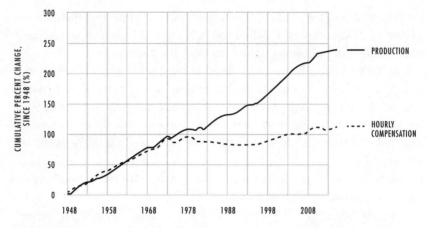

Cumulative change in productivity and real hourly compensation 1948–2015. From data provided by the Economic Policy Institute, "The Productivity-Pay Gap," October 2017, www.epi.org/productivity-pay-gap/.

their plan, many of us who would have retired at sixty-two, or sixty-five, will have to work until sixty-seven or longer—potentially a theft of five years of free time from each worker purely to benefit employers.

Social Security cutters want to reestablish the kind of desperate employment situation that Social Security was created to address. Social Security is a Depression-era program created partly to reduce unemployment among the young. "With 25 percent unemployment and young men riding the rails seen as a potential tinderbox of social unrest," says economic historian Dora Costa, "part of the motivation [for Social Security] was that it was seen as a good idea to get older people out of the workforce."[29] In other words, it was a jobs program, not just a retirement program. With its curtailment or destruction, the number of people seeking jobs will go up, reducing our bargaining power and creating downward pressure on our wages.

Strengthening Social Security

Until now I haven't addressed the obvious problem that Social Security payments are not enough for a decent retirement for many workers, in particular low-waged workers and women. It's not enough to prove the existing Social Security system is healthy, we need to discuss strengthening it. But is this really possible with our current birth rates? Won't we have to settle for the Social Security we have?

Social Security is funded by a percentage of wages and salaries paid to workers. The Social Security system would reflect our society's increases in worker productivity if our wages were reflecting it, but they are not. Our wages have been stagnant or falling since 1970, while our productivity has risen dramatically. For example, if the minimum wage had kept up with productivity gains, it would be over $18 an hour today, rather than $7.25.[30]

The benefits of that increased productivity have not been passed on to wage and salary workers—they've been siphoned off by the rich, whose income is mostly not taxed for Social Security since it is not payment for work, it is investment income. In addition, work income over $128,400 a year is not taxed for Social Security.[31] Forty years of concentration of income at the top means that the share of our national income that is taxed for Social Security is shrinking. Of immediate help would be a substantial rise in the minimum wage, as workers across the country are demanding. But higher wages are exactly the kind of thing employers regard as a national crisis.

Surprisingly, even with the rich vacuuming up national productivity gains, Social Security can meet its obligations to seniors for the reasonably forecastable future. The cap on wages taxed for Social Security rises slightly each year, but if the $128,400 cap were eliminated altogether, we could actually increase Social Security payments. Alternatively, less egalitarian measures could be used. If the payroll tax were raised from 12.4 percent to 14.57 percent, economist Theresa Ghilarducci calculates, the system would be healthy for seventy-five years.[32] From this we can conclude that there is plenty of population and production to support decent retirement for everyone. To improve Social Security, however, we will need to stop all the productivity gains from accumulating at the top.

The fact that the system is surviving even these days of extreme income concentration indicates that there's plenty of room for improvement if the share of resources absorbed by the rich were spread around. We could increase Social Security payments, lower retirement ages, and even consider creative ideas like a universal sabbatical—a paid year off for every seven worked, for every worker—as suggested by the Labor Party in the 1990s.[33]

Defending the "Twenty-Year Paid Vacation"

Increased life spans for everyone are a good thing. We all hope to live to a ripe age. Old age social insurance programs like Social Security are a way for us to "share the wealth" of our newly increased life spans—in free time and fewer births.

But Social Security cutters and privatizers—beholden to corporate interests—know what they want to do with our increased life spans:

If we *insist* on living so long, they want us to spend those extra years working or looking for work. And when our bodies fail, their plan is to try to push the care work, and the economic burdens, back onto the family. "The economy is founded upon profit; in actual fact, the entire civilization is ruled by profit," writes Simone de Beauvoir. "The human working stock is of interest only in so far as it is profitable. When it is no longer profitable it is tossed aside."[34]

Another solution to corporations having to put in money to fund a "twenty-year vacation" is for life expectancy to drop, as it did following the dismantling of the Soviet Union. Could it happen here? There's some evidence that accumulated economic calamity, affecting jobs and wages and hope, caused middle-aged working class whites to experience unprecedented drops in life expectancy starting in the late 1990s.[35] "No other rich country saw a similar turnaround," wrote the authors of a leading study. They blame alcohol and overdoses of painkilling drugs. But alcohol was also blamed in the post-Soviet case, where the despair clearly had economic roots.[36]

Feminist writer Barbara Ehrenreich picked up on the insinuation that there are "too many elderly" during the Bush administration's assault on Social Security:

> A specter is stalking the Western world, and it looks a lot like Grandma. As President Bush has repeatedly put it, the problem with Social Security is that "baby boomers will be living longer." Not "too" long, he's careful to say, but long enough to create a fiscal catastrophe . . . [Will he] confront baby boomers with the question usually addressed to 18-year-old grunts: Are you willing to die for your country? Like maybe right now? Because that's what they want from us, folks, unless we can come up with a better idea.[37]

Who will benefit from the rise in life expectancy? Will we be free to use our extra time in ways of our choosing, or will only corporations and the rich benefit, with us working longer and longer years?

The employing class wants to shed the costs of supporting retired workers. Without Social Security guarantees, and in the face of rapidly disappearing private pensions and laughably small retirement savings, many women (and men) would be back to playing the birth lottery. There's more chance to win if you have more children, so the pressure will be on again, pushing women back into the family as our economic unit of survival and extracting more unpaid work from us.

CHAPTER 7

IMMIGRATION: "INSTANT ADULTS"

Immigration has been described as the "American solution" to the employing class's problem of lower birth rates.[1] Immigrant workers arriving as adults substitute for the children U.S. women didn't produce, and if they settle here permanently, may have children of their own. Establishment Democrats have settled on immigration "for our country's long-term growth strategy" and as "a source of economic vitality and demographic dynamism."[2] Most elite Republicans agree. "Immigrants and their children have made up over half the workforce growth in the country for the last twenty years," said Federal Reserve Bank of Dallas president Robert Kaplan in response to a crackdown on immigrants early in the Trump administration. "Because of aging demographics . . . if we do things that limit sensible immigration, we are likely to slow GDP."[3] Likewise, the Koch brothers, hardly known for their concern for the well-being of immigrants, have been pushing Congress to allow people brought to the U.S. as youngsters to stay.[4]

However, immigration has always caused discomfort as well as joy for the ruling class—a contradiction that has been a recurring theme of U.S. history. As we saw in the 1870s, and again at the beginning of the twentieth century, immigration and the birth rate were often discussed in the same breath: If native-born women don't have more children, we'll be overrun by immigrants. Fear of Slavs, Jews, Catholics, and Chinese have been replaced with fear of Latinos and Muslims, but the alarmist claims endure: They're disloyal, they bring foreign ideas, an alien religion, class conflict, crime, drugs, they won't assimilate, they'll come to outnumber "real Americans." Still, distaste for outsiders always seems to yield when employers need their brain and muscle.

These days, while Democrats largely embrace immigration as an answer to low birth rates, the Republican establishment is split. One faction supports immigration, while the other complains that immigrants will demand government benefits, vote for Democrats, and even bring class war. Even the pro-immigration side worries that the flow of immigrants is unsustainable politically, and lately they have been worrying that the supply will run out due to declining birth rates in the sending countries.

Pro-immigration Republicans are quite candid that they favor immigration to compensate for the low U.S. birth rate. The late Ben Wattenberg, of the pro-corporate American Enterprise Institute, identified immigration as a cheap way to cope with an aging U.S. labor force. "The median age of legal immigrants to the United States is twenty-eight," he writes. "These are men and women who have been raised and educated on someone else's nickel. They typically pay into Social Security and Medicare for about forty years before drawing upon them."

Wattenberg let slip a truth that is often hidden in the immigration debate: Immigration is a colossal rip-off of the labor and resources of the mothers, parents, communities, and countries the immigrants leave behind. This reverses the mainstream narrative that immigrants are a drain on the economy and should be grateful to be here. In fact, Mexico, India, the Dominican Republic, and other sending countries are subsidizing U.S. employers by raising these workers to adulthood.[5]

Wattenberg favors pronatalist tax policies, but they're too slow for him. Even if tax breaks for parents are increased, he writes, "a baby born nine months from now won't even start paying into life's Ponzi scheme for a generation. . . . And that happens only after we spend a lot of money to raise and educate the child. . . . A quicker fix would be 'instant adults.' As it happens, they are available: immigrants."[6]

Former Florida governor Jeb Bush is almost as frank in *Immigration Wars*, a book dedicated to changing U.S. laws to increase immigration: "America's population is shrinking and aging. We need more immigrants to stem that debilitating demographic tide. . . . A demographic time bomb . . . is shaking the sustainability of our savings for retirement, the viability of the entitlement system, and our ability to create robust economic growth."[7]

Bush recognized that much of his party's base opposes increased immigration, but in 2013 he hoped to avoid the venomous split that occurred in 2006, when his older brother, George W. Bush, was president.

Then, the U.S. House passed a bill to punish and expel immigrants who were without the proper papers. Twelve million would have become felons. The Senate favored a program that allowed immigrant workers to stay, while creating expensive hoops for them to jump through—also known as a "path to citizenship."

Bush backed the more pro-immigration Senate bill, which put anti-immigration pundits in a froth. Patrick Buchanan accused the president of allowing an "invasion" and wrote that Bush would be remembered for a "dereliction of constitutional duty that [in an earlier America] would have called forth articles of impeachment."[8]

Fox News host John Gibson waded into the debate by instructing white viewers to "Do your duty. Make more babies! . . . [In Europe] they are not having enough babies to sustain their population. Consequently, they are inviting in more and more immigrants every year to take care of things and those immigrants are having way more babies than the native population, hence Eurabia."[9]

Gibson raised the specter of a Latino majority in the United States: "By far, the greatest number [of children under five] are Hispanic. You know what that means? Twenty-five years and the majority of the population is Hispanic."[10] His logic may have been faulty, but his projection of Fox's racial anxiety was precise.

After he was criticized for racism, Gibson backed off, implying that children of any color were needed: "To put it bluntly, we need more babies . . . or put another way, a slogan for our times: 'procreation not recreation.'"

Along with the Bushes, most corporate owners favored some form of immigration bill and were angry at House Republicans who opposed the Senate bill on "cultural" grounds. *Wall Street Journal* editorial page editor Paul Gigot grumbled that the anti-immigration right "isn't even rational anymore."[11] His wing of the Republican party, more concerned with corporate labor force requirements than the national origin of that labor force, supported a bill that would broaden a work permit system, euphemistically called a "guest worker" program. As long as you are working, you can stay. If you are laid off or fired, you can be deported. Employers thus avoid paying for unemployment insurance for the workers they have discarded, and don't have to face their political protests, either.

Jeb Bush also emphasizes "work-based" immigration and goes further, urging lawmakers to get rid of family reunification as a criterion for immigration. Family reunification makes it possible for immigrants to eventually bring close family members to the United States. But in keeping with their desire to import young adults and avoid paying for children or old people, Bush and his coauthor, Clint Bolick, write:

"Extended family members typically do not produce the economic benefits that work-based immigrants do, and they impose far greater costs.
Many extended family immigrants are children, elderly people, or others
who do not work yet often consume a disproportionate share of social
services such as schooling and health care."[12] Instead, he urges that only
the spouse and children of the immigrant should be permitted to follow
them to the United States. Forget about your family, you're here to work!

Others try to show that "work-based" immigration can create
common ground between employers and xenophobes by assuring everyone that arriving workers would have no rights, no political voice,
and no future guarantees. Daniel Henninger, another *Wall Street Journal*
editor, argued: "I believe the Republicans and the right ought to find a
way to create a guest worker program that is not an amnesty, it does not
necessarily mean [immigrants] become citizens . . . they should be given
temporary status so when the market turns, they can go back where they
came from."[13]

But the differences have been too large to paper over, and immigration bills failed in 2006 and 2007. The drama was replayed in 2013 when
a bipartisan Senate bill was blocked in the House.

For Mexicans, who make up the largest immigrant population in the
United States, being told to "go back where you came from" is nothing
new. Mexican workers have experienced several waves of welcome
and ejection based on the needs of employers. They were welcomed as
laborers during World War I to replace draftees sent to war, but when
unemployment soared, they were ejected: "During the Depression, as
many as a million Mexicans, and even Mexican-Americans, were ousted,
along with their American-born children, to spare relief costs or discourage efforts to unionize," writes journalist Nina Bernstein. "They were
welcome again during World War II and cast as heroic 'braceros.' But
in the 1950s, Mexicans were rebranded as dangerous, welfare-seeking
'wetbacks.'"[14]

It shouldn't surprise us that the treatment of immigrant workers
(like that of U.S.-born workers) reflects the needs of capital. When a boom
comes, employers want access to a big pool of available labor so they can
maximize profits. During an upswing, scarce workers have the power
to demand more in wages. If their employers don't accede, workers
can easily find another job. Employers may pretend indifference to the
demands of workers, but in fact they're very attuned to the balance of
power. Economist Dean Baker writes: "From the standpoint of employers,
life is much easier when the workers are lined up at the door clamoring

for jobs than when workers have the option to shop around for better opportunities."[15]

But recent immigrants, especially if they are undocumented, don't have as many options as U.S.-born workers do, and this gives employers more power. Workers without the right papers can be threatened with deportation if they organize for better treatment or higher wages or a union, and most can't get unemployment insurance or other public assistance if they lose their jobs, so there is even more pressure on them to avoid annoying the boss. "Whenever a worker complained about not being paid their wages, or complained of sexual harassment or tried to form a union, all the employer had to do was call immigration, and they could deport away their problem," explained union organizer Ana Avendano.[16] The U.S. union movement increasingly recognized this phenomenon in the 1990s, and in 2000 the AFL-CIO, the United States' primary union federation, took the position that all workers, no matter their immigration status, must have full rights to organize. They noted, "Newly arriving workers continue to make indispensable contributions to the strength and growth of our unions. These efforts have created new unions and strengthened and revived others, benefiting all workers, immigrant and native-born alike."[17]

Lower Wages?

Some politicians claim that immigration is the main reason wages have been stagnant in the United States for the last three decades. Rick Santorum launched a short-lived bid for the Republican presidential nomination in 2015 making this claim, and Republican Wisconsin governor Scott Walker and even Barack Obama as president have suggested this.[18] In fact there is a vigorous debate among economists about whether immigration lowers wages for U.S.-born workers.

"To many non-economists it seems obvious that a rise in population leads to lower wages," writes David Card, an economist specializing in wage levels.[19] But when economists compare areas with lots of immigration to those with little, they find that the effect of immigration on the wages of the U.S.-born workforce is slight. Card argues that the reason immigration doesn't lower wages for the existing workforce is that immigrants are also spending money and generating demand for goods and services, which creates additional jobs. As a result, the demand for workers goes up, creating upward pressure on wages. Card says the presence of immigrants in an area also attracts employers to build plants or invest in companies. So the general effect of immigration on native wages is neutral, he argues, or positive.[20] (I discuss the relation-ship between wages and population in detail in chapter 9, Cheap Labor.)

Some economists have detected an effect. One study estimated that the pay of low-wage workers was reduced by as much as 9 percent by competition from recent immigrants.[21] But Card argues that low U.S. wages cannot be blamed on immigration, because other forces have been much more powerful.[22] Among these forces are a federal minimum wage that doesn't adjust for inflation, leaving workers perpetually behind; the churning of people from job to job due to automation; periodic recessions that cause lots of unemployment, driving everyone's wages down; and the main determinant of wage levels: worker bargaining power through unions. Wages have been driven down for all U.S. workers by the destruc-tion of unions: 35 percent of the workforce was represented by unions in the mid-1950s, under 11 percent is now. These factors dwarf any effect of immigration.

Immigration is favored by employers, not because it drives down wages for all workers, but because immigrants *themselves* are cheaper to hire.[23] And an influx of immigrants can quickly increase the size of the labor force in boom times, when corporations get desperate for addi-tional workers.

Some employers have used recent immigrants to fill low-wage jobs *after* they destroyed unions. The meatpacking industry is a good example. Starting in the 1930s, meatpacking workers (many of them Eastern European immigrants) were able to improve pay and conditions in their plants by unionizing. By the 1970s, the dominant meatpacking corpora-tions were regulated by union contracts that set wages and safety stand-ards across the industry. But in the 1980s, upstart meatpackers like Iowa Beef Processors built smaller plants in rural areas to compete with big urban facilities. These companies automated more of the process, reduc-ing the need for experienced workers, and kept unions out. In response to this more profitable competition, the big unionized employers started their own union-busting. They closed plants, laid off their longtime union employees, and moved the work to non-union shops with lower pay and a faster work pace.[24] Any unionization efforts were met with brutal retaliation. As conditions in the plants became more dangerous and oppressive, more immigrants hired in while some U.S. workers, who had more options, left. In some cases, plant managers deliberately recruited undocumented workers because they wanted more power over them.

The conditions in many meatpacking plants have returned to the barbaric pre-union days, according to a report by Human Rights Watch.

When the union had power, injuries were in line with other manufacturing, but now meatpacking is the most dangerous factory job in the United States. In any year, one-fifth of workers can expect to be injured or made ill. Workers have to quickly wield sharp knives and operate saws in slippery, cold conditions leading to severe cuts and severed appendages. Forced overtime means exhausted workers are more likely to slip up. Machines designed to grab carcasses can grab the humans trying to clean or unjam them, leading to horrifying deaths, while deadly fumes kill others. Training is minimal—one new hire was told, "Do what the guy next to you is doing"—and safety equipment and procedures are junked to speed production. "Meat and poultry industry employers set up the workplaces and practices that create these dangers, but they treat the resulting mayhem as a normal, natural part of the production process, not as what it is—repeated violations of international human rights standards," Human Rights Watch concluded.[25]

It was the destruction of the unions in meatpacking that resulted in lower pay and the dangerous conditions, not the presence of immigrant workers. The answer is not to kick immigrant workers out, but to bring unions back in, as the workers did after a sixteen-year battle at the giant Smithfield pork processing plant in Tar Heel, North Carolina. In response to the union drive, the employer fired undocumented workers and tried to blame it on African American workers and the union.[26] Despite these divide-and-conquer tactics, the workers won by building unity across lines of language and immigration status. But because U.S. labor law is weak and even the weak laws go largely unenforced, this plant is a brave exception.

Perfect Solution?

For now, U.S. employers seem to have found a partial solution to declining birth rates. Young, healthy adults come to the United States, saving the expense of education and health care. Many are pushed into the low-wage workforce where employers can make maximal profits, while workers on skilled work visas bring down the cost to employers of hiring highly educated workers. When the economy tanks, they can be deported, or at least denied unemployment insurance, food stamps, and Medicaid. For the employing class, what's not to like?

There are problems, however, stated most nakedly by the anti-immigration right. Their fears reflect real interests and cannot simply be ascribed to racial prejudice, although racism adds a certain feverishness to the proceedings.

The first is what employers would call "class war." As the AFL-CIO resolution noted, immigrant workers, including those without papers, have led or contributed to many of the significant labor struggles of the last thirty years: meatpackers in North Carolina, taxi drivers in New York City, janitors in Los Angeles, port truckers in Long Beach, farmworkers in Florida, and domestic workers all over the country, to name a few. Perhaps this is because class consciousness is more prevalent in their countries of origin than it is among U.S. workers, who have been taught from a young age that the United States doesn't have classes, or if there is a working class, it is defined by taste in vehicles and music, rather than common exploitation. Immigrant workers of color additionally can become united around their shared experience of racist mistreatment. This tendency of immigrant workers to organize against rotten conditions is one of the reasons employers are wary of immigration as a solution to their demographic worries.

There's another problem with immigrants, from the standpoint of Republicans. When elections come around, those who can vote (the studies usually focus on Latinos) tend to be pro-labor, anti-war, and more Democrat than Republican. For example, after the 2006 immigration debate, the Latino vote went much more strongly toward Democrats, who were seen as defending the rights of immigrant workers. Anti-immigrant Republicans fear that a growing Latino voting bloc would lead to a permanent Republican minority. John O'Sullivan, *National Review* editor-at-large, made the case: "Of course the Democrats will support legalizing twelve million illegal low-paid workers and bringing in millions more. Low-paid workers vote Democrat. They are simply recruiting new constituents. . . . Democrats will gain something like a net four million new voters within three or four election cycles and millions more with each passing decade."[27]

Then there are power structure fears that the supply of immigrants may run dry. Jeb Bush notes uneasily that "the Mexican birth rate is declining and now is barely above replacement level."[28] He suggests that the United States is in competition with other countries for highly educated immigrants and needs to make it easier for them to come here or they'll go elsewhere, like Canada or Chile.[29] "Relying on immigration to prop up our fertility rate . . . presents several problems, the most important of which is that it's unlikely to last," writes Jonathan Last. He laments that countries with low fertility rates don't usually have a lot of emigrants. "In Latin America, the rates of fertility decline are even more extreme than in the U.S. Many countries in South America are already below replacement level, and they send very few immigrants our way. And every other country in Central and South America is on a steep dive toward the replacement line," Last writes.[30]

Additionally, immigration has created political problems for Republicans among their voters. While these politicians encourage anti-immigrant bigotry in public, their actual policies are more concerned with the workforce demands of large employers. This gap between word and action has left an opening for anti-immigrant demagogues like Donald Trump, who rode anti-immigrant anxiety all the way to the White House, promising a wall to keep out Mexicans and a ban to keep out Muslims.

Conservative parties in other countries have experienced similar punishment from their electorates for their pro-immigration policies. The Christian Democrats in Germany faced losses in 2016 to a right-wing anti-immigration party, the Alternative for Germany, after Chancellor Angela Merkel welcomed war refugees from Syria, Iraq, and other conflicts. French politics have been roiled by the anti-immigrant National Front, which gained support following terrorist attacks in Paris and Nice. In Britain, Conservative Prime Minister David Cameron took the ill-advised decision to call a referendum on his country's participation in Europe. He was hoping to dispatch grumbling from the anti-immigrant wing of his party, but voters unexpectedly forced the country to exit the European Union. The primary complaint driving Brexit voters was unimpeded immigration to Britain from other parts of Europe.

Finally, immigration isn't making up for low birth rates. "In many rich countries, worker-hungry businesses are eager for more immigrants," suggests the *Wall Street Journal*. "But to stabilize the elderly share of advanced countries' population would require an immediate eightfold increase from less-developed countries. . . . This isn't politically feasible given the resistance that even current levels of migration have generated."[31]

While importing workers saves the employing class money, it is also giving them headaches. The basic problem for the establishment is that immigration will not satisfactorily solve their demographic woes. Even now it is causing them messy political problems and, more alarmingly, it may prime the workforce with workers who have greater class consciousness.

CHAPTER 8

REPRODUCTION AND RACE

Are there really unwanted populations in the United States? People can become targets of population control when they occupy land that is coveted by the powerful, as with the sterilization abuse of Puerto Ricans driven off farms to make way for big plantations, as we saw in chapter 5. Native American women's reproductive capacity has been targeted for similar reasons.[1]

But people have also been targeted by the power structure for population control when they show a tendency to organize for their rights, or when they manage to force the system to provide resources for raising children. Both things were true of black people after World War II, as resistance to white supremacy gathered strength and broke down whites-only barriers to schools, hospitals, welfare, and public services. Comedian and civil rights activist Dick Gregory noted the change in power structure policy: "Back in the days of slavery, black folks couldn't grow kids fast enough for white folks to harvest. Now that we've got a little taste of power, white folks want us to call a moratorium on having babies."[2]

Some interpreted attacks on black women's reproduction in the 1960s as attempts at genocide. But it would be an error to assume that the power structure doesn't want black people or other people of color to exist. To get a fuller picture, we need to look at the history of the white ruling class in relation to captured Africans. The powerful have been torn between their fear of political upheaval and their desire for profits from black people's work. In the words of the Black Feminist Working Group, "The United States government has, from its inception, consistently attempted to regulate, scapegoat and profit from the reproductive capabilities of black people."[3]

Children a Commodity

In Colonial times, the white power structure was conflicted about the value of black women's reproductive labor. It needed the labor of Africans to create its wealth, but feared rebellion.

Slave-owners measured in money the reproductive work of the African women they enslaved. Laws like a 1662 Virginia statute decreed that children of enslaved women were automatically enslaved themselves, even if their fathers were free, or white.[4] Children became the property of the mother's owner, and a valuable commodity to be sold to other slave-owners.

The "natural increase" of slaves became the basis for the South's financial system, according to historians Ned and Constance Sublette. The reproduction of enslaved people acted as interest on the owners' wealth, and the wealthy used slaves as collateral for loans and sold them to raise cash fast.[5] Enslaved people didn't just generate wealth, they also *were* the wealth of the South.

After 1808, when the United States made slave importation illegal, slavery became a closed system that could only perpetuate itself through the childbearing of enslaved women, and an even greater premium was put on their maternal labor. Martha Jackson, a freedwoman from Alabama born under slavery in 1850, remembered that her aunt was never beaten because she was regarded as a "breeder woman" who "brought in children every twelve months just like a cow bringing in a calf. [The master gave] orders she can't be put to any strain because of that."[6]

Freedmen and women recalled the lengths to which the slave system tried to reconcile two things necessary to its profitability: the brutality necessary to extract maximum labor from enslaved women, and childbearing by those same women. Freedwoman Lizzie Williams witnessed beatings of pregnant women on a Mississippi plantation. "[The white folks] would dig a hole in the ground just big enough for her stomach, make her lie face down and whip her on the back to keep from hurting the child."[7]

In these unbearable circumstances, enslaved women fought to control their reproduction. black feminist scholars have documented contraception, abortion, and infanticide by women under slavery. Herbal remedies were used as contraceptives and to induce abortion and "Midwives conspired with pregnant slaves to induce and cover up abortions," writes Dorothy Roberts.[8]

Mary Gaffney, a freedwoman who had been enslaved in Texas, recalled that she chewed cotton root as a contraceptive. Her owner thought he "was going to raise him a lot more slaves, but still I cheated [him] . . . he wondered what was the matter. . . . I kept cotton roots and chewed them all the time . . . so I never did have any children while I was a slave."[9] Black men resisted, too. "Slavery shall never own a wife or child of mine," said J.W. Loguen, vowing not to marry until he was free.[10]

But at the same time they wanted maximum reproduction, slave-owners feared that black people might become too numerous and could overwhelm their captors. These fears were stoked by periodic slave uprisings and then, to the horror of enslavers everywhere, the successful Haitian revolution starting in 1791. Historian Gerald Horne writes that George Washington, nervous about the stability of the newly independent United States, lamented the "unfortunate insurrection of the Negroes in Hispaniola," which he declared "both daring and alarming."[11] Washington argued that after the Haitian revolution it was too dangerous to import slaves from the Caribbean—they might bring the flame of insurrection northward. The uprising "should have operated to produce a total prohibition of the importation of slaves," he wrote in 1793. The governor of South Carolina warned that the United States too might one day "be exposed to the same insurrections." One of Washington's associates, Tench Coxe, concerned that blacks would outnumber whites, wrote in 1802 that "the evils of Negro insurrection are so very great, that I hope our legislature will [enact] a naturalization law . . . foreigners with property, professions, and occupations will be a good counterbalance for the blacks."[12]

The Haitian revolution and the various rebellions it supported and encouraged elsewhere were indeed a threat to the slave system, and bolstered abolitionists in England, France, and northern U.S. states, but it would take another seventy years and a bloody war for abolition to reach the South.

Keeping Cheap Labor in Place

After the slavocracy was overthrown, a short period of African American political rights followed. Black men voted and held office. Freed people acquired land and became competitors with whites for farm acreage and business. This period showed precisely what the slave-owners had most feared, not that blacks were unfit for freedom, but that black people were quite capable of governing, all too capable as far as their erstwhile masters were concerned. A fragile period of expanded democracy lasted as long as federal troops remained in the South to secure it, but their withdrawal allowed a long period of backlash against black political and economic independence.

Under slavery, there was a brutal security apparatus to prevent slaves from escaping. But with the end of slavery, big landowners became worried that their black workers might leave, so they passed laws to restrict the movements of freed people, arresting as "vagrants" any who could not prove employment, and making it illegal to relocate if you owed money.[13] First Mississippi and then other southern states enacted Black Codes to prevent black people from owning farmland, carrying weapons, or assembling in groups. While abolishing slavery, the Thirteenth Amendment has one clause allowing involuntary servitude—as punishment for crime—so southern governments made every infraction a crime. Blacks were punished through a system of "convict leasing" that looked a lot like slavery, whereby the state provided convicts to landowners to work for free. Black people were once again given no option but to work for the big landowners.

Nonetheless, blacks did leave in increasing numbers, fleeing economic exploitation and white supremacist terror. Their movement north and west turned into what historians call the Great Migration, "one of the largest and most rapid internal movements of people in history," according to historian Nicholas Lemann.[14] As the Great Migration gained momentum in 1916, the southern power structure mobilized to stop it. "The South was interested in keeping cheap labor . . . they often went to train stations and arrested Negroes wholesale, which in turn made them miss their trains," wrote Harlem artist Jacob Lawrence, who documented the Great Migration in a sixty-painting series.[15]

Georgia's *Macon Telegraph* opined in 1916: "We must have the negro in the South . . . it is the most pressing thing before this State today. Matters of governorships and judgeships are only bagatelle compared to the real importance of this negro exodus."[16]

Troop mobilizations for World War I left northern factories with a labor shortage and employers sent recruiters south to promise jobs. Southern states and cities responded by passing laws against them. Alabama required labor recruiters to pay $750 in every county they operated in, or face a year's hard labor and a $500 fine. In Meridian, Mississippi, the police confiscated copies of the *Chicago Defender*, a black-run paper that they thought might attract people to Chicago.

The southern power structure was desperate to keep black workers in place. "In Brookhaven, Mississippi, authorities stopped a train with fifty colored migrants on it and sidetracked it for three days," historian Isabel Wilkerson writes. "In Albany, Georgia, the police tore up the tickets of colored passengers as they stood waiting to board. . . . In Savannah,

Georgia, police arrested every colored person at the station regardless of where he or she was going. In Summit, Mississippi, authorities simply closed the ticket office and did not let northbound trains stop for the colored people waiting to get on."

Black migrants kept leaving, sometimes purchasing tickets for a station three stops away, and there, where there was less surveillance, buying a ticket to Chicago or Detroit or Pittsburgh or New York.[17]

As during slavery, white landowners and employers needed black workers, whose work made the land productive and the big landowners wealthy. "Black labor is the best labor the South can get," wrote the *Columbia State* of South Carolina. "No other would work long under the same conditions."[18]

It was not only white landowners' racial animus but their desire to keep black people working, and the immense value of their labor, that was foremost in the minds of the homicidal racists who ran the slave South and its Jim Crow successors.

We Charge Genocide

Considering the police shootings of unarmed African Americans, incarceration rates that are off the charts, lower life expectancy, higher maternal and infant mortality, and higher unemployment than whites, it does sometimes look like the U.S. ruling class just wishes black people would disappear.

Has that been the goal? This question was addressed in 1951 by the authors of *We Charge Genocide*, a petition submitted to the United Nations appealing for relief under the UN's 1948 Genocide Convention.

The petition documents an escalation of white terror, north and south, following the end of World War II. The increase in repression was a response to civil rights organizing that had gained momentum during the war and flourished with the demobilization of a million black service members who expected, since they had risked their lives to defend democracy abroad, that they would see a little more of it when they returned home.

Petitioners included leading voices of the black left—W.E.B. Du Bois, Claudia Jones, Harry Haywood, and Paul Robeson—along with widows and family of black men executed on bogus rape charges, and men imprisoned under similar circumstances. The authors document lynchings, jailings, denials of emergency care in hospitals, threats and murders for attempting to vote, and police murders.

"It is sometimes incorrectly thought that genocide means the complete and definitive destruction of a race or people," wrote the authors of the book-length petition. However, "Any intent to destroy, in whole or in part, a national, racial, ethnic or religious group is genocide, according to the [UN's 1948 Genocide] Convention."

"We particularly pray for the most careful reading of this material by those who have always regarded genocide as a term to be used only where the acts of terror evinced an intent to destroy a whole nation," they wrote.[19]

The authors explained that the goal of the genocidal actions they documented was not a decrease in the number of black people but *control*:

> The foundation of this genocide of which we complain is economic. It is genocide for profit. The intricate superstructure of "law and order" and extra-legal terror enforces an oppression that guarantees profit. This was true of that genocide, perhaps the most bloody ever perpetrated, which for two hundred and fifty years enforced chattel slavery upon the American Negro. Then as now it increased in bloodiness with the militancy of the Negro people as they struggled to achieve democracy for themselves. It was particularly bloody under slavery because the Negro people never ceased fighting for their freedom.[20]

Repression goes along with exploitation: the worse the exploitation—and the more people resist—the worse the repression. But the *goal* is the exploitation of people's work, not their elimination. Often, in discussions of racism, the enormous value of black people's work to employers, and to the society at large, remains hidden.

Black Work Matters

Because black workers are generally paid less, it is sometimes implied that their work is worth less than the work of whites. In fact, it is worth *more* to employers: to the extent that black workers are underpaid compared to whites, to that same extent they are providing the employing class additional profits. The same is true for women's lower pay, and it's especially true for black women. Black women's pay gap makes them the most profitable workers from the perspective of employers, which might explain why fast food companies in the United States are so rich while their workers—half of whom are women and 40 percent people of color—are hardly able to survive. The Waltons have accumulated over

$100 billion in personal wealth based on the labor of Walmart's under-paid frontline workforce, mostly women and people of color.

When she was a young staffer with the United Electrical Workers union, Betty Friedan wrote a pamphlet explaining how discrimination benefits employers: "Wage discrimination against women workers exists in every industry where women are employed. It exists because it pays off in billions of dollars in extra profits for the companies. . . . The situation of Negro women workers today is even more shocking."[21]

How much extra profit? Friedan did the math and estimated that in just one year, U.S. manufacturers made $5 billion "in extra profits from their exploitation of women," in 1952 dollars. A current estimate of the premium that goes to employers for discrimination against women is $900 billion a year.[22]

It would also be a mistake to conclude that a higher rate of unemployment among black workers means that they are not valuable to employers, or are simply "throwaways" in a racist system that can no longer use their work. Higher unemployment rates drive down wages, and discrimination takes away options, meaning that black workers, along with Latinos and many recent immigrants, are pushed into the most exhausting, tedious, heavy, dangerous, and dirty jobs. Instead of making those jobs better paid or safer in order to hire or retain workers, discrimination means employers can get away with low wages and dangerous conditions. Employment discrimination isn't a misunderstanding that can be cleared up by "diversity" education, or a blindness on the part of employers to the value of black work—it serves employer interests.

It's worth pausing for a moment to note that an overemphasis on white privilege can distract white people—European Americans—from noticing how their wages and life chances are also undermined by racism. The South, where racism is deepest and the privileges conferred on white skin should therefore be the most pronounced, is actually a depressed region of the country, with the lowest wages, the least social supports, the schools most starved for resources, the unions weakest, and the least environmental and consumer protections.[23] The privilege that whites are alleged to gain from racism turns out to be just another way to jack down living standards for everyone. Yes, white people get advantages over people of color, but whites take the bait of racism at their peril.

Sterilization Abuse

The authors of *We Charge Genocide* attributed the increase in repression to an increase in resistance after World War II. As the civil rights movement grew, that repression started to include forced sterilizations. This was new; there had not been much special attention paid to African American birth rates, as distinct from whites, until the Great Depression. Black people had largely been spared the eugenicist's scalpel because public welfare programs had mainly been whites-only, as were the institutions where doctors did most involuntary sterilizations. Eugenics was mostly about "improving" the white race and black people weren't even on the radar.[24]

Indeed, birth control campaigners within the black community had to make great efforts to win rights to the same level of access to birth control clinics that white women had. But after World War II, as black organizing increased, and as African Americans won access to programs from which they had been previously excluded, the white power structure suddenly became concerned that the black birth rate was too high.

In the South, another factor was at work: The labor-intensive cotton farming system was ending due to mechanization. The change was driven by the labor shortage during World War II, and by white fears of returning black GIs. Nicholas Lemann quotes a planter's impassioned letter to the local cotton industry association in 1944: "I strongly advocate the farmers of the Mississippi Delta changing as rapidly as possible from the old tenant or sharecropping [system]. . . . Mechanized farming will require only a fraction of the amount of labor which is required by the share crop system thereby tending to equalize the white and negro population which would automatically make our racial problem easier to handle."

First, mechanical pickers were brought in, replacing the picking job but leaving the task of chopping (removing weeds). Plantations started to kick their resident workers out, hiring day labor for the chopping jobs. Lemann writes that as black war veterans returned to Mississippi and tried to register to vote, the white plantation owners got even more nervous because African Americans outnumbered whites and could easily outvote them, in some places three to one. "The idea of getting the numbers of blacks and whites in the Delta a little closer to equilibrium began to seem attractive to whites on political as well as economic grounds," Lemann writes. Then in the late 1950s, planters started to use herbicides to keep down the weeds, eliminating the chopping job.[25] This explains the quick about-face of the southern white power structure—from trying to prevent black workers from leaving, to forcibly sterilizing black women.

"They'll Head for Chicago"

At the height of the battle over federal civil rights law, while Mississippi's James Eastland and seventeen other southern senators were launching a filibuster of the Civil Rights Act in March of 1964, the Student Nonviolent Coordinating Committee published *Genocide in Mississippi*. This twelve-page pamphlet brought national attention to a law passed by the Mississippi House of Representatives which made having a second child out of wedlock a felony punishable by one to three years in prison (the original bill had stipulated punishment upon the birth of a first child). In lieu of prison, the mother (and father, if apprehended) could opt for sterilization. SNCC showed that the law was aimed at black people, reporting statements by the bill's supporters that "the measure would cut down the rise of illegitimate children on the welfare rolls and force many Negroes to leave the state." Representative Stone Barefield said during the debate, "When the cutting starts, they'll head for Chicago."[26]

While SNCC's exposure of the bill stopped it from passing the Mississippi Senate, sterilization of black women was already unofficial policy among white Mississippi doctors. Fannie Lou Hamer, the brilliant tactician of the Mississippi Freedom Democratic Party, had been sterilized when she went to the hospital to get a uterine tumor removed in 1961. The doctor who inflicted the unnecessary hysterectomy neither asked her consent nor informed her afterward. In 1965, Hamer estimated that Sunflower County's hospital, in the heart of Delta cotton country, had forcibly sterilized 60 percent of black women who had been admitted to give birth. The practice was so common it was called a "Mississippi appendectomy."[27]

A 1974 lawsuit exposed widespread official support for the practice, not just in Mississippi. In 1973 doctors sterilized two African American sisters in Montgomery, Alabama, ages twelve and fourteen, when their mother thought she was consenting to experimental contraceptive shots. The Relf family lawsuit, combined with a lawsuit by the National Welfare Rights Organization, revealed that "Although Congress has been insistent that all family planning programs function on a purely voluntary basis, there is uncontroverted evidence . . . that an indefinite number of poor people have been improperly coerced into accepting a sterilization operation under the threat that various federally supported welfare benefits would be withdrawn unless they submitted."[28] District Court Judge Gerhard Gesell found that sterilizations were very common, 100,000 to 150,000 women had been sterilized annually. It is unclear how many were coerced or forced, but a disproportionate 50 percent were black.[29] To 1960s black liberationists and many feminists, incidents of forced sterilization of black women looked like a continuation of population control policies abroad, applied to the black population here in the United States.

It's hard to overstate the elite panic caused by mobilizations of black people in the 1960s. When it wasn't demands for the vote and school integration, it was demands for jobs and housing. Welfare mothers conducted sit-ins at politicians' offices demanding increased benefits. Black Panthers called for a multiracial revolution taking inspiration from Marx, Lenin, and Mao. Black nationalists called for an independent black state in the South. Urban riots—or uprisings—took place in sixty-two cities in 1967, panicking the Johnson administration which sent in troops, infiltrated black organizations with police spies, and impaneled commissions to recommend appeasement measures in the form of poverty relief. When Martin Luther King Jr. was assassinated in 1968, dozens more uprisings filled the country's biggest cities with smoke. At the same time, Puerto Rican, Chicano, and Native American movements were gaining strength, and the U.S. military was failing to subdue the Vietnamese. Population size may not have been the cause of the rebellions, but thinning out these restive populations, here and overseas, must have seemed like a plausible strategy to some members of a ruling class that was losing control.

Population control sentiment came from the top; it wasn't just a few rogue doctors. The U.S. government "eventually will have to do something about this country's rapidly growing population," said Donald Rumsfeld, then White House counselor to Richard Nixon, in 1971. The government "will have to decide about persuading or coercing its citizens to have fewer children."[30]

Doctors all over the country sterilized black women, Latinas, and white welfare recipients without their knowledge or consent when they went to hospitals to deliver babies. An obstetrician writing in 1973 for the journal *Contemporary Ob/Gyn* explained why he participated in sterilizing patients against their will: "The welfare mess, as it is called, cries out for solutions, one of which is fertility control."[31]

While women on public assistance, and in particular black women, were being targeted for sterilization, non-poor women who wanted to be sterilized faced something called the "120 rule," instituted by most hospitals in the 1950s. Hospital administrators multiplied your age by the number of children you had. If you were thirty and had four children, or forty and already had three children, the operation might be permitted. But if the total were lower than 120, the hospital board would refuse the operation. Some hospitals used a 150 rule or a 175 rule. Poet Adrienne Rich recalled that in the 1950s she "had to plead and argue for sterilization after bearing three children." She had to present a letter "counter-signed by my husband" and give her rheumatoid arthritis as "a reason acceptable to the male panel who sat on my case; my own judgment would not have been acceptable."[32] As feminism got going again, women started suing hospitals that had refused to help them. After decades of denials, they got the rules thrown out.[33]

By 1969, forced or coerced sterilization was a known threat aimed at black women and any low-waged or unemployed woman. A white testifier at the 1969 Redstockings Abortion Speakout said that she had been offered a deal by one of the several hospitals to which she applied for a legally sanctioned abortion: She could have the abortion if she agreed to be sterilized. She was twenty years old.[34]

Both black and white radicals in the newly emerging feminist movement were denouncing forced sterilization at the same time they were fighting for abortion rights.[35] Some scholars later claimed that majority-white feminist groups didn't address this until the late 1970s, but the written record contradicts this.[36] For example, Redstockings' 1969 letter to new women says: "The most fundamental rights to life and body are denied women. Laws against abortion in every state force us to bear children against our will and cause thousands of us to die each year. At the very same time, others of us are being denied the right to have children. Many women in the 'land of the free' are being forcibly sterilized."

An International Women's Day flier from 1970 produced by Florida's Gainesville Women's Liberation group demanded: "Free and safe abortions on demand; and an end to forced sterilization—the genocide of black and brown people."[37]

While sterilizations were being forced on some women, others who were pregnant and didn't want to be were suffering injuries or death from illicit abortions. Women of color bore the worst of it.

There were some splits among feminists over sterilization based on women's different experiences. In Los Angeles in the late 1960s and early 1970s, hundreds of Mexican American women were sterilized against their will at the county hospital, often just after they gave birth. They had signed consent forms, but the signatures were extracted while they were in labor. The women recalled threats: they would be denied painkillers, or they were told they would die, if they didn't sign the form. Because of this practice, feminist Gloria Molina recalled, Latinas were campaigning to require a waiting period between signing the consent form and the operation. White feminists, who more often faced obstacles to getting sterilized, viewed this as just another barrier and wanted sterilization with no waiting.[38]

A 1975 flier produced by the New York Wages for Housework Committee summed up their analysis of the reasons for involuntary sterilizations at the same time birth control and abortion were denied:

> In the USA it is welfare women and Black women in particular who are the main target of the government sterilization policy. . . . When they need more workers, we women are forbidden any form of contraception and we are condemned to uninterrupted maternity, or we are forced to resort to back street abortionists. . . . When the workers we produce are not disciplined enough, or when we claim some money for the cost of raising them—that is, when *we* are not disciplined enough, they sterilize us.[39]

What about Now?

There is evidence that the nervousness among the powerful about "overproduction" of black children faded in the early 1970s as the general overpopulation craze passed and as the most revolutionary parts of the black liberation movement were crushed, with many leaders assassinated, imprisoned, or exiled.

Fannie Lou Hamer and SNCC, the National Welfare Rights Organization, the Black Panthers, the Relf family, and the fast-growing women's liberation movement (including black-led feminist organizations like the SNCC Black Women's Liberation Committee) were exposing the power structure's racist sterilization policies at a time when newly independent countries in Africa were looking carefully at whether to align with the United States, be neutral, or ally with socialist countries. International power games meant the U.S. government needed to fix its racist ways, or at least appear to do so. At the same time, the birth rate in the United States was plunging. Some combination of these factors led the coercive sterilizers to back off.

Protests caused Medicaid to institute consent rules for sterilization in 1976. No longer could women be induced to sign consent forms during labor, and no one under twenty-one or who was institutionalized could be sterilized. Initially there was a seventy-two-hour waiting period after written consent; in 1978 the waiting period was extended to thirty days. Now there is evidence that waiting periods and consent forms have become an obstacle to getting the operation under Medicaid. A recent study found that sixty-two thousand women annually have requested sterilization under Medicaid but have not been able to obtain it. Medicaid does pay for twice that number of sterilization operations each year.[40]

Current federal and state policies seem to be mainly aimed at coercing the production of babies regardless of race. The Hyde Amendment has stopped Medicaid from covering abortion since 1977. While seventeen states now fund some abortions through Medicaid, bypassing Hyde restrictions, not one of these states is in the South where more than half of African Americans reside.[41] Medicaid enrollment is 41 percent white, 22 percent black, 25 percent Latino, and 12 percent other people of color. If the white power structure were making it a priority to reduce births among people of color, these barriers would have fallen.[42]

Hyde restrictions also hit military women, 47 percent of whom are women of color, with 31 percent African American.[43] Unbelievably, until 2013, the military exceptions were even narrower than Hyde. A servicewoman (or a military spouse or dependent) could only get an abortion under her military health plan if the pregnancy endangered her life. Since 2013 the regulations have provided exceptions for rape and incest, but still deny abortion for the most common reason—not wanting to be pregnant.[44]

In Mississippi, where SNCC exposed involuntary sterilizations in the 1960s, there is only one abortion clinic. But the state is beset by anti-abortion Crisis Pregnancy Centers (thirty-eight by one count) dedicated to manipulating women into carrying their pregnancies to term.[45] Mississippi state law requires that doctors lie to their patients that abortion will increase their risk of breast cancer; and they face a twenty-four-hour waiting period after this "counseling," a required ultrasound, and if underage, notification of both parents. Of the states with the highest teen pregnancy rates, seven are in the South, including Mississippi, Louisiana, Alabama, and Texas.

Nor should we get confused by welfare policies that seem to be aimed at reducing births but are really more about saving money and rationalizing the resulting suffering. Take "family caps," which were permitted under the 1996 welfare reform and apply in fifteen states, including much of the South.[46] These laws say that if you conceive a child under the current welfare program, Temporary Assistance for Needy Families, your welfare check will not increase to help you care for the new child. The regulation is justified by the idea that women on welfare were having children to increase their checks, which is ridiculous when you look at how long the checks generally last (two years maximum with a lifetime limit of five years) and how little they would increase per child (from $20 more a month in Wyoming to $130 more a month in California).[47] The caps are in reality just another cut to welfare, another way to push the

REPRODUCTION AND RACE   117

work and expense of young children entirely onto their impoverished families. If you are pregnant and *don't* want to bear a child, as we've seen, in most states Medicaid won't pay for your abortion.

While national policies have tended toward coercing births among women of all races, there are outbursts of racist population control. The most far-reaching was the promotion in the 1990s of long-acting contraceptives Norplant and Depo-Provera, aimed at young black women. Norplant, a long-acting contraceptive implanted under the skin, was approved by the FDA in 1990 and shortly after that promoted in black-majority high schools in Baltimore. Its use spread from there. Lawsuits over its side effects eventually led its maker to withdraw it from the U.S. market. Depo-Provera, a contraceptive shot, has been similarly promoted to young women of color, even though it carries worrisome side effects. In 2004 the U.S. Food and Drug Administration recommended against using it for longer than two years because of risks to bone density.[48]

Partly because women of color have continued to organize against them, and partly because the power structure isn't as enthusiastic about population control, these efforts are more limited than in the 1960s. Some rely on private funding. A pernicious private program called Project Prevention (originally "CRACK") emerged in 1997 that "bribes women who have a substance abuse problem to be sterilized." For $300, women could "cash in their reproductive rights," according to INCITE! Women of Color Against Violence. In a classic population controller argument, "They blame women of color for social problems rather than government and corporate policies that have led to increased poverty in communities of color." Instead of the $300, INCITE! called for "Free and low-cost drug treatment for pregnant and parenting women that offer[s] neo-natal care, pre-natal care and childcare."[49] But the effort persisted in 2010.[50]

Black feminist theoretician and organizer Loretta Ross, of SisterSong Women of Color Reproductive Justice Collective, has argued that U.S. restrictions on birth control serve to push white women to produce more babies, in part to balance out the political power of people of color. "Many of the restrictions on abortion, contraception, scientifically-accurate sex education, and stem cell research are directly related to an unsubtle campaign of positive eugenics to force heterosexual white women to have more babies," Ross writes.[51] A recent example is the Colorado legislature blocking funds that would have continued a small program to provide free or cheap IUDs and contraceptive implants to low-income young women in Colorado, mostly white. The teen birth rate dropped, saving the state more money that it would have spent on the program, but that did not convince the Colorado legislature to fund it.[52]

While white babies are encouraged, Ross writes: "In contrast, children of color are often deemed unwanted, excessive and perceived as a threat to the body politic of the United States by being described as a 'youth bulge' creating a dysfunctional education system, economic chaos, environmental degradation, and a criminal underclass."[53]

Is the racist rhetoric identified by Ross an indication that the powerful want to stop black women from having children? Dorothy Roberts, in her book *Killing the Black Body*, writes:

> Although some Blacks believe that white-controlled family planning literally threatens Black survival, I take the position that racist birth control policies serve primarily an ideological function. The chief danger of these programs is not the physical annihilation of a race or social class. . . . Rather, the chief danger of these policies is the legitimation of an oppressive social structure. Proposals to solve social problems by curbing Black reproduction make racial inequality appear to be the product of nature rather than power.[54]

Of course there are racists who would like to reduce the number of people of color relative to white people, or who fear a "majority minority" country, in which European Americans are projected to be less than 50 percent of the population by 2050. We met some of them in our discussion of immigration, and Donald Trump's 2016 presidential campaign was pitched to voters with those anxieties. But those running the country face the same contradictions we saw in slavery days and in ongoing immigration fights—needing an abundant oppressed workforce, but uneasy about the political implications.

The racist ideology identified by Ross and Roberts no doubt influences the actions of doctors, welfare administrators, and others in petty positions of power, resulting in eruptions of racist population control. But on balance it seems the command to "make more babies" currently covers women of all races. What is clear is that women's reproductive capacity continues to be controlled and exploited, and black women and other women of color have suffered, and are still suffering, the worst violations of their reproductive freedom.

The range of reproductive coercion and the lack of decent conditions for raising children, which hit women of color hardest, have led Ross and others in SisterSong to organize around a program they call "reproductive justice," which includes fixing the racist, sexist, and capitalist injustices that make raising children so hard, while expanding reproductive rights to include full access to reproductive health, health care, and a healthy community, not just birth control and abortion.[55]

Ross writes: "A woman cannot make an individual decision about her body if she is part of a community whose human rights as a group are violated, such as through environmental dangers or insufficient quality health care." She criticizes the tendency to fight for abortion rights as a single issue. "Reproductive justice addresses issues of population control, bodily self-determination, immigrants' rights, economic and environmental justice, sovereignty, and militarism and criminal injustices that limit individual human rights because of group or community oppressions."[56] Winning the right to not have children is only one part of the battle—we all need healthy social conditions in which to bear and raise them.

CHAPTER 9

CHEAP LABOR

I s it really true that the fewer workers there are, the higher their pay will be, and the more workers there are, the lower their pay will be? This seems to be what the financial press is insisting when they warn of higher labor costs due to low birth rates. It's a simple case of supply and demand, they seem to be saying. But is it true? The idea goes back at least to Adam Smith, the "father of economics." Smith, writing in Scotland in 1776, thought that the "invisible hand" of the market controlled the price of labor by determining the survival of children. The greater the supply of laborers, he reasoned, the lower the price of labor. He writes that "poverty, though it does not prevent the generation, is extremely unfavourable to the rearing of children. The tender plant is produced, but in so cold a soil and so severe a climate, soon withers and dies. It is not uncommon, I have been frequently told, in the Highlands of Scotland for a mother who has borne twenty children not to have two alive."[1]

Smith argues that when workers are scarce, employers are forced to increase their pay, allowing families to live in better conditions and more children to survive to adulthood. The resulting increase in workers leads wages to fall again, starving some and restoring a macabre equilibrium:

> The reward of labor must necessarily encourage in such manner the marriage and multiplication of laborers. . . . If the reward at any time should be less than what was requisite for this purpose, the deficiency of hands would soon raise it; and if it should at any time be more, their excessive multiplication would soon lower it to this necessary rate. . . . It is in this manner that the demand for men, like that of any other commodity, necessarily regulates the production

of men; quickens it when it goes on too slowly, and stops it when it advances too fast.[2]

Nearly a hundred years later, Karl Marx argued against this view, saying that the survival rate of children could in no way account for the rapid fluctuations in the demand for labor, along with fluctuations in the price of labor, which he saw all around him in 1860s industrial Europe.

Corporate owners hire more people when there is paying demand for their products, the boom part of the boom-and-bust cycle characteristic of capitalism. When demand becomes slack, they lay them off. Since the boom-bust cycle takes place every ten years or so, Marx argued, population cannot be a factor leading to these wild swings, because population cannot be produced that rapidly.[3]

Instead of blaming the workers for having too many children, Marx blamed the tendency of capital to make more than it could sell, because it failed to pay the workers enough to buy the product of their own labor. Needed goods piled up in warehouses because people didn't have enough money to purchase them. Workers lined up desperate for employment, not because they were too numerous, but because capital developed a periodic incapacity to use them.

This "overproduction" problem came to full flower in the United States and worldwide with the crash of 1929 and the Great Depression following it. It was not a sudden abundance of workers that was at fault, but the sudden inability of capital to employ them. Unemployment was so prevalent it could no longer be blamed on individual workers' alleged lack of motivation, training, or education.

In the United States, the Depression led to a deep questioning of the system, as well as to the militant labor organizing which resulted in the reforms of the New Deal. But ordinary rates of unemployment under capitalism, Marx argues, are essential to maintain the power of the employing class. The presence of a "reserve army of the unemployed" weakens the power of all workers, employed and unemployed. The more unemployed people there are, the less power employed workers have, and the lower wages can be driven: "The general movements of wages are exclusively regulated by the expansion and contraction of the industrial reserve army . . . not . . . by the variations of the absolute numbers of the working population, but by the varying proportions in which the working class is divided into active and reserve army," Marx wrote.[4]

Depressions and recessions, with their high unemployment, weaken the power of the working class to resist wage cuts. We can see examples of this in recent times. As unemployment rose after the great financial crisis of 2008, wages dropped for those who still had jobs.[5] Recalling British Prime Minister Margaret Thatcher's drastic cuts in government spending in the 1980s and the layoffs that resulted, a conservative commentator wrote in an unguarded moment: "Raising unemployment was a very desirable way of reducing the strength of the working classes."[6] This is when bosses tell workers, so sorry, because of the economy, we have to cut your pay, and by the way, I have a stack of applications for your job on my desk.

So does the overall population matter at all to wages? The employing class cannot rely on sheer numbers alone to undermine the power of workers, because the boom and bust cycle still determines the employment rate. But a stable or falling population narrows their range of motion. It's harder to maintain a pool of unemployed people when the working-age population is shrinking, as it has started to do in Japan and China.

But perhaps more importantly, a stable or falling population creates the specter of a shrinking economy. It seems likely that capitalism requires growth to function. In past eras, this meant bringing new areas under capitalist control, but these are largely exhausted. The devastation of war can create new markets, as we saw with the demand for goods and services after World War II, to rebuild destroyed factories and cities. And so can population growth, like the postwar baby boom in the United States, with growing families requiring food, clothing, housing, and transportation. But can capitalism cope with stable or declining populations? This is a new problem, and mainstream economists are not sure what to make of it. Liberal economist Paul Krugman writes, "The Census projects that the population aged eighteen to sixty-four will grow at an annual rate of only 0.2 percent between 2015 and 2025. Unless labor force participation not only stops declining but starts rising rapidly again, this means a slower-growth economy."[7] Krugman and others have suggested that the two decades of stagnation afflicting the Japanese economy have been due to its low birth rate, and they argue that it is a warning to other societies which will soon have shrinking workforces.

How to Suppress Wages

The growth of the economy is a long-term worry, but in the short term, employers have lots of tactics to increase the pool of potential workers when the demand for labor is high. Part of the motivation for "ending welfare as we know it" during the Bill Clinton administration was that unemployment was low and wages were rising as a result. Pushing mothers of small children onto the job market was a quick way to bring down wages, because it increased the pool of workers who needed jobs.

Indeed, increasing unemployment is the standard method used by the U.S. Federal Reserve to curb inflation, by which the Fed mostly means a rise in the price of labor.[8] When unemployment gets "too low" (jobs are easy to get) and wages threaten to rise, the Fed raises interest rates, making it more expensive for businesses to borrow money. The effect is to slow down the economy and sink millions of people into unemployment and desperation, blaming themselves for the loss of their jobs. And because all workers lose leverage, their wages go down.

This is why employers want to increase the number of people available for work—to increase the size of that "reserve army of the unemployed"—though not so much that it will cause a questioning of the whole system, as it did in the 1930s. Once there's a pool of unemployed workers with no other way to survive, employers can gain the upper hand.

How do they increase the labor pool without paying more? They need quick ways—having more kids is too slow. Importing workers has its own problems, as we've seen, which is why employers like "guest worker" programs so they can deport workers when unemployment rises again. We've already discussed cutting welfare. Then there's unemployment insurance that is inadequate and quickly runs out. Another way is to raise the retirement age, or make pensions so inadequate that people can't afford to retire and need to keep working. Then there's lowering the working age. If there is any doubt that employers would hire children if it weren't illegal, we need only look at U.S. agriculture, where child labor is legal and five hundred thousand U.S. children, as young as six, help support their farmworker families by working in the fields.[9] Maine governor Paul LePage has pushed for his state to lower the working age to twelve.

A less-noted way to increase the reserve army of unemployed people is to intensify the work process, a method known as "lean production." When a nurse has to take care of eight patients instead of five, or when an autoworker on an assembly line is forced to be in motion fifty-five seconds of every minute as opposed to forty seconds, they are really doing the jobs of more than one person. This allows employers to lay off workers. Conversely, when workers have more control over their work process, they slow it down, leading to more jobs at a more humane pace. Today, even in unionized jobs, the fight over the work process has largely been lost, as labor scholars Kim Moody and Charles Post have documented.[10] (An exception is union nurses, who have fought vigorously to increase nurse-patient ratios, which is good for both the nurses and the patients.) Lengthening the workday and requiring overtime have the same effect, bumping up unemployment.

This is an answer to those people who are perennially predicting the "end of work"—the idea that a combination of automation or offshoring means that unemployment will rise and never fall again.[11] This prediction is often accompanied by the assertion that the working class in the United States is no longer needed, and therefore the employing class doesn't have any reason to concern itself with our numbers or our needs.

The "end of work" idea is hauled out when unemployment rises or when some technological development results in a mass of people losing their jobs. There are too many people, they say, using unemployment as evidence—the working class is obsolete. But unemployment is a constant feature of capitalism, it's not evidence of a fundamental shift. At the height of the postwar manufacturing boom, in the 1950s, unemployment *already* plagued Detroit autoworkers as plants closed, or moved to the suburbs or the South to avoid unions. Historian Thomas Sugrue quotes Ford Motor Company president Henry Ford II in this connection: "Obsolescence is the very hallmark of progress."[12] The normal operations of capitalism make sure there are lots of people unemployed, but that doesn't mean the employing class doesn't need workers anymore.

Employers *will* hire as few workers as they can get away with, so in reality creating jobs requires struggle, over the length of the workday, over the intensity of the work, over the weekend, over holidays and paid leave and the age of retirement and whether we get to have a childhood before we go to work.

Another way to fight back against the power of employers and to blunt the effects of unemployment on everyone's wages is to enact government programs that make unemployment less miserable. So we've struggled over the size and duration of unemployment insurance and welfare, guaranteed health care whether you have a job or not, free college with stipends, and even the idea of a guaranteed annual income, which feminists called for in the 1960s and which seems to be making a comeback as an idea, although it never seems to make it to reality in capitalist countries.[13]

Remarkably, one proposal for a type of guaranteed annual income came from the Richard Nixon administration, which picked up proposals developed under a Johnson administration panicked by urban unrest. The story of the Family Assistance Program (FAP) is a great example of employers opposing government assistance because it can give workers more power—both economic and political. This principle explains employer opposition to programs that support individuals independent of their jobs and beyond the power of their employers.

Nixon wanted to woo working-class white voters, especially southerners, and thought that a payment program to benefit low-wage workers would attract them to the Republican party. The FAP was a wage supplement that would phase out for workers with higher incomes. Women with preschool-age children, those over sixty-five, or those who had unemployed husbands would also get the pay. But the plan had an unanticipated flaw, as Nixon soon discovered.

Southern politicians had always insisted on locally administering welfare programs so that they could manipulate the workforce. According to congressional hearings, southern welfare officials cut off payments during cotton picking season so that plantation owners could avail themselves of cheap labor. Similar tactics were used during civil-rights-era voter registration campaigns when "county officials cut African Americans off the welfare rolls, suspended commodity [food] distributions, and warned they would only restore their benefits when blacks 'surrendered their uppity ideas about changing the local balance of power.'"[14]

What Nixon hadn't anticipated was that the whole system of control over southern workers was put in jeopardy by a guaranteed wage supplement. "The FAP funds would raise the entire southern wage base and provide southern workers, especially black workers, an opportunity to refuse demeaning, low-wage work," writes sociologist Jill Quadagno in her book *The Color of Welfare*. "There's not going to be anybody left to roll these wheelbarrows and press these shirts," complained Georgia representative Phillip Landrum, who voted against the bill.

The bill passed the House overwhelmingly in 1970 but came to a halt as the Chamber of Commerce and southern senators pushed against it. Nixon wasn't winning the friends he had hoped and dropped the bill.[15]

This is a small illustration of why employers oppose public assistance programs on principle, even when they're not paying for them through taxes. Sometimes we hear that employers like Walmart are happy that their workers can get food stamps or Medicaid to supplement the low wages and spotty hours endured by their enormous retail workforce. But in fact, while employers do encourage workers to rely on these programs, at the same time they'd rather see them cut, and take an active role in lobbying to cut them, because anything that makes workers independent of employers increases their bargaining power when they go to look for a job. For example, Walmart has helped fund the American Legislative Exchange Council, which opposed expansion of Medicaid in 2015 arguing that, "expanding Medicaid to childless adults could lower the likelihood of working by up to 10 percentage points [and] could cause 2.6 million Americans to drop out of the labor force entirely."[16]

It's not cruelty that causes employers to organize against government programs for workers but their need to tame the power of the working class.

Malthus and the Neo-Malthusians

Nowadays, it is not Adam Smith or Karl Marx who is most associated with arguments about population and wages. That prize goes to Thomas Robert Malthus, an Anglican minister who in 1798 wrote *An Essay on the Principle of Population*. Malthus thought that unchecked human reproduction would inevitably outstrip agricultural production. People could either marry later and be abstinent, or infant mortality, starvation, and disease would wipe out the resulting overpopulation.

"From this somber analysis," write historians Will and Ariel Durant, "Malthus drew surprising conclusions. First, there is no use raising the wages of working men, for if wages are increased the workers will marry earlier and will have more children . . . and poverty will be restored." And there was no use providing unemployment funds, because that would just encourage unemployed people to be idle and have larger families, outstripping food supplies.[17]

Malthus's argument encouraged British conservatives in the view that they shouldn't raise wages or pay taxes for the unemployed. Prime Minister William Pitt had introduced a poor relief bill to encourage growth in the population with "liberal allowances for children." But as a result of Malthus's essay, Pitt withdrew the bill.[18]

Malthus opposed contraceptives as "improper arts," instead advocating sexual restraint and late marriage. Nineteenth-century advocates of birth control nonetheless called themselves Malthusians (and later neo-Malthusians) to associate themselves with what was widely thought to be irrefutable scientific doctrine. Malthusians believed that unemployment was a result of more workers than jobs, and that to reduce unemployment and conquer low wages, workers needed to have fewer children.[19]

Workers themselves thought this. Francis Place, a tailor who had fathered fifteen children, campaigned for birth control on this basis in

1822: "If means were adopted to prevent the breeding of a larger number of children than a married couple might desire to have, and if the laboring part of the population could thus be kept below the demand for labor, wages would rise so as to afford the means of comfortable subsistence for all, and all might marry."[20] This became the standard argument of neo-Malthusian birth control advocates, whose number included feminists, freethinkers, and various stripes of socialists. Their pamphleteering and agitation substantially weakened anti-contraceptive laws in Britain and spread information about birth control techniques.

Even before Marx, some socialists argued against Malthus that it was not a glut of workers that led to destitution but that "workers' misery was due to the unequal and unjust distribution of the world's goods." But they employed a moral or religious argument against Malthus. "His name was already spitten upon by almost every decent and religiously-minded man and woman in the country," wrote one critic. "To doubt that 'God sent food for every mouth which he sent into the world' was blasphemous; to inquire further was obscene."[21] Marx provided a better explanation that included not just the number of workers but their potential and actual power.

German Birth Strike Debate

Clashes between neo-Malthusians and Marxists became particularly sharp in the period before World War I in Germany, where there was a large and vigorous socialist movement led by the German Social Democratic Party. Some neo-Malthusians in the party trumpeted birth control as the key to ending capitalism, and called for a "birth strike." While many grassroots women were interested, women leaders of the party argued against it, even calling two mass meetings titled "Against a Birth Strike" (Gegen Den Geburtstreik). A radical U.S. paper described the scene in 1913:

> The Socialists held a meeting recently in Berlin, Germany, to discuss the position that they should take in relation to the proposed birth strike of Socialist women. Rosa Luxemburg and Clara Zetkin, the two most famous women leaders of the Socialists, strongly opposed the birth strike or the proposition to make the question one of the big topics on the programme of the party convention.[22]
>
> Miss Zetkin declared that the reduction of cannon food for the Government would also effect a reduction in the number of revolutionists. If individual families decided to limit the number of

children, she said, it was a personal matter, but she was opposed to making it party policy.

Dr. [Julius] Moses [a Berlin family physician and Social Democrat] came out in a vigorous defence of the birth strike. He declared that it would be the quickest, most effectual and most certain way of raising the status of the working classes. He told of attending working mothers who had fifteen or eighteen children, while ten or twelve children in the family of a working woman were numerous. He declared that leaving out of consideration the physical ruin of mothers[,] no workingman could even halfway rear, feed and educate such a number of children in the present conditions.[23]

The Berlin meetings were packed and brought out many more women than regular party gatherings. Margaret Sanger quotes a Dr. Robinson, who gave this eyewitness account:

The interest of the audience was intense. One could see that with them it was not merely a dialectic question, as it was with their leaders, but a matter of life and death. I came to attend a meeting AGAINST the limitation of offspring; it soon proved to be a meeting very decidedly FOR the limitation of offspring, for every speaker who spoke in favor of the artificial prevention of conception or undesired pregnancies, was greeted with vociferous, long-lasting applause; while those who tried to persuade the people that a limited number of children is not a proletarian weapon, and would not improve their lot, were so hissed that they had difficulty going on. The speakers who were against the . . . idea soon felt that their audience was against them.[24]

Some birth control promoters did get carried away with what they imagined to be the revolutionary potential of a lowered birth rate. Berlin doctor and Social Democrat Alfred Bernstein "announced that the decline in births was sapping capitalism's vital strength: 'If we do not recruit the objects of exploitation, if we do not increase the army, then capitalism is at an end.'"[25]

More sober birth strike advocates suggested that fewer births among working-class women would make it easier for them to study and participate in the political movement. Contemporary reports say that Julius Moses "denied having tried to elevate [the birth strike] to the status of a 'revolutionary weapon'; rather, it was merely one of the possible remedies for the proletariat's physical recovery."[26]

Sanger caricatures the debate, saying Marxists wanted more reproduction to fill the ranks of the revolutionary forces.[27] In fact, most Social Democrats supported birth control as a right, but opposed calling a birth strike as a political tactic. They pointed to France's lower birth rate as evidence that capitalism could happily accommodate itself to fewer workers without raising wages or making working-class life more bearable.

Russian revolutionary leader V.I. Lenin took the side of those who opposed a birth strike as a revolutionary tactic, while supporting the right to contraceptives and abortion: "It goes without saying that [we want] the unconditional annulment of all laws against abortions or against the distribution of medical literature on contraceptive measures, etc. . . . Freedom for medical propaganda and the protection of the elementary democratic rights of citizens, men and women, are one thing. The social theory of neomalthusianism is quite another."[28]

These distinctions on the left were lost on the German ruling class, which blamed the socialist movement for a reprehensible drop in the birth rate. Dr. Jean Bornträger, a Düsseldorf doctor and government councilor, published a 1912 polemic against the Social Democrats for their promotion of birth control. He suggested banning any mass publication that discussed contraception, along with any meeting on the subject, and proposed nudging men to marry by imposing extra taxes and military duty on single men.[29]

Bornträger also suggested reforms to assist large families of small means—including housing and food subsidies. While the Social Democrats were arguing among themselves about whether a birth strike would have an effect, the ruling class was already worried that it had, and was debating whether to pitch in some resources to reverse the trend.

When the German legislature in 1914 proposed outlawing contraceptive use, the Social Democrats put aside their differences and united to defend birth control. They denounced the law as "state birth compulsion."[30]

By 1917, the feminists had won the argument for birth control as a right within the socialist movement, at least for a while. Russian revolutionary leaders Alexandra Kollontai and Nadezhda Krupskaya stood for the "elementary democratic rights" to birth control and abortion, and instituted both shortly after the Bolshevik victory.

Modern-Day Malthusians

This debate is valuable to recall because there are still Malthusians among us, arguing that birth control will alleviate poverty—though not by raising general wage levels. As with old-time Malthusians, the argument surfaces when liberals promote the benefits of birth control. "Giving low-income women more control over their own fertility . . . promotes economic security, educational attainment, income mobility and more stable environments for American children," writes *Washington Post* columnist Catherine Rampell. "Children brought into the world before their parents were financially or emotionally ready for them are likewise disadvantaged before they're even born, no matter how loved they are." And, she says, think how much money will be saved in public expenditures— "two-thirds of unplanned births are paid for by public insurance programs," she claims, and describes government spending on family planning as having a "high return on investment."[31] These commenters never explain how it is that more people getting an education won't just mean more people with master's degrees laboring over deep fryers for the minimum wage, which in fact is what has happened as the population has gotten more educated.[32] Women who recently completed four years of college have seen their wages go down to the level of the mid-1990s.[33]

There is no guarantee that a couple with low wages or unstable employment, who have a child at eighteen, would be more "financially ready" to have children when they're twenty-eight. As the Albuquerque reproductive justice group Young Women United points out, teen pregnancy prevention efforts often get the direction of causality wrong, blaming poverty on young parenthood. "Teen pregnancy prevention campaigns extoll delaying parenting as a key to 'breaking the cycle of poverty,' yet research shows that the cycle continues unabated . . . whether people parent as adolescents or not." Instead of blaming teen parents, Young Women United suggests that "positive change in the lives of young people is rooted in equal access to educational opportunities, living-wage jobs, affordable health care and safe housing."[34] In reality, the lack of paid leave and expensive health care and childcare means that few people are "financially ready" to have a child.

Then there are the racist versions of modern Malthusianism, as when the *Philadelphia Inquirer* published an editorial in 1990 saying "the main reason more black children are living in poverty is that people having the most children are the ones least capable of supporting them."[35] The paper suggested that the government pay women on welfare to get the newly approved contraceptive implant Norplant. Outrage eventually forced the paper to apologize but, Dorothy Roberts writes, *Newsweek*, the *New Republic*, and the *Washington Post* all said basically the same thing within the following year.[36]

Roberts believes that this position on the part of opinion makers is not really aimed at reducing the birth rate among the low-waged and African Americans. Instead, she says, it serves an ideological function—much as Malthus's original essay did. "By identifying procreation as the cause of Black people's condition, they divert attention away from the political, social, and economic forces that maintain America's racial order."[37] And, we could add, its class order.

Is a Birth Strike Malthusian?

Recalling "the ancient battle of Marx against Malthus," as Sanger called it, can help us distinguish Malthusianism from a theme of this book, that U.S. women are on a birth strike and that there is potential power in it.[38] When we suggest that U.S. women are staging a reproductive slowdown or strike, we do not assume that better conditions will automatically follow—clearly they haven't. Struggle is also necessary.

Although pressure from women having fewer children has caused governments to increase the social wage in European countries and others—and could here, too—that is not the same thing as saying poverty is caused by too many children. The United States has the lowest birth rate it has ever had, and our poverty rate is still off the charts for a developed country.[39]

Poverty is caused when a select few control the products of everyone's labor, and by a capitalist production system geared to generate profit rather than meet human needs. A birth slowdown or strike, accompanied by feminist organizing and protest, might pressure the power structure to provide better working conditions for reproductive work, but the problem isn't too many children to begin with.

This can be confusing because in the United States it is indeed true that people get poorer when they have kids. But that's because bearing and raising them is expensive, not, as Adam Smith would have it, because the supply of their labor is outstripping demand by employers, or, as Malthus would have it, because there is not enough food being produced to feed them.

Parents, particularly mothers, become poorer because they are not properly compensated for the contribution they're making to the continuation of society by bearing and raising children. And they are certainly not being compensated for the contribution they make to the wealth of the employing class by supplying them with a steady stream of young workers.

Having children doesn't have to plunge parents into financial distress. We could tax those who have gained enormous wealth from the lopsided income distribution of the last fifty years and institute universal programs: childcare, health care, paid family leave, education through college, and child allowances that assist parents in providing their off-spring with appropriate food, clothing, and shelter.

Another solution is to eliminate profit-making businesses entirely, and run the society on a nonprofit basis, with all goods and services provided as public amenities. Those who live off profit would object, so they try to stamp this idea as unworkable, but there's no good reason they should get the last word.

Although some establishment thinkers seem to be worried that low birth rates will drive up wages, it's not possible for women to produce children quickly enough to fill their needs for the next upswing, so in general, higher birth rates are not an effective weapon to keep wages low. Anyway, employers have many tactics more easily matched to the business cycle. The fight over the birth rate is mainly aimed at extracting another type of cheap labor: that of bearing and rearing children.

CHAPTER 10

CANNON FODDER

O ne hundred years ago, it was common for feminists and the left to charge that the ruling class wanted women to have lots of children to provide "cannon fodder" for national expansion and imperial wars. Perhaps this seemed self-evident then, when a single day in the Battle of the Somme during World War I consumed fifty-seven thousand British troops, and the five-month offensive was responsible for a million casualties. It really did seem that the cannons were hungry for humans. But what about now? Could the supply of military-age recruits—and thus the birth rate—still be a concern for modern nations, and specifically for U.S. planners? Surprisingly, the past two decades of war have provided substantial evidence for this, along with a matching worry: the expense of recruitment. Conservative Jonathan Last summed up the dual concerns: "Low-fertility societies . . . cannot project power because they lack the money to pay for defense and the military-age manpower to serve in their armed forces."[1]

National Aggrandizement

Early in the twentieth century, U.S. feminists argued that women were being induced to have children to provide troops for an insatiable military machine. Sociologist Leta Hollingworth wrote in 1916 of various "devices" used to impel U.S. women "to produce and rear families large enough to admit of national warfare being carried on, and of colonization." The primary device she listed was the "drastic" Comstock Law.[2]

Theodore Roosevelt provided grounds for this feminist accusation. As president he urged women to have children as a patriotic duty. Later he blamed notoriously modest French birth rates for World War I, arguing that if the French had kept up with the Germans in population, the Germans would not have dared to attack.[3] He expressed related fears for the United States: "If our birth rate continues to diminish we shall by the end of this century be impotent in the face of powers like Germany, Russia or Japan; we shall have been passed by the great states of South America," he wrote.[4]

Legendary women's rights movement leader Susan B. Anthony wrote of Roosevelt in 1908, "His ideas on race suicide are those of a soldier, who looks upon human beings either as possible soldiers or possible mothers of soldiers. . . . There is nothing new in the propositions advanced by the President. They are as old as the patriarchs, who, I believe, had families large enough to suit even Mr. Roosevelt."[5]

The carnage of World War I led feminist novelist Charlotte Perkins Gilman to write: "The women bear and rear the children. The men kill them. Then they say: 'We are running short of children—make some more.'"[6]

In 1917, Margaret Sanger wrote: "In the present soul-trying crisis, the flower of European manhood has been sacrificed on the altar of Tyranny. The rulers of Europe are begging, imploring, crying to woman, using every subterfuge to induce her to breed again. . . . Soon the war lords of America will be echoing the same plea. To all these entreaties the working woman must answer No! She must deny the right of the State or Kingdom hereafter to make her a victim of unwilling motherhood, and the handmaiden of militarism."[7]

Feminists abroad had long associated crackdowns on birth control with militarism. French feminist Nelly Roussel wrote in 1904: "Beware, oh society! The day will come . . . when we will refuse to give you, ogres, your ration of cannon-fodder, of work-fodder, and fodder for suffering! The day, at last, when we will become mothers *only when we please*."[8]

"The bosses have need of man-power and cannon-fodder: the law punishes abortion implacably," wrote Russian revolutionary Victor Serge in 1926.[9]

In 1929 Martha Ruben-Wolf, a leftist and feminist doctor in Berlin, wrote a widely circulated pamphlet, *Abortion or Contraception?*, which was published in at least six editions and translated into Swedish. She wrote:

> In virtually all capitalist states, abortion is punished by severe penalties. . . . Bourgeois doctors and lawyers . . . explain the necessity of maintaining the penalties against abortion as (1) the interests of

morality, (2) the interests of public health, and (3) the interest of the population stock. But the true reason is and remains that the ruling classes of all capitalist states need cannon-fodder for their imperialistic wars and an industrial reserve army with whose help they can put down the demands of the working class.[10]

Ruben-Wolf fled Germany when the Nazis took power.

Militarists the world over showed the same pattern. In Japan in the 1920s "militarist ideology increasingly took hold in throughout Japanese society," writes Australian scholar Mark McLelland.[11] "Opposition to birth control was not based on religious or ethical grounds, but rested ultimately on the issue of national power."[12] In 1922, a militarist Japanese government yanked Margaret Sanger's visa when she was to speak there at the invitation of women's groups demanding birth control.[13] By 1937, the government cracked down on public advocacy of birth control, seeking increased reproduction "in order to secure large reserves of man power for the armed forces and for the exploitation of the occupied areas [Korea and Manchuria]."[14]

Most women's liberationists of the 1960s steered away from the "cannon fodder" argument, perhaps judging it to be an historical relic or an Old Left cliché. The Boston Women's Health Book Collective, in an early edition of *Our Bodies, Ourselves*, described the Comstock Law as the product of a post–Civil War desire to increase reproduction to replace the war dead. But they gave other explanations for the anti-abortion laws they were trying to change in 1971. The same pattern appears in Linda Gordon's 1976 history of birth control. She gives credence to the military motive for restrictions on birth control and abortion at the beginning of the twentieth century, when Theodore Roosevelt "first expressed fears for the birth rate . . . during his campaign to justify seizure of the Philippines by the United States." But Gordon blamed U.S. religiosity for current laws.[15] Gordon is asking us to believe that material interests were the overriding concern a century ago, but cultural interests are now primary. This seems unlikely given that the U.S. population is less religious, less prudish, and less sexist than it was in 1900, though arguably it is more militaristic.

Still, some second-wave feminists did echo earlier feminist and left charges about cannon fodder. Barbara Segal, a British correspondent for *Off Our Backs* reporting on the 1974 United Nations Bucharest population conference, wrote: "A brief look at the history of the developed countries—both capitalist and socialist—over the past fifty years will confirm that it is always the women who are expected to adjust their fertility to the need for labor or cannon-fodder, never the economy which must adapt to an increasing or decreasing birthrate."[16] Kathie Sarachild of Redstockings briefly gives a military motive in a 1971 article. When New York legislators attacked abortion coverage under Medicaid, she wrote, "The men at the top . . . insure that the section of the population from which comes the bulk of their work force and military rank and file will continue to produce generations of cheap labor and human cannon fodder for the ruling elite."[17]

Without a Draft, Troops Cost More

The U.S. military makes fabulous promises to its recruits, and it even keeps some of them. What other job is available to a person without a college education or specialized training that provides access to full health care, a pension, funds for college, housing, and even comprehensive childcare?

It was not always true. The price of military labor has been driven higher by popular opposition to the draft, both among draftees and the general public. Antiwar outrage ended the draft in 1973, toward the end of the U.S. war in Vietnam. Officers agreed the draft wasn't working, given rising "draftee recalcitrance and malevolence," which included numerous incidents of soldiers killing their own officers. Soldiers even pooled their money for bounties to put on the heads of hated commanders, ranging from $50 to $1,000, and in one case $10,000.[18]

When the draft ended in 1973 it was the first time since 1940 that the United States had no conscription.[19] Without a draft, substantial expenditures became necessary to entice young people to join the military. The military raised wages and increased benefits, what historian Jennifer Mittelstadt calls "the rise of the military welfare state."[20]

Military and political leaders find themselves in a quandary. If they reinstitute a draft the next time there's a big war mobilization, the public will pay closer attention to how troops are used, stimulating more political opposition. But without a draft, recruitment for military interventions and the endless, borderless "war on terror" will continue to be expensive. Establishment planners are worried about how to maintain U.S. military dominance in the face of these pressures. Phillip Longman of the centrist New America Foundation writes: "Today the U.S. thinks of itself as the world's sole remaining superpower. . . . But as the cost of pensions and health care consume more and more of the nation's wealth, and as growth of the labor force vanishes, it will become more and more difficult for the United States to sustain its current levels of military spending, let alone maintain today's force levels."[21]

The British weekly the *Economist* is worried that Europe's aging population is leaving it defenseless:

> Since the end of the cold war, Europe and America have made different calculations about where to spend public money. America has put more into defence; Europe has spent more on social programmes. The result is a familiar military imbalance. America spends about twice as much on defence as the entire European Union . . . thus maintaining its preponderant military might. Europeans intermittently promise to spend more in order to narrow the military gap, recognising the dangers to the NATO alliance if they fail to pull their weight, but population trends will sap their determination.[22]

In other words, rather than keeping up their part of policing the world for the benefit of the ruling elite, European governments have been spending some of their money for the well-being of their citizens. It's either "guns or grannies," says the *Economist*, coming down on the side of guns.

The late Peter G. Peterson framed the question as "weapons or walkers" in 2004 when he was chair of the Council on Foreign Relations, a think tank of bankers, politicians, and ex-secretaries of state: "Washington's foreign friends . . . will face the wrenching dilemma of whether to fund weapons or walkers even more than the United States will. . . . And leaders will grow even more reluctant than they are already to commit public resources to U.S.-led military actions or nation-building operations."[23]

Why? Peterson blames the incapacity of European governments to cut pensions because the people will be in the streets protesting and striking: "Of course, [European] political leaders can propose trimming benefits, but . . . they will encounter stiff resistance, because the elderly in these countries are so dependent on public benefits, which in turn are vigorously defended by powerful trade unions and their political allies."

Focusing back on U.S. birth rates, Peterson writes, "It now seems nearly certain that the aging of America's population—which would pose a massive fiscal challenge over the next few decades itself—will unfold in an era of large additional commitments to our national security agenda."

Why so many "additional commitments"? The United States spends more on the military than the next seven biggest-spending countries combined, accounting for 37 percent of the world's total.[24] It seems fair to ask, in a country with 4.4 percent of the world's population, why is a military of such extraordinary size and expense necessary?

End of the Cold War

People in the United States could be forgiven for believing that the end of the Cold War would bring peace and a smaller, less expensive military. The Cold War included two protracted hot conflicts, in Korea and Vietnam, each involving an extensive draft. In each case the number of U.S. active duty military personnel swelled to three million (2,933,000 in 1955, 3,063,000 in 1970).[25] The Cold War also involved an astonishingly expensive arms race. All this blood and treasure was expended to "stop the spread of communism," we were told.

But instead of peace, the break-up of the Soviet Union and the end of the Cold War has been followed by a proliferation of overseas U.S. troop deployments.

From 1950 to 1989, the U.S. Army had ten significant deployments (and three of those were to quell urban uprisings in Los Angeles, Detroit, and Chicago). From 1990 to 1996 there were twenty-five significant deployments, including Panama, Iraq, Yugoslavia, Somalia, Haiti, and Bosnia.[26] After 2001 it became hard to keep track, with interventions large and small in Afghanistan, Iraq, Somalia, Yemen, Libya, Syria, Pakistan, and drone attacks in an unknown number of countries.

The United States now maintains permanent military bases in eighty countries; up from forty in 1989. The number of overseas bases doubled too, from 800 to 1,600.[27] We are perhaps familiar with the large garrisons in Germany, Japan, South Korea, and the Philippines. But what about Colombia, Kenya, Australia, and Bulgaria?[28]

Why was there such a drastic increase in deployments and installations after the Cold War? In 1992, a secret memo billed as "Definitive guidance from the Secretary of Defense"—then Dick Cheney—was leaked to the *Washington Post*. "The new memo gives central billing to U.S. efforts to prevent emergence of a rival superpower, a diplomatically sensitive subject that has not been prominent in public debate," the *Post* reported.

> That objective, the document states, "is a dominant consideration underlying the new regional defense strategy and requires that we endeavor to prevent any hostile power from dominating a region whose resources would, under consolidated control, be sufficient to generate global power. These regions include Western Europe, East Asia, the territory of the former Soviet Union and Southwest

Asia." The document . . . contemplates use of American military power to preempt or punish use of nuclear, biological or chemical weapons, "even in conflicts that otherwise do not directly engage U.S. interests."[29]

The memo was directed at the incoming Bill Clinton administration, because some Democrats in Congress were making noises about a peace dividend. *Post* reporter Barton Gellman wrote: "The new draft continues to make the case for the [George H.W.] Bush Administration's concept of a 'base force' military of 1.6 million uniformed troops and rejects calls in Congress for a greater peace dividend that could be derived from deeper military cuts."

This desire to blunt the "global power" of other nations partly explains why the collapse of the United States' main rival didn't lead to peace: Other countries must also be kept in their place. This bloody work has involved deterring or removing governments that insist on using their land, resources, and labor to provide for domestic development and human needs. It is painful to consider, but supported by innumerable examples, that U.S. military intervention abroad has been most consistently employed in the service of corporate power against the power of working people. It is not about defending the U.S. people.[30]

What is the goal of all this military might? Listen to neoconservative Harvard professor Stephen Peter Rosen: "Our goal is not combating a rival, but maintaining our imperial position, and maintaining imperial order. . . . The maximum amount of force can and should be used as quickly as possible for psychological impact—to demonstrate that the empire cannot be challenged with impunity. . . . We are in the business of bringing down hostile governments and creating governments favorable to us."[31]

When we are told that being an empire is necessary to provide "American prosperity" or the "American way of life," we should ask, whose way of life is being protected? Generals and oil company executives seem to be doing well, but U.S. infrastructure and social supports are a shambles. Programs that would benefit working people are laughed off as unbelievably expensive while unbelievably expensive weapons systems and aggressive wars are funded without question.

An increased military budget for 2018 passed with overwhelming bipartisan support and authorized even more spending than the Trump administration had requested. Contrast this to the political response to climate change, which threatens U.S. lives and infrastructure more than any foreign rival. If the protection of people were the top priority, the U.S. government would be meeting the current destruction and future menace of climate change with a military-budget-sized response.

Smarter Bombs and Fewer Troops?

After the 1991 Gulf War with its allegedly smart bombs, there was talk in the military that overwhelming technological superiority would be the deciding factor in future wars, not large numbers of troops. This doctrine foundered during United States and NATO actions in the Balkans. "The recent past provides a convincing example in the NATO deployment to Bosnia . . . the NATO peace plan ultimately required a large, visible contingent of U.S. ground troops." To achieve U.S. objectives around the world, the army argued in a planning document, troops would be needed in ever-larger numbers: "With the end of the Cold War, a prominent theory arose that there would no longer be a need for large land forces, that power projection and national military strategy could primarily be carried out through precision strikes using technologically advanced air and naval forces. This 'standoff' approach would reduce the level of U.S. involvement and commitment and thus the requirement for large land forces. Reality proved that theory to be invalid."[32] To carry out U.S. government objectives, troops are still needed and cannot be replaced with technology.

U.S. military experience in the long occupations of Iraq and Afghanistan has further cemented the lesson. In 2005, several architects of the U.S. war in Iraq wrote, "There is abundant evidence that the demands of the ongoing missions in the greater Middle East, along with our continuing defense and alliance commitments elsewhere in the world, are close to exhausting current U.S. ground forces . . . after almost two years in Iraq and almost three years in Afghanistan, it should be evident that our engagement in the greater Middle East is truly, in [Secretary of State] Condoleezza Rice's term, a 'generational commitment.'"[33] Rosen explains: "Conventional international wars end and troops are brought back home. Imperial wars end, but imperial garrisons must be left in place for decades to ensure order and stability."[34]

The desire for a larger military force crosses the political aisle. When he was running for president in 2007, Barack Obama called for adding 65,000 troops to the army and 27,000 more to the Marines.[35] Hillary Clinton, while a senator from New York, advocated increasing the size of the army by 80,000, in line with neoconservative proposals.[36]

The Obama administration's 2015 budget proposed increasing military spending by $26 billion and by $115 billion for 2016–2019.[37] "It is an ironic fact that the president who won a Nobel Peace Prize for his soaring disarmament rhetoric is the same president who has laid out [a] $1 trillion plan to modernize every aspect of the U.S. nuclear arsenal over the next thirty years," noted Harvard nuclear proliferation specialist Matthew Bunn.[38] The military accounts for 54 percent of discretionary federal spending, but in the Senate only Bernie Sanders on the left and a couple of libertarian Republicans are willing to vote against these giant military appropriations that put every other budget item in the shade.[39]

It is generally agreed among military brass that the Iraq war stretched the military to the breaking point. Army tours overseas were extended from twelve months to fifteen months in 2007.[40] Troops were returned to war zones three and sometimes four times. Men and women who thought their military service was over were prevented from returning to civilian life through the military's "stop-loss" program. Jobs formerly done by military personnel were contracted out to mercenary outfits like Blackwater, a company so notorious it changed its name to "Xe" and then two years later to "Academi," trying to shed its corrupt and brutal reputation.

National Guard troops were used for extended periods, leaving jobs and families at home. Reworking the Army National Guard recruiting slogan, "One Weekend a Month, Two Weeks a Year," troops stuck overseas on long deployments responded with their own version, "One Weekend a Month, My Ass!"[41] When National Guard troops were overseas and unable to assist after hurricanes Katrina and Rita devastated New Orleans and the Gulf Coast in 2005, a new sign appeared at peace rallies, "Bring the troops home, we have a Gulf crisis here!" In 2012, Army Chief of Staff Ray Odierno announced the intention to increase the National Guard's annual commitment during peacetime from two weeks to seven weeks of annual drilling and training.[42]

The military understandably had trouble meeting its recruitment goals during a shooting war, and increased the use of waivers to admit those who had a criminal conviction, a health problem, or failed to finish high school.[43] Despite offering increased enlistment bonuses (up to $40,000 up front and $65,000 toward college), recruiters were rebuffed and fell short of their targets. Commanding officers put intense pressure on recruiters and recruiters in turn bullied, threatened, and lied to potential recruits, which resulted in mental breakdowns among the recruiters themselves, including suicides.[44] It became such a crisis that the military ordered a national stand-down for all recruiters in 2005 to get a handle on the misconduct, which a CNN report delicately labeled "inappropriate sign-up methods."[45]

It's probably not a coincidence that in 2011 the United States stopped kicking gays and lesbians out of the military and in 2015 permitted women to take all combat roles. Of course there was a great deal of struggle to get these more equitable policies, but it's also likely that the opposition within the military was weakened by the need for troops, and that helped push activist demands forward. In 2016 the military accepted transgender service members.[46]

All young men in the United States ages eighteen to twenty-five have to register with the Selective Service System in case a draft is called. The army's chief of staff and the commandant of the Marine Corps told Congress in 2016 that since women are being integrated into combat positions, they should be required to register too. Adding women will double the pool of available young people if a draft is called again. But the more likely reason it is being considered now is that registering serves as an advertisement to women that the military is a possible job, with the goal of increasing the number of women who may volunteer for the military. Democratic Missouri Senator Claire McCaskill said during a hearing, "Asking women to register as we ask men to register would maybe possibly open up more recruits as women began to think about, well, the military is an option for me."[47]

While it may seem wild to claim that raw numbers of available recruits could be an issue for an active-duty military of 1.5 million in a country of 320 million, it appears that at least during big mobilizations, the military is finding it difficult to fill its ranks.[48]

Since 2001, it is no longer seriously debated whether the United States constitutes an empire. "American Empire (Get Used to It)" blared a red, white, and blue *New York Times Magazine* cover in 2003.[49] The only thing debated is whether it is a benevolent one. A military large enough to run a world empire requires enormous resources. Not only is the sweat and blood of young people needed, the treasure of the nation is needed. This is where U.S. women's de facto birth strike clashes with the needs of empire. "Generational commitments," as then–Secretary of State Condoleezza Rice put it, require the generation of more people.

CHAPTER 11

CONTROLLING THE MEANS OF REPRODUCTION

If we reproduce the very workers we work with, who fill the slots emptied by the retiring, the very workers who help to supply us with food, housing, shelter, medical care, highways, services, art, history . . . why aren't we paid for the production of reproduction? Since unions constantly seek better wages, better conditions for workers—pay for their production—why not for women for reproduction production?[1] —Judith Brown

Women in the United States are staging a production slowdown, a baby boycott, in response to bad conditions. Determining that the burdens are unfairly piled on us as women, we're deciding to have fewer children or none at all. All our individual decisions taken together have put pressure on our economic and political system, whether we have been conscious of it or not.

But, if our reproductive work is so important, why haven't we won more concessions? Leaving aside the advances made in countries that had socialist revolutions, we haven't even won the advances they have in other capitalist countries, where birth slowdowns are leading to more collective support for childbearing and childrearing—in Sweden, France, Germany, and Canada for instance. It's not that high U.S. immigration rates are making up the difference. Sweden, Germany, and Canada have more immigrants than the United States does. So what's missing here?

One reason we haven't won more is that for the last thirty years, our birth rate has been higher than in comparable countries. Experts observed this phenomenon, but they struggled to explain it. "America is the world's great demographic outlier," said Hania Zlotnik of the United

Nations Population Division in 2002.[2] "It's a mystery, we can't figure it out," said Susan McDaniel, a social demographer at the University of Lethbridge in Alberta, Canada, in 2012.[3]

Nicholas Eberstadt of the pro-corporate American Enterprise Institute labeled this phenomenon American "demographic exceptionalism," while *Washington Post* columnist Robert Samuelson credited "greater optimism, greater patriotism and stronger religious values." Samuelson even claimed that "American society better mixes child rearing and jobs than do other societies that provide greater child subsidies."[4]

Eberstadt disagreed. "Pro-natalist government policies cannot explain it: The United States has none. Nor do U.S. labor patterns seem especially 'family-friendly': Americans work longer hours and enjoy less vacation time than any of their European friends." He settles on the "religiosity gap between America and Europe" as an explanation.

Some assumed that the unexpectedly high U.S. fertility rate was due to more births among immigrant women who arrive in the United States during their childbearing years and may come from rural areas where larger families are prized. But even U.S.-born women have been bearing more children than women in comparable countries.

Comparing the United States' higher birth rate to Canada's, a Canadian news report credited "religiosity [which] . . . also tends to include sticking to a traditional family structure, with men as the breadwinning head of household and women primarily as nurturers of children." In other words, pushing the family as the unit of survival, by making it harder for women to have independent lives, may be a factor. But the report also noted that Canadians used "more effective contraception" than U.S. women.[5]

So here's an explanation for our higher birth rate that is rarely mentioned: U.S. women have more difficulty getting access to birth control and abortion. We've been getting pregnant when we don't want to more frequently, and we're having the baby more frequently. According to the Guttmacher Institute, 45 percent of U.S. pregnancies were unplanned in 2011 with 18 percent never wanted and 27 percent "mistimed." Of those unintended pregnancies, 58 percent ended in a birth; the rest ended in abortion.[6]

When we compare the United States to Europe, with its lower birth rates and wider availability of contraception and abortion, we find that U.S. women have more unintended pregnancies, and our rate of abortion is lower. So the overall rate of women bearing children they didn't intend is higher in the United States than in comparable countries. In one international comparison, 50 percent of all U.S. pregnancies were unintended, with 23 percent of all pregnancies resulting in unplanned births (the rest were abortions or miscarriages).[7] In Western Europe, 33 percent of all pregnancies were unintended, with 12 percent of all pregnancies resulting in unplanned births (with the rest abortions or miscarriages).[8] This means that for women in Europe, only 12 percent of their children are unplanned, whereas in the United States, 23 percent of our children are unplanned. (Some studies say closer to 37 percent are unplanned in the United States.[9])

It's not because we have more sex. In a cross-national study of teen pregnancy, the authors found that young people in the United States have sex at the same rate as the other countries studied. Yet we use birth control less. Why? The study's authors suggest several reasons: "Easy access to contraceptives and other reproductive health services in Sweden, France, Canada, and Great Britain contributes to better contraceptive use and therefore lower teenage pregnancy rates than in the United States." National health care systems in these countries provide everyone with care. As a result, "adolescents know where to obtain information and services, can reach a provider easily, are assured of receiving confidential, nonjudgmental care and can obtain services and contraceptive supplies at little or no cost."[10] Teens in the United States face health insurance obstacles, high costs, judgmental adults, and a government uninterested in their goals and desires.

Most damning, many U.S. women can't get abortions because they don't have the money. A study comparing states where Medicaid covers abortion to those that don't concluded that every year tens of thousands of women are prevented from getting abortions they want due to the cost.[11] Regulations targeting abortion providers add to those costs: waiting periods now in force in twenty-seven states add more time off work and travel, while laws that force abortion clinics to shut down add travel time and expense.

If one in four of our births is unintended, with our intentions thwarted by lack of contraception and restricted abortion rights, then the U.S. birth rate is being kept up by a coercion quotient much larger than that in other countries. Explanations about religiosity, optimism, and patriotism are unnecessary: if we had the same high rate of successful contraceptive use they have in Europe, our birth rate would drop to the levels that have panicked some European governments into providing universal childcare and other programs.

Indeed, there is recent evidence that unintended pregnancies and births are going down in the United States, especially among teenagers, not because of a crisis of religious faith but as a result of better distribution of contraceptives.[12] Scholars attribute the drop to more women using IUDs and contraceptive implants, which are more effective than the pill or barrier methods but are more expensive up front. Another factor may be that more women know about, and have easier access to, the morning-after pill since it went over-the-counter. And while the official abortion rate has been declining, abortion pills—now readily available without a prescription from gray-market internet purveyors—may account for this as more women have abortions "off the books."

Still, even before this recent drop in our birth rate, we were not having babies at replacement, nor were the rates high enough to satisfy the establishment. If we had been, they would not be warning about economic stagnation and fiscal collapse, and there wouldn't be a faction of Republicans suggesting tax breaks and even cash incentives like Ross Douthat's tiny baby bonus, and Democratic candidates claiming to support twelve weeks of paid family leave. We have some leverage as a result.

There is a lot that can be done to increase our leverage, but I'm going to focus on four areas. Readers will, I'm sure, think of others.

1. We need to bring the hidden fight over the birth rate out into the open by raising consciousness about it, and make explicit what has been concealed: our birth slowdown is due to bad conditions. When we understand the true value of our unpaid work and turn our justified rage at those responsible for our lousy conditions, we'll have a chance to make fundamental changes.

2. Using the leverage of our birth strike, we need to make bold, universal demands that target those who are benefitting from our reproductive work but not contributing to it. In this way we can win better working conditions when we do have children.

3. We need to sharpen our strike weapon so that no woman has to bear a child because she couldn't get safe, effective birth control or abortion.

4. We need to fund our own organizations and not rely on corporate foundations and the establishment think tanks and politicians they fund.

1. Make the Hidden Fight Open

Our media encourage us to see kids as luxury goods requiring ample time and money. So when we have children and are having a rough time, we are supposed to believe it is our fault. "We blame ourselves because we wanted kids and we knew it would be hard," said one of our testifiers.

"Well, I can't ask for help, I made this individual choice. I decided to do it of my own free will. I can't even let on that it's a struggle," said another. And when we make the decision *not* to have children, even when we want them, that too feels like an individual decision, and sometimes an individual failure.

To get the things that we need to make childbearing and childrearing fair, we will need to see that we're not just making bad choices within a fundamentally sound system. It is not our *individual* failures to get an adequate job or relationship, the right kind of health insurance, or the right childcare arrangement; it is a *systemic* failure to provide the things that mothers and all parents need to carry out the necessary work of bearing and raising children. And it's not a failure in the sense of an oversight: It is a carefully maintained economic arrangement in which a powerful class of rich people benefit from our work but do not contribute to it.

That consciousness will increase the pressure we're already bringing to bear on the system through our millions of individual decisions to postpone, trim back, or give up on having children. But the propaganda is very thick. How do we break through? The method the 1960s women's liberation movement used was consciousness-raising, and it spread new understandings very fast. (We saw an example of it in chapter 3.)

The term "consciousness-raising" is now used to mean any increase in understanding, but it was coined in 1967 to describe a particular type of political meeting, in which women went around the room answering a question about their lives and then compared the data and drew conclusions based on the testimony. The feminist radicals who originated it got the idea from participating in the southern civil rights movement, where testifying and "telling it like it is" about racist conditions—often in large public gatherings—were important to developing the unity required to confront white supremacy.[13]

Consciousness-raising allows us to investigate our own conditions and compare them. Through it, we come to understand that our misery is not the result of personal failings or bad decisions. We may hear from others who tried individual strategies we haven't tried, and we learn that they aren't the solution either. For example, we may think we should have quit our jobs to take care of our kids, but because we didn't, we face an impossible time crunch. In consciousness-raising, we hear from women who *did* quit their jobs and discovered themselves in a dependent relationship with their breadwinning spouse and driven nuts by unrelenting care work. And we hear from those who tried to shoot the rapids by going part-time, only to discover that they still did most of the work at home and had less money to boot. Those who are single parents may assume that two-parent families have it made, until they hear from those in that situation that it's no solution either. By comparing our experiences, we discover that, even in the *best* cases, the answers are not available within our system. We have to change the system to get free. A million self-help books *can* be wrong: there is no personal key to liberation, only collective struggle and society-wide solutions.

Carol Hanisch of Redstockings described some of their early consciousness-raising discoveries in 1969: "The bad things that are said about us are either myths (women are stupid), tactics women use to struggle individually (women are bitches), or are actually things that we want to carry into the new society and want men to share too (women are sensitive, emotional)."[14]

Based on consciousness-raising, women's liberation organizers developed what they called the "Pro-Woman Line." Women are not dumb, weak, damaged, or lacking ambition. Instead we face external obstacles, including discrimination and exploitation. Far from being passive, women are struggling all the time against bad conditions, using whatever individual tools we have. "Women have developed great . . . techniques for their own survival . . . which should be used when necessary until such time as the power of unity can take its place," Hanisch wrote.[15] But when we struggle alone, we can be easily pushed back into line. Individual struggle is not enough to stop the exploitation and oppression we experience in our lives—we need to act collectively.

The Pro-Woman Line said that women's actions weren't the source of the problem. Therefore the personal changes that were always being urged on us—self-help books, therapy, self-esteem exercises, assertiveness training, increased efficiency—were just more ways to blame women and distract from the source of the problem. What women needed was a feminist revolution to overthrow the unjust privileges enjoyed by men and the power structure.

This feminism clashes with that promoted by Sheryl Sandberg's *Lean In: Women, Work, and the Will to Lead*, which at its core exhorts women to higher individual effort. Sandberg acknowledges that women face external obstacles, but, she says, "internal obstacles deserve a lot more attention in part because they are under our own control. We can dismantle the hurdles in ourselves today."[16] She recommends strategies to get a raise, get a promotion, and bear and rear children while working. The Pro-Woman Line tells us that women are already trying various strategies, but that we face real obstacles that no amount of leaning in, willpower, or self-confidence can overcome. Women are smart and brave—if there were an individual solution, we'd all be doing that.

Consciousness-raising is not just about comparing our experiences; it's also about analyzing together who benefits and who pays. Who benefits when we can't plan our pregnancies? Who benefits when we spend eight hours at work and then another eight hours buying groceries, cooking, and doing dishes, laundry, and childcare? (I've included consciousness-raising questions in the Appendix for anyone who would like to start their own group.)

2. Make Bold Demands of Those Who Benefit

Consciousness-raising allows us to direct our rage toward the source of the problem rather than at each other (as in the so-called mommy wars) or, more typically, at ourselves where it may condense into depression.

The consciousness that our pain and struggles are not individual but systemic has been helped by the increasing exposure of what Redstockings calls "Myth America": "Far from being 'number one,' the U.S. lags way behind other countries in taking the burden of unpaid care work off women." As more international comparisons are sneaking into the consciousness of U.S. people, there has been a deeper questioning of the system.[17]

Redstockings made the case in a signature ad in the National Organization for Women's newspaper in 2004:

> In dozens of other countries, women have more economic independence from men, regardless of their marriage or employment status, and more time for themselves. This is because they have:
> - national health care for everyone, health care that is not dependent on a job or a husband
> - universal free quality childcare and eldercare
> - paid parental leave for both parents
> - shorter working hours (with no reduction in pay)
>
> Many countries have all of these programs; others have some of them. Our government doesn't guarantee any of them. Who takes up the slack here? Women. We take care of children, husbands, boyfriends, parents, even husbands' parents. Because we lack these universal programs in the U.S., we are tracked into unpaid care work and made dependent upon men and employers. On top of that, people in the U.S. now work the longest hours in the industrialized world.[18]

Two hundred feminists signed it, including Betty Friedan, who punctured the myth of America's "liberated women" in 1963.

The details are telling. The United States is not just behind a few exceptional countries like Sweden and France, it's astonishingly backward by world standards. While we once again are debating whether paid family leave is really possible in the U.S., national paid leave laws are in force in 185 of the 193 countries of the United Nations. The suggestion that all workers get twelve weeks of paid family leave has brought howls of indignation from U.S. employers. But fifty nations provide paid leave of *six months or more*.[19] We should be insulted by the suggestion of twelve weeks. Are we really going to sell our reproductive labor that cheaply?

In making our demands, we must be conscious of the balance of forces. Women have more power than we know, as evidenced by our ability to alarm the employing class through our birth slowdown. But the opposition is a formidable collection of financial and political elites. In order to defeat them, or even extract worthwhile concessions, we need to make demands that unite the 99%. So we should avoid going for timid half measures or trying to sound "reasonable" in a completely unreasonable state of affairs.

Means-tested programs—provided only to those whose income and assets are below some government-determined threshold—are a patented way for the power structure to divide people: the vast majority of struggling people who don't qualify against the even more struggling group of people who do. They also require an expensive bureaucracy to determine who qualifies, usually in the most invasive and time-consuming way, because it is alleged that it would be a disaster if someone gets a benefit they don't "deserve." (Somehow it is never seen as a disaster if someone who could qualify goes without food or shelter.)

With universal programs, by contrast, there's no question whether someone is "deserving" or "qualifies." Everyone is and everyone does.

Means-testing ensures that government programs will only be used by the most oppressed in the society, with the expected results: Inconvenient, cash-strapped services with frazzled, underpaid staff and demeaning all-day waits that say, "your time is worth nothing."

When budget-cutting time comes, means-tested programs are more vulnerable to cuts because the beneficiaries are few and for this reason alone have little political power. Programs that everyone expects to benefit from, like Medicare or Social Security, have a much broader base to defend them. These programs unite the many to defend against the attacks of the 1%.

Opposition to universal proposals is sometimes disguised as a populist attack on the privileges of the rich. Hillary Clinton assailed Bernie Sanders during the presidential primary in 2015 when he proposed free tuition at all public universities. "I'm a little different from those who say free college for everybody. . . . I am not in favor of making college free for Donald Trump's kids," Clinton said, proposing for her part another complicated means-tested method to fund college tuition.[20] But if millionaires like Donald Trump were finally forced to pay proportionate taxes, they would pay in plenty more than they would get out, so why shouldn't the program be for everyone? Social Security is a good example. High-income people get Social Security just like everyone else. We should extend to all our demands the slogan used by advocates of health care for all, "Everybody in, nobody out," which conveys the power as well as the justice of universal programs.[21]

We can apply this principle to childcare. In the absence of public spending, parents are paying a lot for childcare. But just because childcare is expensive, doesn't mean childcare workers are well paid. In fact, childcare workers are the lowest-paid profession in the United States, with high turnover among teachers as they struggle to pay their bills. As childcare teacher organizers in the Worthy Wages Campaign put it a few years ago, "Parents can't afford to pay, teachers can't afford to stay, there has to be a better way." And there is a better way, public funding of childcare as a national system, like the public schools, in which the teachers are paid on the same scale and are unionized. As it stands now, childcare teachers are subsidizing the stingy U.S. child production system with their low pay, just as parents are with their unpaid work. Childcare teachers and parents are natural allies, but they are pitted against each other by the fact that most parents are personally paying for childcare.

Existing programs split rather than unify parents. Childcare vouchers for low-wage parents are a classic dodge. Rather than creating a quality system that works for everyone, we get a program only for those who can prove their low income, splitting the constituency that could fight for a fully funded childcare system and leaving those with vouchers to chase spots in ridiculously underfunded and fragmented system. Head Start, which provides preschool and other services to children whose parents have low wages, has this same Achilles' heel. The tempting logic is that children of low-income and unemployed workers are under extra duress and should have extra help. But because it is then defined as a poverty program, it is always under attack by budget cutters, who use racism and resentment among those who are not eligible to undermine support. As a result, the teachers in Head Start, including those with bachelor's degrees, make half what kindergarten teachers make in the public schools. Many of them leave, finding they can't afford to do this valuable work. These systems stigmatize and segregate the children of low-waged workers rather than guaranteeing every child a quality spot as a right.

This is not to knock the work of those who are fighting to save these programs, or who have worked hard to push through the first paid parental leave laws in California, New Jersey, Connecticut, and New York. Making any progress against such a powerful and well-funded opposition is difficult. But the job of the movement is to expose whose interests are being served by the status quo, and to expand the possibilities by raising hell, not by making "reasonable" proposals that get you a seat at the table in some government taskforce where you fight a losing battle to keep your reasonable proposal from being further watered down.

Radicals are forever being counseled to be reasonable and not ask too much. A longtime campaigner for living wages once cautioned me that when campaigning for a higher minimum wage you had to pick a wage that "passed the laugh test." If people laughed upon hearing your proposal, it was too high. I'm grateful that the union-led Fight for $15 campaign didn't follow this logic—it would have been a Fight for $9.12 or a Fight for $8.75. The bolder wage demand galvanized a broad range of people because they thought, OK, this isn't just crumbs. This could actually make a difference in my life. Now I think if nobody is laughing at how foolish your demand is, you're not demanding enough. Of course, when politicians and corporate lobbyists get hold of any proposal they'll weaken it. Our role is to set the bar high and demand something that is worth the fight and benefits as big a constituency as possible.

This leads to another lesson from countries that have won both reproductive rights and tax-funded childcare and parental leave programs. In Europe, when the feminist movement arose in the late 1960s, it was able to make good on demands for free abortion and birth control because labor and socialist movements had already won national systems providing health care to everyone. Abortion and contraception were simply included. Here in the United States, the feminist movement won us the legal right to these things, but with our health care system still in the hands of private interests, our access is blocked by cost. Similarly, in other countries, tax funds for childcare, paid leave, and other social wage programs were extracted from employers not just by feminists, or by birth strikes, but by a strong labor movement. The battered and besieged state of the U.S. labor movement means employers can do what they want when it comes to family and sick leave, health insurance, even whether they pay taxes.

As SisterSong points out in their program for reproductive justice, our conditions for bearing and rearing children are determined by our jobs, our wages, our relationships, and how much power we really have in our communities. Women and all working people need drastic changes in the prevailing conditions in the United States. The birth rate is just one leverage point among many—at work, at home, in the streets, in the media, and in the political arena—and we will need all of them to win.

3. Sharpen Our Strike Weapon

While feminists have been struggling valiantly to defend our reproductive rights, we have only vaguely sensed *why* the power structure wants to control our reproductive lives. We confront the clash of cultural or religious views when we defend abortion clinics from protesters. But these are just the visible stalks and leaves produced by a hidden root: the struggle over the price of our reproductive labor. Obstacles to abortion are keeping our reproductive labor cheap. In light of this, we need to stop thinking about birth control and abortion as just individual choices or "our most personal health care decisions" and start thinking about them as a *tool of political power* that women, the childbearing workforce, must control.[22]

Surgical abortions are generally faster and may be less painful than pill abortions, and should be the gold standard for what we want, with more medical personnel being allowed to perform them, at any stage of pregnancy, and covered, along with all other methods of birth control, through a tax-funded national health care system that provides all care to anyone who wants it.[23] But when developing a strategy for the next phase of the struggle, we should take into account how medical advances have made at-home abortions much safer than they were before *Roe v. Wade*, when many women faced life-threatening injuries or infections from back-alley procedures or attempts to end their own pregnancies.

Medical abortions—done with pills—became available in the United States in 2000 when the FDA approved the abortion pill mifepristone (Mifeprex), originally developed in France as RU-486. Used in combination with misoprostol (Cytotec), this is now the method used in 30 percent of abortions in the United States.[24] Yet the abortion pill was only allowed into the United States on condition that it be just as expensive and inconvenient as surgical abortion. It cannot be prescribed like an ordinary drug that one goes into a retail pharmacy to pick up. It has to be dispensed by the provider, who has to pass a special certification and have a relationship with the supplier. These precautions are aimed at restricting abortion access and serve no medical purpose. A group of doctors recently reviewed the data and concluded, in the *New England Journal of Medicine*, that abortion pills are unnecessarily burdened by regulations that were designed for the most dangerous drugs.[25] With a concerted campaign, feminists and other defenders of reproductive rights could make abortion pills available in pharmacies, dramatically increasing the number of medical practitioners who can prescribe them.[26]

Even with existing restrictions, the abortion pill has made it harder for legislatures to choke off the supply of abortions, although they're trying. Legislatures in thirty-seven states have dictated that only doctors can dispense the pills, although the World Health Organization says that nurse practitioners should be able to do so. When clinics tried to increase access by having doctors consult by video conference and dispense the medicine remotely, nineteen states responded by outlawing telemedicine consultations.[27]

As always with abortion, women are taking matters into their own hands. Misoprostol, the second part of the combination used by clinicians for medical abortions, induces abortions on its own in 80 to 85 percent of cases. It's available over-the-counter in Latin America, and by prescription in the United States, to protect against ulcers.[28] People buy it in Mexico, and it shows up in border states like Texas, where women find it at flea markets.[29] In the United States, "an underground network of midwives, doulas and activists" are distributing misoprostol to women in need, according to reporter Phoebe Zerwick. "If I got caught with this stuff, I could be facing twenty-five years to life," one underground activist told her. "I have a seven-year-old. Going to jail is a scary thought. But I can't just sit around and wait for things to change."[30]

Authorities are responding by threatening criminal charges against women who are suspected of aborting using pills they obtained on their own—or arresting women who helped. In one case in rural Pennsylvania, a mother of three who obtained the pills online for her pregnant sixteen-year-old daughter was sentenced to nine months in jail. The nearest abortion clinic was seventy-five miles away, and both transport and cost were obstacles. And because of the legislatively mandated waiting period, a legal abortion would have required two trips.[31] The pills they received in the mail worked, but the daughter's painful cramping led the two to go to a hospital emergency room, and someone there reported them to the police. (If you are in a similar situation, it's important to know that an abortion caused by pills has the same symptoms as a spontaneous miscarriage and, in the unlikely event that you have complications, the same treatment. So it is not necessary to disclose to medical personnel that you used pills.[32])

Taking advantage of the technological advance of the abortion pill, the Netherlands-based direct-action organization Women on Waves in 2006 launched its Women on Web project, which mails abortion pills to women who request them from countries where abortion is illegal.[33] Sometimes the packages are stopped by customs, but more often they get through. The group doesn't send pills to the United States, instead concentrating on countries where abortion is much more restricted. Even so, Women on Web got six hundred requests in 2015 from U.S. women frantic for help.[34] In 2018, Women on Web's founder Rebecca Gomperts set up a separate entity, Aid Access, to distribute pills in the United States. But the FDA claims that Aid Access, while it provides a long-distance consultation and a prescription, violates the agency's extra regulations.[35]

In the United States, several dozen organizations in the National Network of Abortion Funds (NNAF) collect donations and provide money and lodging for women seeking abortions and in some cases birth control. Recognizing that the real solution is to abolish unfair laws and funding restrictions, NNAF and several other feminist organizations are focused on repealing the Hyde Amendment, which would allow federal funds to be used for abortion, and cover abortions for those who get their insurance through Medicaid. But even if we manage to repeal Hyde, states are likely to mount court challenges to the requirement that they provide abortion funding—like half the states did when the Affordable Care Act expanded Medicaid coverage. In thirty-two states in 2017 both houses of the legislature were majority anti-abortion, along with thirty governors.

The political scene is not promising. State legislatures have passed an appalling 668 restrictions on reproductive rights since 2000.[36] In 2016, the Supreme Court finally struck down two drastic measures passed by Texas—laws that had already closed half the clinics in the state. But the Court has been silent while states order doctors to recite scaremongering scripts, force women to undergo unnecessary ultrasounds, gag state-funded workers from mentioning abortion services, fund anti-abortion groups posing as clinics, and restrict second-trimester abortions.

A political breakthrough is desperately needed. If history is any guide, breakthroughs will come when women organize and escalate, based on understanding our new conditions. Feminists could follow Margaret

Sanger's lead and openly distribute abortion pills here. Repression would follow, but so could a real debate that asks, Who is it that wants to force us to have babies against our will? And why?

An effective birth strike requires that *every* woman be able to control her reproduction. Knowing this should lead us to the conclusion that solidarity is urgently required. If any woman can be denied control, our collective power is weakened. "We must subject every proposal for change and every tactic to the clearest feminist scrutiny," cautioned abortion rights leader Lucinda Cisler in 1970 as new abortion laws were being written, and "demand only what is good for *all* women, and not let some of us be bought off at the expense of the rest."[37]

4. Fund Our Own Organizations

Instead of paying their taxes into the public till, many billionaires start foundations to keep control of their money. These foundations tend to study problems to which the solutions are completely obvious but are being blocked by the same billionaire class. The reason we haven't booted private insurance companies out of our health care, for example, is not that we don't know how to solve such a complicated problem. In fact a universal system has worked in every other country that has tried it, and it even works just fine here in the form of Medicare for those over sixty-five. The reason we don't have it here is that insurance companies (and their banks) don't want to give up their profits from selling health insurance. So in the early 2000s, we had the Kaiser Family Foundation and others puzzling over how to "cover the uninsured." That framing of the problem led us directly to the Affordable Care Act (Obamacare), which did indeed cover, minimally, some of the uninsured, but left insurance companies gatekeeping our access to care. This is why movement organizations cannot be dependent on corporate foundations. When we ask "Who benefits?" as we do in consciousness-raising, foundations would not like the answer.

Sheryl Sandberg, chief operating officer of Facebook and author of *Lean In*, is a case in point. A grim occasion for higher consciousness arose when Sandberg's husband died in 2015 and she was left a single parent. Even with $1 billion in personal wealth and a top management job, she acknowledged that she was having a hard time, and had been too glib in her book. "Before, I did not quite get it," she wrote a year after her husband's death. "I did not really get how hard it is to succeed at work when you are overwhelmed at home." Calling for more community support, she wrote, "Single moms have been leaning in for a long time—out of necessity and a desire to provide the best possible opportunities for their children."[38] But does Sandberg support the taxes on her wealth that would be required to put in place such community supports? Certainly part of the problem is Facebook's strategy of avoiding $5.8 billion in U.S. taxes using the stock option loophole, and another $2.8 billion by moving money around between European countries.[39] These unpaid taxes would make a nice contribution to starting a universal childcare system, and Facebook is just one corporate tax evader among many. One group estimates that offshore tax havens alone allow big corporations to avoid $100 billion in federal taxes annually.[40]

Not surprisingly, corporate foundations favor solutions that carry no danger of altering the balance of power or their accumulation of capital. Indeed, many foundations, while claiming to act in the public interest, tip the balance of power further in favor of corporations and against working people. The entire foundation-led education "reform" movement, from the Gates and Walton foundations laundering the profits of Microsoft and Walmart to Sandberg's own Facebook throwing around $100 million in Newark, New Jersey, is aimed at reducing the power of teachers through their unions.[41] Corporate foundations like a "reform" unless it shifts power away from the rich toward working people.

The foundation approach carries over to government, with boutique solutions that dispense a voucher here and a scholarship there, but never provide a broad vision that the majority of people could unite around and own as real progress. Feminist writer Katha Pollitt nailed this general outlook in a review of Hillary Clinton's 1996 book It Takes a Village: "For every problem she identifies, a study, a foundation, a church, a business or government-funded pilot project is already on the case. . . . Some of these programs sound terrific, but none of them are on remotely the same scale as the problems they confront. . . . For H.R.C. the state itself becomes a kind of pilot project, full of innovation but short on cash, and ever on the lookout for spongers."[42]

Hillary Clinton's 2016 approach to childcare suffered from the same problems. She proposed a thicket of acronyms for each piece of her plan—but examined up close they dissolved into nothingness. The boldest of her initiatives started out well, "Make preschool universal for every four-year-old in America." But then the details emerged: "she will work to ensure that every four-year-old in America has access to high-quality preschool in the next ten years." Access? Apparently the access will be backed up by a pledge that "no family in America will spend more than ten percent of its income on childcare." This is to be done by "significantly increasing the federal government's investment in childcare subsidies and providing tax relief for the cost of childcare."

She recognizes that childcare workers are poorly paid and that it results in turnover, so there's the "Respect and Increased Salaries for Early Childhood Educators (RAISE) initiative," which will "fund and support states and local communities that work to increase the compensation of childcare providers and early educators and provide equity with kindergarten teachers by investing in educational opportunities, career ladders, and professional salaries." The initiative already undermines itself by suggesting that the problem is that childcare workers don't have enough education to deserve a worthy wage. The reality is that until the wages are higher, teachers who have managed to get higher degrees won't be able to afford to stay in those jobs. Further, Clinton's campaign materials made it sound like all the federal government can do is "work to increase" compensation. Childcare workers earn median hourly pay of $9.77.[43] What would really increase their compensation is a $15 an hour federal minimum wage.

Then there's the SPARK program, which addresses the fact that one quarter of students are parents by providing "scholarships of up to $1,500 per year to help as many as one million student parents afford high-quality child care." Rather than proposing a national childcare program that all children qualify for, student-parents will compete for a small stipend to pay for a fraction of their childcare bill. And there are the locutions suitable for advertising: "up to $1,500" and "as many as" one million student parents. This kind of program is easily junked because the people who are supposed to benefit mostly don't even know it exists.

Hillary Clinton conceded that her approach might have been flawed in her post-2016 campaign book *What Happened*. She observed: "Democrats should reevaluate a lot of our assumptions about which policies are politically viable. These trends make universal programs even more appealing than we previously thought. I mean programs like Social Security and Medicare, which benefit every American, as opposed to Medicaid, food stamps, and other initiatives targeted to the poor." She recalled her opposition to Bernie Sanders's plan for free public college, and reflected, "It's precisely because they don't benefit everyone that targeted programs are so easily stigmatized and demagogued.... Democrats should redouble our efforts to develop bold, creative ideas that offer broad-based benefits for the whole country."[44] But she couldn't resist characterizing Sanders's serious proposals for universal programs as

"America should get a pony" and still regards her means-tested hodge-podges as "more efficient and progressive."[45]

The movement is supposed to provide a counterweight to this mess, demanding broad change that's worth fighting for. This is why the foundation-led outlook is not a side issue but central to our effectiveness. When feminist organizations are reliant on corporate foundations for their livelihood, they tend to provide stopgap services or fight for small "winnable" programs rather than organize for power to change hands.

Our organizations need to be accountable to us, but they won't be as long as someone else is paying the bills. We need to engage in a lot more of what Redstockings calls "dues-paying feminism."[46] But what if you're really poor? Then aren't dues elitist or classist? Serious, radical organizations of the poor such as the Philadelphia/Delaware Valley Union of the Homeless collect dues—at one point they had six thousand dues-paying members.[47] Money to organize will always come from somewhere—out of organizers' pockets or from public fundraisers, from dues, or from corporate foundation grants. Too often in our movement the answer has been foundations, binding us to boutique project organizing along with more obvious taming effects.[48]

●

Feminists have contended that it is women's reproductive capacity that made us targets of oppression. Some saw pregnancy and nursing as a burden or disability that made us unable to defend ourselves against men's prehistoric power grab. Some thought control of our reproductive capacity was the ongoing motive for that oppression—that women were corralled into patriarchal families to produce babies for war or conquest, or to increase the family's workforce. But it has been unclear how women's capacity to reproduce could translate into political power—it seemed to be perpetually used against women, blocking us from education, keeping us out of desirable jobs, and making us dependent on fathers and husbands. Women were exempted from military service because of our value as reproducers, but even this has cut both ways. Our dangerous service was in childbirth, with a death rate comparable to soldiering until the twentieth century. But then men got benefits due veterans that we could only access through marriage.

It's a relatively new development that women have had both the motive and the means to so strictly control our reproduction that we are not replacing the population. The results are just now being felt in countries with the lowest birth rates, first as working-age populations decrease, and then as total populations shrink. Feminist movement understanding and strategies are only now adjusting to these new conditions and many questions remain.

For example, we don't know how capitalist economies, with their imperative to grow, will cope with decreasing populations. Some have suggested that capitalism must grow to stay viable: "The insatiable need to increase profits cannot be reformed away," said the authors of the Belem Ecosocialist Declaration. "Capitalism can no more survive limits on growth than a person can live without breathing."[49] Until now, population growth has been a large part of capitalist growth. Is it an essential part? As the birth slowdown progresses, it is likely to reveal new things about the nature of the system.

Feminists landed some solid punches during the 1960s, gaining greater economic independence and reproductive control. In response, the elite is punching back with curtailments of our right to motherhood at our own discretion. The more clearly the battle lines are drawn, the more women, and all working people, have a chance to win. We are the majority and we are the ones who will decide how many or how few people are needed to make our society run, and run in the interests of the many, not the few.

CONSCIOUSNESS-RAISING QUESTIONS

Below are suggested questions to use if you want to start a consciousness-raising group. They are mostly related to the issues in this book, but you can create additional questions to discuss any area of life. It helps to investigate something you're truly curious about. Resist the temptation to put your expected conclusion in the question—you may be surprised! It also helps if your group includes a diversity of ages, jobs, races, orientations, and backgrounds—the broader the group of women, the deeper the conclusions can be. (But don't let this be an obstacle to getting together—you can also reach important conclusions in a homogeneous group.)

At the beginning, set a time to start conclusions—at least thirty minutes is recommended. For conclusions, you can start by listing the commonalities and differences. Differences, or contradictions, can be particularly illuminating, because you have a chance to look for a common root. Some conclusions won't occur to participants until days later. Make sure to discuss who is benefitting from the situations you describe.

To prepare, we highly recommend Kathie Sarachild's essay, "Consciousness-Raising: A Radical Weapon," in Redstockings' *Feminist Revolution*, available for download from the Redstockings Women's Liberation Archives for Action at www.redstockings.org.[1]

If you want help, National Women's Liberation can provide guidance. Write us at NWL@womensliberation.org or go to womensliberation.org. There you can also find a reading group guide to this book for your organization or book club.

Children and Care Work

1. **How many kids did your great-grandmothers have? Grandmothers? Mother? You?**
   - What factors do you or did you weigh when considering whether to have or not have kids? How have your views changed over time?

2. **What are your reasons for wanting children? For not wanting them?**
   - Has your thinking on this changed? Are your parents' lives a factor in your thinking?
   - Do you experience pressure from anyone on the subject?

3. **Have you ever participated in child rearing (as a parent, step-parent, grandparent, family member, childcare teacher, etc.)?**
   - What do/did you like about it? What do/did you not like about it?

4. **What do you want from society in terms of child rearing?**
   - What do you want from men in terms of child rearing?
   - For those who have done parenting work: When does this work feel like an individual or nuclear family responsibility? When does it feel like a collective (community, society-wide, national) responsibility?

5. **What have you and/or your family gotten from the current health care system that you needed?**
   - What have you needed that you haven't gotten?
   - What would change in your life if you had guaranteed health care?

6. **What care work do you do (child rearing, care for sick or frail family members, or others in your life needing care)?**
   - What care work do the men in your life do?
   - Have you tried to get them to do more? What happened?

Abortion and Birth Control

1. **What kind of birth control do you use or have you used?**
   - Do you like it? Why or why not?
   - How did you find out about it?
   - How do you pay for it?

2. **Have you ever had an unplanned pregnancy or pregnancy scare?**
   - What happened?
   - What role did your partner play?

- What would you do if you got pregnant now?

3. **What restrictions or obstacles have you faced when trying to access birth control or abortion services?**
   - How did these restrictions or obstacles affect you? What did you do?
   - Are these restrictions acceptable to you? Why or why not?

4. **How does birth control, abortion, or childcare affect your life?**
   - What obstacles do you face? What role do men play?
   - What role does your insurance company play? What role does your employer play?
   - How would having full and free (no-cost) birth control, abortion, and childcare affect your life?

General Feminist

1. **Have ever you felt something or someone has challenged your bodily autonomy or policed your exercise of it? What did you do? What happened?**

2. **Have you experienced pressure to meet certain milestones in your life, such as marriage or having children?**
   - From whom or what did you receive pressure?
   - How did it affect you?

3. **Are you, or do you want to be, married (or its equivalent)?**
   - If so, why? If not, why not?
   - What are the advantages in your particular decision about the question?
   - What are the downsides?

4. **When have you had a close, trusting relationship with another woman?**
   - Has a lack of trust or sense of competition ever interfered with your relationship with another woman?
   - How was the relationship affected? What happened?

5. **How has your relationship with your mother changed over time?**
   - How has she influenced you?
   - How are you like her? How are you different?

- When did you first see your mother as a woman beyond her role as a mother?
- To your knowledge, was your mother ever unhappy or rebellious in her roles?
- How did this affect you?

6. **What have you gotten from the women's liberation movement or feminism?**
   - Have those things made it worthwhile to make contributions (time, money, etc.)? Why or why not?
   - What have you contributed?
   - What would have to happen in order for you to do more?

ACKNOWLEDGMENTS

The genesis of this book is a research assignment on birth control history from Redstockings of the Women's Liberation Movement for a larger think-tank project. It began to crystallize into its present form from Kathie Sarachild's observation in her Redstockings essay "Beyond the Family Wage: A Women's Liberation View of the Social Wage," (2001) that women in the U.S. are on a spontaneous birth strike. It certainly described my case at the time, as a woman in my mid-thirties without stable employment or reliable health insurance, and a spouse in similar circumstances. As I tried figure out how I would manage if I had a child, the pieces seemed expensive and impossible to assemble: work that paid enough to raise a child but was flexible, childcare, after-school programs, and, looming large, health care.

Given my situation, I was inspired by Sarachild's argument that birth slowdowns or strikes have given force to feminist demands for increased "social wages" in other countries—the very supports that would have made it feasible for me to have a child. Her essay was part of a Redstockings book she and I coedited with Amy Coenen, *Women's Liberation and National Health Care: Confronting the Myth of America*. Simultaneously, I was working on mobilizing feminists for national health insurance, and working with Gainesville (Florida) Women's Liberation on gaining over-the-counter access to the morning-after pill. We found that there was majority support for both reforms, but opposition from the two major political parties. The groundswell for universal "single-payer" health insurance was deflected into a compromise, the Affordable Care Act, with its giant deductibles and still-high premiums—a giveaway to health insurance companies. Our campaign for the morning-after pill did finally gain a victory in 2013, but thanks to a judicial ruling, not the Democratic administration, which resisted almost as vigorously as the Republicans had.

Bipartisan establishment opposition to national health insurance and hostility to effective contraception seemed connected, so drawing many guiding ideas from Redstockings, particularly Sarachild, and with financial support from the group, I volunteered to draft what we thought would be a short essay. Other priorities intervened, but in 2016 National Women's Liberation commissioned me to finish this longer work.

Collaboration between Redstockings and Gainesville Women's Liberation goes back to the 1960s. Gainesville became a center of feminist ferment in 1968 when Beverly Jones, a civil rights activist, faculty wife and mother, and Judith Brown, a civil rights activist in the Congress of Racial Equality and a student left leader, collaborated to write *Towards a Female Liberation Movement*. It spread rapidly, becoming known as "The Florida Paper," and was soon recognized as a foundational call to action for the new movement. At a meeting in Sandy Springs, Maryland, in June 1968, Brown and her recruit, Carol Giardina, met Sarachild and Carol Hanisch of New York Radical Women, from which Redstockings developed as a radical feminist action group.

Brown, Sarachild, and Hanisch were all civil rights movement veterans, and they recognized in each other a similar outlook even when they disagreed, which they sometimes did vigorously. The women started an intense collaboration, with frequent correspondence, long-distance phone calls (made free through various shenanigans), and visits for precious face-to-face time. The New York women passed on to Brown and Giardina a technique that New York Radical Women had been developing for analyzing women's oppression that the group called "consciousness-raising." The four women's gripping correspondence, as they further developed consciousness-raising, "sisterhood is powerful," "the personal is political," the "pro-woman line," and other founding ideas of the women's liberation movement, is available in Redstockings' microfilm publication *Redstockings' Women's Liberation Archives for Action, 1940s–1991* (Primary Source Media/Cengage). The history is also recounted in Carol Giardina's *Freedom for Women: Forging the Women's Liberation Movement, 1953–1970*.

Like nearly all of the germinal Women's Liberation groups of the 1960s, Gainesville Women's Liberation flew apart by 1970. Redstockings also disintegrated, but some of its members quickly regrouped in a tighter formation, incorporated in 1973, and in 1975 published *Feminist Revolution*, a work analyzing the experience of the movement—its impressive victories and its rapid derailment. In the mid-1980s, Brown and Giardina restarted Gainesville Women's Liberation and began to work with Redstockings again. In 1991, while Brown was dying of breast cancer, she pushed the two groups into closer collaboration. She saw the necessity of our unity despite renewed disagreements. Through the years, Redstockings has specialized in developing the theory and history, with Gainesville Women's Liberation teaching classes and organizing women through campaigns. Our fight to win the morning-after pill without a doctor's prescription, one of the few recent victories on reproductive rights among a flood of setbacks, was a result of this collaboration. Another result is the group National Women's Liberation, which now has members all over the country.

I represent a younger generation of Gainesville Women's Liberation. My father remembers being locked in a sweatbox jail cell in 1963 in St. Augustine, Florida, with Judith Brown's husband Julian and others protesting racist segregation. In 1969, when my mother expressed interest in attending a Gainesville Women's Liberation meeting, my father responded, "Off to join the ball cutters, eh?" She didn't go to the meeting, though she did get a divorce a couple of years later.

I started working with GWL in 1987, and then in 1989 I traveled the well-worn road from Gainesville to New York when Sarachild recruited me to work on the first catalog of the newly public Redstockings Women's Liberation Archives for Action, with the slogan "Building on what's been won by knowing what's been done." As an impatient youngster biased toward action and prone to charging ahead without regard for what had gone before, working in the Redstockings Archives showed me that archives really could be "for action." Instead of outdated ideas, I found that 1960s materials were *more* radical and *more* insightful than the later, allegedly improved radical feminism I had encountered. This led me to a decades-long dedication to the Archives and to teaching about its treasures. Our efforts have paid off. Since that first 1989 catalog, the radical 1960s roots of women's liberation have gradually been unearthed, founding papers have been reprinted in countless anthologies, pioneers have been rediscovered, and common misinterpretations of second-wave feminism have been dented, if not defeated. I've tried to incorporate Archives lessons about "history for activist use" in the present work.

It is not an exaggeration to say this book is a group effort. The present book emerged from three conferences, three extended study groups, several rounds of feedback, many consciousness-raising sessions, and innumerable arguments among dozens of feminist activists and organizers, from long-time leaders to the newest members. It also relied on the practice Redstockings promotes with its slogan "dues-paying feminism." The funds to write it came from the hard-earned dollars of women, not from corporate money laundered through foundations.

Hard work and thinking, patient and impatient explanations and corrections were provided by 1960s Redstockings Kathie Sarachild and Myrna Hill, and Gainesville Women's Liberation cofounder Carol Giardina. Their insights shone through the fog.

Early feedback came from members of the Redstockings Allies and Veterans Social Wage Committee in New York: Allison Guttu, Erin Mahoney, and Annie Tummino, and from Amy Coenen, Alexandra Leader, Kelly Mangan, and Stephanie Seguin in Gainesville. Later drafts were reviewed by National Women's Liberation, with special contributions from Ayn Cheema, Candi Churchill, Andrea Costello, Paulina Davis, Lydia Devine, Brooke Eliazar-Macke, Pennie Foster (rest in power, sister), Francie Hunt, Meggan Jordan, Hazel Levy, Natalie Maxwell, Diana Moreno, Zoharah Simmons, Lori Tinney, and Kendra Vincent, and Redstockings Marisa Figueiredo, Nicole Hardin, Adrielle Munger, and Jen Sunderland. Additional feedback came from Birth Strike study groups conducted by National Women's Liberation chapters in New York and Florida in 2018. The Women of Color Caucus of National Women's Liberation, in particular, provided sharp understandings.

Although we didn't end up agreeing on a number of points in the manuscript, we agreed that it represented some developments in our understanding that were urgent to share with the movement. As we continue to research, argue about, and organize with these ideas, I expect our understanding to deepen and our strategic aim to improve. I hope that despite its errors and oversights, the present work adds insights useful to women's liberation and the general movement for human liberation. The responsibility for errors, blind spots, and misjudgments is my own.

Thanks are also due to Frances Beal for her important questions and criticisms, to Nancy Folbre for her stimulating objections, and to Michael Pollak for his sharp edits.

Thanks to Joey Paxman, Ramsey Kanaan, and the rest of the crew at PM Press—you are a joy to work with. For the cover, many thanks to John Yates at Stealworks, and for interior graphics I'm indebted to Charlotte von Hardenburgh.

Finally, I am filled with gratitude for my family, Joe, Joye, Barbara, and Michael. Your love makes everything worthwhile.

NOTES

INTRODUCTION

1   See Lucinda Cisler, "Unfinished Business: Birth Control and Women's Liberation," in *Sisterhood Is Powerful*, ed. Robin Morgan (New York: Vintage, 1970), 245–89; Shulamith Firestone, *The Dialectic of Sex* (New York: William Morrow, 1970); Betty Friedan, "NOW's Statement of Purpose."

2   The report also notes: "The rate among Hispanic women fell below the replacement level of 2,100 for the first time (2,092.5). The Black [Total Fertility Rate] has been below replacement since 2009, and the White TFR has been below 2,100 every year since 1990." David Drozd, "Highlights from January 31, 2018 National Center for Health Statistics Report Titled 'Births: Final Data for 2016' with Comparison to Prior Data on Births," Center for Public Affairs Research, University of Nebraska Omaha, https://www.unomaha.edu/college-of-public-affairs-and-community-service/center-for-public-affairs-research/documents/highlights-from-2016-births-report.pdf.

3   The 2007 Gonzales v. Carhart decision banned D&X procedures, so-called partial birth abortion. The 2016 Whole Woman's Health v. Hellerstedt decision rejected two restrictions passed by Texas that required doctors to have admitting privileges at nearby hospitals and clinics to be ambulatory surgical centers. Most restrictions still stand.

4   Providers are defined as those that do more than four hundred abortions a year. Esmé Deprez, "Abortion Clinics Are Closing at a Record Pace," *Bloomberg Businessweek*, February 24, 2016.

5   Daniel Grossman et al., "Knowledge, Opinion and Experience Related to Abortion Self-induction in Texas," Texas Policy Evaluation Project Research Brief, November 17, 2015, https://liberalarts.utexas.edu/txpep/_files/pdf/TxPEP-Research-Brief-KnowledgeOpinionExperience.pdf.

6   As reported by Shannon Brewer, director of the Jackson (Mississippi) Women's Health Organization, "Abortion Access Collides with Pro-Life Activists in the Deep South," interview by Leonard Lopate, WNYC, June 10, 2016.

7   Andrea Rowan, "Prosecuting Women for Self-Inducing Abortion: Counterproductive and Lacking Compassion," *Guttmacher Policy Review* 18,

no. 3 (2015), https://www.guttmacher.org/gpr/2015/09/prosecuting-women-self-inducing-abortion-counterproductive-and-lacking-compassion.

8   Amanda J. Stevenson et al., "Effect of Removal of Planned Parenthood from the Texas Women's Health Program," *New England Journal of Medicine* 374, no. 9 (March 3, 2016): 853–60.

9   Our unplanned birth rate is 30 percent of all births, compared to 18 percent in France, and 16 percent in Sweden according to "Abortion in Context: United States and Worldwide," *Issues in Brief 1999 Series*, no. 1, Allan Guttmacher Institute. The Centers for Disease Control estimates that 37 percent of U.S. births are unintended. W.D. Mosher et al. "Intended and Unintended Births in the United States: 1982–2010." National Health Statistics Reports, no. 55 (Hyattsville, MD: National Center for Health Statistics, 2012).

10   The pill is more effective the sooner it is taken after sex, so the prescription requirement made it difficult to use effectively by adding the time and costs of a doctor visit.

11   Heather Boonstra, "Emergency Contraception: Steps Being Taken to Improve Access," *Guttmacher Policy Review* 5, no. 5 (December 1, 2002), https://www.guttmacher.org/gpr/2002/12/emergency-contraception-steps-being-taken-improve-access.

12   Under the brand name Plan B One-Step™ the morning-after pill is a one-time dose of hormonal contraceptive, equivalent to about four birth control pills, but because it is not taken on a sustained basis, the risks from regular birth-control pills are not present. Around one in five women experience brief nausea or jitteriness.

13   Jackie Calmes and Gardiner Harris, "Obama Endorses Decision to Limit Morning-After Pill," *New York Times*, December 8, 2011, https://www.nytimes.com/2011/12/09/us/obama-backs-aides-stance-on-morning-after-pill.html.

14   In the middle of this, our groups founded a new organization, National Women's Liberation, womensliberation.org. Jenny Brown and Stephanie Seguin, National Women's Liberation, "How We Won the Fight on the Morning-After Pill," *Huffington Post*, June 22, 2013, http://www.huffingtonpost.com/jenny-f-brown/how-we-won-the-fight-on-t_b_3134796.html.

15   Tummino v. Hamburg, filed by the Center for Reproductive Rights, joined by the Partnership for Civil Justice Fund and Southern Legal Counsel, Inc. No. 12-CV-763 (ERK)(VVP), United States District Court E.D.N.Y. 2013.

16   See, for example, Thomas Frank, *What's the Matter with Kansas? How Conservatives Won the Heart of America* (New York: Henry Holt, 2004).

17   W.D. Mosher and J. Jones, "Use of Contraception in the United States: 1982–2008." National Center for Health Statistics. *Vital Health Statistics* 23, no. 29 (2010).

18   Judith M. DeSarno and Marilyn J. Keefe, "Weathering the Storm: Federal Legislative and Regulatory Action On Reproductive Health in 2005," (Report) National Family Planning and Reproductive Health Association, January 13, 2006, https://www.nationalfamilyplanning.org/document.doc?id=178.

19   Cecile Richards, "They're Even Anti-Contraception," October 19, 2006, letter from Planned Parenthood.

20   These are total fertility rates. Based on current births, they estimate how many children each woman is likely to have during her childbearing years. The 0.1

in the 2.1 "replacement" rate accounts for those children who don't survive to childbearing age themselves.

21   Sabrina Tavernise, "U.S. Fertility Rate Fell to a Record Low, for a Second Straight Year," *New York Times*, May 16, 2018, A11. See also Brady E. Hamilton et al. *Births: Provisional Data for 2017, Vital Statistics Rapid Release*, no. 4 (Hyattsville, MD: National Center for Health Statistics, May 2018), https://www.cdc.gov/nchs/data/vsrr/report004.pdf.

22   Steven Philip Kramer, *The Other Population Crisis: What Governments Can Do about Falling Birth Rates* (Washington, DC: Woodrow Wilson Center, 2014), 6–7.

23   Phillip Longman, *The Empty Cradle: How Falling Birthrates Threaten World Prosperity and What to Do about It* (New York: Basic Books, 2004), 4.

24   Ben Wattenberg, *Fewer: How the New Demography of Depopulation Will Shape Our Future* (Chicago: Ivan R. Dee, 2004), 116. Earlier he wrote *The Birth Dearth* (New York: Pharos, 1987).

25   Greg Ip, "The World's New Population Time Bomb: Too Few People," *Wall Street Journal*, November 24, 2015, A1.

26   Eduardo Porter, "Coming Soon: The Vanishing Work Force," *New York Times*, August 29, 2004, http://www.nytimes.com/2004/08/29/business/coming-soon-the-vanishing-work-force.html.

27   Ross Douthat, "More Babies Please," *New York Times*, December 1, 2012, SR11.

28   The first wave is the nineteenth-century women's rights movement.

29   Katha Pollitt, *Pro: Reclaiming Abortion Rights* (New York: Picador, 2014), 137.

30   Pollitt, *Pro*, 139.

31   Linda Gordon, *The Moral Property of Women: A History of Birth Control Politics in America* (Champaign: University of Illinois Press, 2002), 90–91.

32   Gordon, *Moral Property of Women*, 304.

33   Michelle Goldberg, *The Means of Reproduction: Sex, Power, and the Future of the World* (New York: Penguin, 2009), 207, quoting David Willetts, *Old Europe? Demographic Change and Pension Reform*, London: Centre for European Reform, September 2003.

34   Goldberg, *Means of Reproduction*, 219–20.

35   "Report on the Economic Well-Being of U.S. Households in 2014," Board of Governors of the Federal Reserve System, May 2015, Washington, DC, 18.

36   Goldberg, *Means of Reproduction*, 222.

37   Michelle Goldberg, "Texas Is Hell-Bent on Ending Reproductive Health Care Access for Poor Women," *Slate*, October 19, 2015, http://www.slate.com/blogs/xx_factor/2015/10/19/texas_cuts_planned_parenthood_out_of_medicaid.html.

38   Amanda Marcotte, "As the GOP attacks on birth control increase, a new paper demonstrates its economic value," *Salon*, June 7, 2017, http://www.salon.com/2017/06/07/as-gop-attacks-on-birth-control-increase-new-paper-demonstrates-its-economic-value.

39   Adele M. Stan, "Anatomy of the War on Women: How the Koch Brothers Are Funding the Anti-Choice Agenda," *RH Reality Check*, November 5, 2013. https://rewire.news/article/2013/11/05/anatomy-of-the-war-on-women-how-the-koch-brothers-are-funding-the-anti-choice-agenda/. (*RH Reality Check* has since been renamed *Rewire*).

40   For second-wave writing, see Silvia Federici and Arlen Austin, eds., *The New York Wages for Housework Committee 1972–1977: History, Theory, Documents* (Brooklyn: Autonomedia, 2018) and Marlene Dixon, *The Future of Women* (San

Francisco: Synthesis, 1980), 3–13. For recent organizing, see Every Mother is a Working Mother Network, http://www.everymothernetwork.net and Bill the Patriarchy, https://www.billthepatriarchy.com.

41 Kathie Sarachild, "A Program for Feminist Consciousness-Raising," (November 1968) in *Feminist Revolution*, ed. Redstockings (New York: Redstockings, 1975; New York: Random House, 1978), 202–3.

42 Redstockings, *The Redstockings Manifesto* (New York: July 7, 1969), Redstockings Women's Liberation Archives for Action, http://redstockings.org/index.php/rs-manifesto.

CHAPTER 1: INTERNATIONAL COMPARISONS

1   CIA World Factbook "Total Fertility Rate (2017 estimates)," https://www.cia.gov/library/publications/the-world-factbook/fields/2127.html.

2   Greg Ip, "The World's New Population Time Bomb: Too Few People," *Wall Street Journal*, November 22, 2015, http://www.wsj.com/articles/how-demographics-rule-the-global-economy-1448284890.

3   "Breaking the Baby Strike," *Economist*, July 25, 2015, http://www.economist.com/news/international/21659763-people-rich-countries-can-be-coaxed-having-more-children-lazy-husbands-and.

4   Kathie Sarachild observed this phenomenon in 1971, comparing then-similar French and U.S. birth rates. "In France . . . the government openly describes the birth rate as dangerously low and not only forbids abortions but pays family allowances to encourage women to have children." Sarachild, "The Myth of Abortion Law Repeal," *Woman's World* 1, no. 1 (April 15, 1971): 10. Redstockings Women's Liberation Archives.

5   Rachel Martin, "Germany Frets about Women in Shrinking Workforce," *Morning Edition*, National Public Radio, May 24, 2006, http://www.npr.org/templates/story/story.php?storyId=5427278.

6   Anne Chemin, "France's Baby Boom Secret: Get Women into Work and Ditch Rigid Family Norms," *Guardian* (UK), March 21, 2015, http://www.theguardian.com/world/2015/mar/21/france-population-europe-fertility-rate.

7   *Economist*, "Breaking the Baby Strike."

8   Stephanie Mencimer, "The Baby Boycott," *Washington Monthly*, June 2001, http://www.washingtonmonthly.com/features/2001/0106.mencimer.html.

9   Martin, "Germany Frets."

10 Max Fisher, "Japan's Sexual Apathy Is Endangering the Global Economy," *Washington Post*, October 22, 2013, https://www.washingtonpost.com/news/worldviews/wp/2013/10/22/japans-sexual-apathy-is-endangering-the-global-economy/.

11 Leo Lewis, "Japan: Women in the Workforce," *Financial Times*, July 6, 2015, http://www.ft.com/intl/cms/s/0/60729d68-20bb-11e5-aa5a-398b2169cf79.html#axzz3wByujfqS.

12 Philip Brasor and Masako Tsubuku, "Want More Daycare? Pay Workers More," *Japan Times*, November 2, 2012, http://blog.japantimes.co.jp/yen-for-living/want-more-daycare-pay-workers-more/; Isabel Reynolds, "Japan's Childcare Backlog Hampers Abe Push to Put Women to Work," *Bloomberg*, September 30, 2015, http://www.bloomberg.com/news/articles/2015-09-30/japan-s-childcare-backlog-hampers-abe-push-to-put-women-to-work.

13   Max Fisher, "Japanese Politician Wants to Boost the National Birthrate by Banning Abortion," *Washington Post*, February 26, 2013, https://www.washingtonpost.com/news/worldviews/wp/2013/02/26/japanese-politician-wants-to-boost-the-national-birthrate-by-banning-abortion/.

14   Enda Curran and Connor Cislo, "Japan Opens Up to Foreign Workers (Just Don't Call it Immigration)," *Bloomberg*, October 25, 2016, https://www.bloomberg.com/news/articles/2016-10-25/a-wary-japan-quietly-opens-its-back-door-for-foreign-workers.

15   Chris Buckley, "China Ends One-Child Policy, Allowing Families Two Children," *New York Times*, October 29, 2015, http://www.nytimes.com/2015/10/30/world/asia/china-end-one-child-policy.html.

16   Nie Jing-Bao, *Behind the Silence: Chinese Voices on Abortion* (Lanham, MD: Rowman and Littlefield, 2005), 52.

17   Therese Hesketh, Li Lu, and Zhu Wei Xing, "The Effect of China's One-Child Family Policy after 25 Years," *New England Journal of Medicine* 353, no. 11 (September 15, 2005): 1171–76.

18   Jing-Bao, *Behind the Silence*, 55ff. Abortions for sex-selection purposes are strictly forbidden. See also U.S. Department of State, "Country Reports on Human Rights Practices," Bureau of Democracy, Human Rights, and Labor, March 31, 2003, http://www.state.gov/j/drl/rls/hrrpt/2002/18239.htm.

19   Dexter Roberts, "Behind China's Labor Unrest: Factory Workers and Taxi Drivers," *Bloomberg*, February 20, 2014, http://www.bloomberg.com/bw/articles/2014-02-20/behind-chinas-labor-unrest-factory-workers-and-taxi-drivers.

20   Buckley, "China Ends One-Child Policy."

21   Haining Liu, "Xi Has Not Undone the Sorrows of China's One-Child Policy," *Financial Times*, November 2, 2015, 9; Patti Waldmeir, "A Silver Lining to China's One-Child Policy," *Financial Times*, October 27, 2015, 8.

22   Buckley, "China Ends One-Child Policy."

23   U.S. Census Current Population Reports, May 2014, https://www.census.gov/prod/2014pubs/p25-1140.pdf.

24   "Decree on the Legalization of Abortions of November 18, 1920," in *The Family in the USSR: Documents and Readings*, ed. Rudolf Schlesinger (London: Routledge, 1949), 44ff.

25   William M. Mandel, *Soviet Women* (New York: Doubleday, 1975), 75; H. Kent Geiger, *The Family in Soviet Russia* (Cambridge, MA: Harvard University Press, 1968), 100.

26   The government's official history says, "In 1936, in view of the rising standard of welfare of the people, the government passed a law prohibiting abortion, at the same time adopting an extensive program for the building of maternity homes, nurseries, milk centres and kindergartens." *History of the Communist Party of the Soviet Union (Bolsheviks) Short Course* (New York: International Publishers, 1939), 340.

27   Richard Stites, *The Women's Liberation Movement in Russia: Feminism, Nihilism and Bolshevism, 1960–1930* (Princeton, NJ: Princeton University Press, 1978), 386.

28   Geiger, *Family in Soviet Russia*, 167, 195.

29   Nicholas Eberstadt, "Drunken Nation: Russia's Depopulation Bomb," *World Affairs*, Spring 2009, http://www.worldaffairsjournal.org/article/drunken-nation-russia%E2%80%99s-depopulation-bomb.

30 "Russia Reverses Birth Decline—but for How Long?" *Moscow Times*, June 22, 2014, http://www.themoscowtimes.com/news/article/russia-reverses-birth-decline-but-for-how-long/502325.html.

31 "Vladimir Putin Reveals Plan to Boost Russia Birth Rate," *BBC News*, April 20, 2011, http://www.bbc.com/news/business-13143523.

32 Tom Parfitt, "Vladimir Putin Calls on Russian Families to Have Three Children," *Telegraph* (UK), December 12, 2012, http://www.telegraph.co.uk/news/worldnews/vladimir-putin/9739678/Vladimir-Putin-calls-on-Russian-families-to-have-three-children.html.

33 Fiona Clark, "Russia Ponders Restrictions on Abortion Rights," *Deutsche Welle*, June 14, 2015, http://www.dw.com/en/russia-ponders-restrictions-on-abortion-rights/a-18509939.

34 Dan Bilefsky and Sebnem Arsu, "Women See Worrisome Shift in Turkey," *New York Times*, April 25, 2012, https://www.nytimes.com/2012/04/26/world/europe/women-see-worrisome-shift-in-turkey.html.

35 "Turkey Unveils Plan for More Babies, Offers Incentives to Parents," *Agence France-Presse*, January 9, 2015, http://www.ndtv.com/world-news/turkey-unveils-plan-for-more-babies-offers-incentives-to-parents-724587.

36 Jonathon Burch, "Turkey Readies Incentives to Halt Falling Birth Rate," Reuters, January 31, 2013, http://www.reuters.com/article/us-turkey-population-idUSBRE90U14I20130131.

37 Arash Ahmadi, "Turkey PM Erdoğan sparks row over abortion," *BBC News*, June 1, 2012, http://www.bbc.com/news/world-europe-18297760.

38 Burch, "Turkey Readies Incentives."

39 *Agence France-Presse*, "Turkey Unveils Plan for More Babies."

40 Selcan Hacaoglu, "Turkey Abortion Law: Women Protest Plans to Curb Abortion," June 3, 2012, Associated Press, http://www.huffingtonpost.com/2012/06/03/turkey-abortion-law-women-protest_n_1566007.html

41 Redstockings goes into feminist objections to the fringe benefits system in greater detail in Kathie Sarachild, Jenny Brown, and Amy Coenen, *Women's Liberation and National Health Care: Confronting the Myth of America* (New York: Redstockings, 2001).

42 Katrin Bennhold, "The Female Factor In Germany, a Tradition Falls, and Women Rise," *New York Times*, January 18, 2010, http://www.nytimes.com/2010/01/18/world/europe/18iht-women.html.

43 Bennhold, "Female Factor in Germany."

44 Susan Gal and Gail Kligman, eds., *Reproducing Gender: Politics, Publics, and Everyday Life after Socialism* (Princeton, NJ: Princeton University Press, 2000), 118.

45 West Germany had a fertility rate of 1.45 in 1990 and 1.39 in 1993.

46 John Caldwell and Thomas Schindlmayr, "Explanations of the Fertility Crisis in Modern Societies: A Search for Commonalities," in *Population and Society*, ed. Frank Trovato, 2nd ed. (Oxford: Oxford University Press, 2012), 204–5.

47 Emma Pearse, "Germany in Angst over Low Birthrate" *Women's ENews*, April 11, 2005, www.womensenews.org/articl.cfm/dyn/aid/2253/context/archive.

48 Pearse, "Germany in Angst."

49 Henry Chu, "For Germany, Refugees are a Demographic Blessing as Well as a Burden," *Los Angeles Times*, September 10, 2015, http://www.latimes.com/world/europe/la-fg-germany-refugees-demographics-20150910-story.html.

50   Chu, "For Germany, Refugees."
51   Fernand Braudel, *The Structures of Everyday Life* (New York: Harper & Row, 1979), 55.
52   United Press International, "French Birth Rate Falling; Government Plans Campaign for Larger Families," *Chicago Tribune*, September 14, 1969; United Press International, "'Make More Babies' campaign being launched in France," *Eugene Register-Guard*, September 14, 1969.
53   UPI, "French Birth Rate Falling,"; UPI, "'Make More Babies' campaign."
54   The declaration was initially printed in *Nouvel Observateur*, April 5, 1971, then translated and reprinted in the United States in the *Socialist Worker*, and from there reprinted in the Women's Liberation newspaper *Woman's World* 1, no. 2 (July–August 1971): 5. Redstockings Women's Liberation Archives for Action, Redstockings.org.
55   Chemin, "France's Baby Boom Secret."
56   Laura Addati, Naomi Cassirer, Katherine Gilchrist, *Maternity and Paternity at Work: Law and Practice across the World*, International Labour Organization, May 13, 2014, 155.
57   Chemin, "France's Baby Boom Secret."
58   Sissela Bok, *Alva Myrdal: A Daughter's Memoir* (Reading, MA: Addison-Wesley, 1991), 117.
59   Bok, *Alva Myrdal*, 117.
60   Asa Lundqvist, *Family Policy Paradoxes: Gender Equality and Labour Market Regulation in Sweden, 1930–2010* (Bristol: Policy Press, 2011), 27.
61   Bok, *Alva Myrdal*, 102.
62   Lola Akinmade Åkerström, "10 Things That Make Sweden Family-Friendly" (Swedish government site), January 4, 2016, https://sweden.se/society/10-things-that-make-sweden-family-friendly/.
63   Uri Friedman, "Sweden: The New Laboratory for a Six-Hour Work Day," *The Atlantic*, April 9, 2014, http://www.theatlantic.com/international/archive/2014/04/sweden-the-new-laboratory-for-a-six-hour-work-day/360402/.

CHAPTER 2: SMALL GOVERNMENT, BIG FAMILIES

1   Feminist economist Nancy Folbre argues that U.S. cash supports for parents—such as the earned income tax credit—are not really that low when compared to other countries, but the "United States stands out in its level of programmatic complexity and inconsistency. The distributional effects are perverse: many affluent families receive benefits that are surprisingly similar, in absolute terms, to those that poor families receive. Middle-income families typically receive less." Nancy Folbre, *Valuing Children: Rethinking the Economics of the Family* (Cambridge, MA: Harvard University, 2008), 139.
2   Kelly Alfieri, "How Much Your Pregnancy Will Really Cost You," The Bump, http://www.thebump.com/a/how-much-pregnancy-costs.
3   If your workplace has under 50 employees, or you haven't already worked there for six months, or you don't work enough hours, you won't qualify for unpaid family leave. California provides paid Family and Medical Leave up to 12 weeks, but the same exclusions apply.
4   Danielle Paquette, "The Shocking Number of New Moms Who Return to Work Two Weeks after Childbirth," *Washington Post*, August 19, 2015, https://

www.washingtonpost.com/news/wonk/wp/2015/08/19/the-shocking-number-of-new-moms-who-return-to-work-two-weeks-after-childbirth/.

5   Peter Holley, "Why Desperate Mothers Are Turning to Crowdfunding to Pay for Maternity Leave," *Washington Post*, April 16, 2016, https://www.washingtonpost.com/news/parenting/wp/2016/04/16/why-desperate-mothers-are-turning-to-crowdfunding-to-pay-for-maternity-leave/.

6   Helena Lee, "Why Finnish Babies Sleep in Cardboard Boxes," *BBC News*, June 4, 2013, http://www.bbc.com/news/magazine-22751415.

7   Nancy Folbre, "The Present Value of Producing Future Taxpayers," *New York Times*, March 29, 2010, http://economix.blogs.nytimes.com/2010/03/29/the-present-value-of-producing-future-taxpayers/.

8   Megan Erickson, "The Privatization of Childhood," *Jacobin*, September 3, 2015, https://www.jacobinmag.com/2015/09/children-testing-schools-education-reform-inequality/. The USDA figures are a low estimate, according to Nancy Folbre in *Valuing Children*, 70-78.

9   Noah Berlatsky, "Why Are Liberals Obsessed With Using Contraception to Fight Poverty?" *New Republic*, October 2, 2015, http://www.newrepublic.com/article/122992/why-are-liberals-obsessed-using-contraception-fight-poverty.

10 Brigid Schulte and Alieza Durana, *New America Care Report* (Washington, DC: New America Foundation, 2016, https://www.newamerica.org/in-depth/care-report/introduction/.

11 Jonathan Chait, "Working Mom Arrested for Letting Her Daughter Play Outside," *New York Times Magazine*, July 15, 2014, http://nymag.com/daily/intelligencer/2014/07/mom-arrested-for-letting-daughter-play-outside.html.

12 Donna St. George, "Maryland Parents Who Allowed Their 'Free Range' Children to Walk Home on Their Own Cited for Neglect," *Washington Post*, March 4, 2015, http://news.nationalpost.com/news/world/maryland-parents-who-allowed-their-free-range-children-to-walk-home-on-their-own-cited-for-neglect.

13 Dorothy Roberts, *Shattered Bonds: The Color of Child Welfare* (New York: Civitas Books, 2009), 92. The Every Mother is a Working Mother Network has been organizing against this horrifying regime as "a national multi-racial grassroots network of mothers, other carers and supporters campaigning to establish that raising children is work and that caring work has economic value, entitling us to welfare and other resources." http://www.everymothernetwork.net/.

14 Elaine Sorensen et al., "Assessing Child Support Arrears in Nine Large States and the Nation," Urban Institute, July 11, 2007, 3, 68, http://www.urban.org/research/publication/assessing-child-support-arrears-nine-large-states-and-nation/view/full_report.

15 Frances Robles and Shaila Dewan, "Skip Child Support. Go to Jail. Lose Job. Repeat," *New York Times*, April 19, 2015, http://www.nytimes.com/2015/04/20/us/skip-child-support-go-to-jail-lose-job-repeat.html.

16 Robles and Dewan, "Skip Child Support."

17 See, for example, Elinor Burkett, *The Baby Boon: How Family-Friendly America Cheats the Childless* (New York: The Free Press, 2000).

18 Jessica Deahl, "Countries around the World Beat the U.S. on Paid Parental Leave," *All Things Considered*, National Public Radio, October 6, 2016, https://www.npr.org/2016/10/06/495839588/countries-around-the-world-beat-the-u-s-on-paid-parental-leave. Several states recently introduced paid parental leave, though not all workers are covered: California provides six weeks at

55 percent of salary, New Jersey offers six weeks at two-thirds of salary, New York is gradually phasing in twelve weeks at two-thirds of salary by 2021 (but capped around $750 a week) and Rhode Island provides four weeks, at 60 percent of salary.

19   Ross Douthat and Reihan Salam, "The Party of Sam's Club," *Weekly Standard*, November 14, 2005, http://www.weeklystandard.com/the-party-of-sams-club/article/7501.

20   Ross Douthat, "Author: GOP Needs to Refocus on the Working Class," interview by Robert Siegel, *All Things Considered*, National Public Radio, November 18, 2005, https://www.npr.org/templates/story/story.php?storyId=5019085.

21   Douthat and Salam, "Party of Sam's Club." The Quebec program has since been scrapped in favor of improved paid parental leave.

22   Robert Stein, "Tax Reform to Strengthen the Economy and Lighten the Burdens Families Bear," in *Room to Grow: Conservative Reforms for a Limited Government and a Thriving Middle Class*, YG [Young Guns] Network, 2014, 33–38.

23   Elizabeth Bruenig, "Marco Rubio and Mike Lee Want You to Have Kids—Unless You're Poor" *New Republic*, March 4, 2015, https://newrepublic.com/article/121216/rubio-lee-tax-plan-features-penalties-poor-families; Matt Bruenig and Elizabeth Bruenig, "Republicans and Democrats Both Claim to Be Pro-Family. Here's How They Can Prove It," *The New Republic*, April 20, 2014, https://newrepublic.com/article/117453/monthly-child-allowance-best-way-support-strong-families.

24   Leta Hollingworth, "Social Devices for Impelling Women to Bear Children," (1916) in *Pronatalism: The Myth of Mom and Apple Pie*, eds. Ellen Peck and Judith Senderowitz (New York: Thomas Y. Crowell, 1974), 24.

25   Patrick Buchanan, *The Death of the West: How Dying Populations and Immigrant Invasions Imperil Our Country and Civilization* (New York: St. Martin's Griffin, 2002), 36–37.

26   Buchanan, *Death of the West*, 28.

27   Bryce Covert, "Why America Gave Up on the Fight for a Family-Friendly Workplace, and Why It's Starting Again," *ThinkProgress*, July 31, 2014, https://thinkprogress.org/why-america-gave-up-on-the-fight-for-a-family-friendly-workplace-and-why-its-starting-again-54f536b27572/.

28   Covert, "Family-Friendly Workplace."

29   Buchanan, *Death of the West*, 42 (pompous capitalization in the original).

30   Santorum, who calls public schools "government-run schools," was caught enrolling his children in a publicly-funded cyber charter school in a district where he no longer resided—so in his case it took more than one village. Stephanie Mencimer, "Rick Santorum's School Scandal: How the Public-School-Loathing GOP Candidate Used Pennsylvania's Taxpayer Dollars to School His Kids in Virginia," *Mother Jones*, January 4, 2012, http://www.motherjones.com/politics/2012/01/rick-santorums-school-scandal.

31   "Even with its flaws, it was a critical first step to reforming our nation's welfare system. . . . I agreed that [Bill Clinton] should sign [the welfare bill] and worked hard to round up votes for its passage," writes Hillary Rodham Clinton in *Living History* (New York: Simon & Schuster, 2004), 368.

32   Laura Bassett, "Jeb Bush in 1995: Unwed Mothers Should Be Publicly Shamed," *Huffington Post*, June 9, 2015, http://www.huffingtonpost.com/2015/06/09/jeb-bush-1995-book_n_7542964.html.

33   Matt Bruenig, "Promoting Marriage Has Failed and Is Unnecessary to Cut Poverty," *Demos*, December 4, 2015, http://www.demos.org/blog/12/4/15/promoting-marriage-has-failed-and-unnecessary-cut-poverty. Bruenig's analyses can be found at People's Policy Project, http://peoplespolicyproject.org.

34   Bruenig, "Promoting Marriage."

35   John Merline, "Why Are So Many Workers Refusing to Apply for Jobs?" Investors.com, April 20, 2015, http://www.investors.com/job-openings-are-up-but-labor-participation-is-down/.

36   Rick Santorum, *It Takes a Family: Conservatism and the Common Good* (New York: Open Road Media, 2014), 34.

37   Santorum, *It Takes a Family*, 36–37.

38   Ruth Conniff, "Rick Santorum's America," *Progressive*, October 2005, http://progressive.org/mag_conniff1005

39   Linda Bear, letter to the editor, *Pittsburgh Post-Gazette*, July 14, 2005.

40   Eileen R. Sisca, letter to the editor, *Pittsburgh Post-Gazette*, July 13, 2005.

41   Kathie Sarachild, "Beyond the Family Wage: A Women's Liberation View of the Social Wage," in *Women's Liberation and National Health Care: Confronting the Myth of America*, eds. Kathie Sarachild, Jenny Brown, and Amy Coenen (New York: Redstockings, 2001), 22.

42   Patrick Buchanan says the 1964 Civil Rights Act, by chipping away at discrimination in employment, "Turned the new Equal Opportunity Employment Office into a siege gun against the family wage," *Death of the West*, 36. Not very effectively, though. Among full-time year-round workers, women's pay is 79 percent of men's.

CHAPTER 3: IS IT A BIRTH STRIKE? WOMEN TESTIFY

1   Christine Emba, "Paul Ryan's Recipe for a Robust Economy: Have More Babies," *Washington Post*, December 15, 2017, https://www.washingtonpost.com/opinions/paul-ryans-recipe-for-a-robust-economy-have-more-babies/2017/12/15/dcd767b4-e1dc-11e7-89e8-edec16379010_story.html.

2   Stassa Edwards, "Paul Ryan Would Like You to Have More Babies," *Jezebel*, December 14, 2017, https://theslot.jezebel.com/paul-ryan-would-like-you-to-have-more-babies-1821293804.

3   There is more on consciousness-raising—what it is and isn't—in the final chapter of this book. The meeting, organized with Redstockings, was held May 17, 2015, in Gainesville, Florida.

4   This testimony is not intended as a representative sample—consciousness-raising among many more women is necessary to draw full conclusions about our common situation and our response to it. For example, this group had more college education than average, no one was at that moment involuntarily unemployed, and everyone who wanted an abortion was able to obtain one. In consciousness-raising, the greater the range of experiences and circumstances represented, the deeper and truer the conclusions.

5   An incision in the perineum, between the vaginal opening and the anus during childbirth to speed up passage of the baby, now generally considered to be medically unnecessary.

CHAPTER 4: COMSTOCKERY TO THE BABY BOOM

1   The birth rate dipped during the war, and recovered after it, but only to up to the declining trend line. Civil War deaths are estimated at between 620,000 to 750,000 out of a population of 31 million. Herbert S. Klein, *A Population History of the United States* (Cambridge: Cambridge University Press, 2012), 109.

2   Comstock Law, March 3, 1873. It's clarifying to read the text: "Whoever . . . shall sell, or lend, or give away, or in any manner exhibit . . . or shall otherwise publish or offer to publish in any manner, or shall have in his possession, for any such purpose or purposes, any obscene book, pamphlet, paper, writing, advertisement, circular, print, picture . . . or any cast, instrument, or other article of an immoral nature, or any drug or medicine, or any article whatsoever, for the prevention of conception, or for causing unlawful abortion, or shall advertize the same for sale, or shall write or print or cause to be written or printed, any card, circular, book, pamphlet, advertisement, or notice of any kind, stating when, where, how, or of whom, or by what means, any of the articles in this section hereinbefore mentioned, can be purchased or obtained, or shall manufacture, draw, or print, or in any wise make any of such articles, shall be deemed guilty of a misdemeanor, and, on conviction thereof in any court . . . shall be imprisoned at hard labor in the penitentiary for not less than six months nor more than five years for each offense, or fined not less than one hundred dollars nor more than two thousand dollars, with cost of court."

3   L.D. Griswold, Toland Jones, and Henry West, "Additional Report from the Select Committee to Whom was Referred S.B. No. 285," (Ohio Senate committee), *Journal of the Senate of the General Assembly of Ohio*, vol. 63, 1867, 235.

4   James C. Mohr, *Abortion in America: The Origins and Evolution of National Policy* (Oxford: Oxford University Press, 1978), 208–9.

5   Mohr, *Abortion in America*, reproduces such ads, 51, 56, 57.

6   Mohr, 89.

7   Mohr, 161

8   Horatio R. Storer, *Why Not? A Book for Every Woman* (Boston: Lee and Shepherd, 1866), 62.

9   Storer, *Why Not?* 63, 64.

10   Edwin M. Hale, *The Great Crime of the Nineteenth Century* (Chicago: C.S. Halsey, 1867), 4.

11   Mohr, *Abortion in America*, 180–81

12   Marilyn Irvin Holt, *The Orphan Trains: Placing Out in America* (Lincoln: University of Nebraska Press, 1992), 24. A PBS documentary film, *The Orphan Trains*, further exposed this hidden history in 1995.

13   Claudia Nelson, *Little Strangers: Portrayals of Adoption and Foster Care in America, 1850–1929* (Bloomington: Indiana University Press, 2003), 29.

14   Nicola Kay Beisel, *Imperiled Innocents: Anthony Comstock and Family Reproduction in Victorian America* (Princeton, NJ: Princeton University Press, 1998), 53.

15   N.E.H. Hull and Peter Charles Hoffer, *Roe v. Wade: The Abortion Rights Controversy in American History* (Lawrence: University of Kansas Press, 2001), 36.

16   "Race" in this context was used to mean anything from native born to Protestant to Anglo-Saxon (as opposed to recent southern and eastern European immigrants, Catholics, and Jews), but Roosevelt was mostly worried about national population, at a time when the United States was becoming an empire. See

Roosevelt's article "Birth Control—From the Positive Side," October 1917 in *Metropolitan* magazine, 5, where he defines native stock: "I use the term with elasticity to include all children of mothers and fathers born on this side of the water." Elsewhere in the article, he speaks of increasing white birth rates in the South and is clearly not interested in Black birth rates.

17   Theodore Roosevelt, "On American Motherhood," Address to the National Congress of Mothers, Washington, DC, March 13, 1905, http://www.bartleby.com/268/10/29.html. High child mortality may account for his assertion. Twenty percent of children born in the U.S. in 1900 died before their fifth birthday.

18   The quote is actually from the editors of *American Medicine* in their review of Sanger's article "Why Not Birth Control Clinics in America?" *American Medicine*, March 1919, 164-67. Sanger's original article is available from the New York University Margaret Sanger Papers Project: https://www.nyu.edu/projects/sanger/webedition/app/documents/show.php?sangerDoc=320522.xml. For examples of misattribution of this quote, see Jonathan V. Last, *What to Expect When No One's Expecting* (New York: Encounter Books, 2014), 53 and Margaret Forster, *Significant Sisters: Grassroots of Active Feminism* (New York: Knopf, 1985), 271. SisterSong Women of Color Reproductive Justice Collective has compiled a useful corrective to the distortions. See Anna Holley, "Margaret Sanger and the African American Community," Trust Black Women, July 2010, https://www.trustblackwomen.org/2011-05-10-03-28-12/publications-a-articles/african-americans-and-abortion-articles/26-margaret-sanger-and-the-african-american-community-.

19   David Kennedy, *Birth Control in America* (New Haven, CT: Yale University Press, 1970), 16.

20   Margaret Sanger, Frederick A. Blossom, and Elizabeth Stuyvesant, "To the Men and Women of the United States," *Birth Control Review* 1, no. 1 (February 1917): 3.

21   Kennedy, *Birth Control in America*, 32.

22   "To Fight in Court for Birth Control," *New York Times*, September 5, 1915, 8.

23   Jesse M. Rodrique, "The Black Community and the Birth-Control Movement," in *Unequal Sisters: A Multicultural Reader in U.S. Women's History*, eds. Ellen Carol DuBois and Vicki Ruíz (New York: Routledge, 1990), 333-44.

24   Rodrique, "The Black Community," 335, 338.

25   Jeffrey B. Perry, ed., *Hubert Harrison Reader* (Middletown, CT: Wesleyan University Press, 2001), 2; W.E.B. Du Bois, *Darkwater: Voices from Within the Veil* (New York: Harcourt Brace, 1920; Mineola, NY: Dover Thrift Edition, 1999), 96.

26   Rodrique, "The Black Community," 338.

27   Michele Mitchell, *Righteous Propagation: African Americans and the Politics of Racial Destiny after Reconstruction* (Chapel Hill: University of North Carolina Press, 2005), 230.

28   W.E.B Du Bois, "Black Folks and Birth Control," *Birth Control Review* 16 (June 1932): 166-67.

29   Emma Goldman, letter to Margaret Sanger, May 26, 1914. Emma Goldman Papers, University of California at Berkeley, http://emmagoldmanpapers.tumblr.com/post/115237727585/the-birth-strike.

30   Alice Wexler, *Emma Goldman in America* (Boston: Beacon, 1984), 215.

31   Mary Ware Dennett, *Birth Control Laws: Shall We Keep Them, Change Them, or Abolish Them?* (New York: Frederick H. Hitchcock, the Grafton Press, 1926), 19-21.

32   Dennett, *Birth Control Laws*, 19-21.

33   Leta Hollingworth, "Social Devices for Impelling Women to Bear Children" (1916) in *Pronatalism: The Myth of Mom and Apple Pie*, eds. Ellen Peck and Judith Senderowitz (New York: Thomas Y. Crowell, 1974), 24.

34   Hollingworth, "Social Devices," 24-26.

35   Crystal Eastman, "Birth Control in the Feminist Program," *Birth Control Review*, January 1918, 3.

CHAPTER 5: POPULATION PANIC TO THE BABY BUST

1   Betty Friedan, *The Feminine Mystique* (New York: Dell, 1963), 175.

2   Friedan, *Feminine Mystique*, 12.

3   Donald Critchlow, *Intended Consequences: Birth Control, Abortion, and the Federal Government in Modern America* (Oxford: Oxford University Press, 2001), 9. John D. Rockefeller III was the brother of Nelson Rockefeller, New York governor then U.S. vice president, and of banker David Rockefeller.

4   Betsy Hartmann, *Reproductive Rights and Wrongs: The Global Politics of Population Control* (Boston: South End Press, 1995), 106.

5   Hartmann, *Reproductive Rights and Wrongs*, 106.

6   William Paddock and Paul Paddock, *Famine, 1975! America's Decision: Who Will Survive?* (Boston: Little, Brown, 1967).

7   See, for example, Amartya Sen, *Poverty and Famines: An Essay on Entitlement and Deprivation* (Oxford: Oxford University Press, 1982).

8   For a definitive feminist analysis of U.S. population control measures, see Hartmann, *Reproductive Rights and Wrongs*.

9   Frances Beal, "Double Jeopardy: To Be Black and Female" (1969). Redstockings Women's Liberation Archives for Action.

10   Nelson Denis, *War Against All Puerto Ricans: Revolution and Terror in America's Colony* (New York: Nation Books, 2015), 139.

11   Annette B. Ramírez de Arellano and Conrad Seipp, *Colonialism, Catholicism, and Contraception: A History of Birth Control in Puerto Rico* (Chapel Hill: University of North Carolina, 1983), 33-34.

12   Hartmann, *Reproductive Rights and Wrongs*, 247. For a fuller account, see Ramírez and Seipp, *Colonialism, Catholicism*.

13   Critchlow, *Intended Consequences*, 36; Victor S. Clark et al., *Porto Rico and Its Problems* (Washington, DC: *Brookings Institution*, 1930), http://quod.lib.umich.edu/p/philamer/agd9090.0001.001.

14   *La Operación*, film directed by Ana María García, 1982, http://www.dailymotion.com/video/xpu79i_la-operacion_shortfilms.

15   Ramírez and Seipp, *Colonialism, Catholicism*, 131, 146.

16   Hartmann, *Reproductive Rights and Wrongs*, 248.

17   *La Operación*, directed by Ana María García, 1982.

18   Hartmann, *Reproductive Rights and Wrongs*, 247; Ramírez and Seipp, *Colonialism, Catholicism*, 143.

19   Caroline Bird, *Born Female: The High Cost of Keeping Women Down* (New York: David MacKay, 1968; New York: Simon & Schuster, 1969), 39.

20   Remarkably, the Pill was one of Margaret Sanger's later projects. She and a wealthy heiress, Katherine McCormick, conspired to fund the research that

developed it. See Bernard Asbell, *The Pill: A Biography of a Drug That Changed the World* (New York: Random House, 1995).

21   Critchlow, *Intended Consequences*, 150, 153.

22   J. Joseph Speidel et al., "Making the Case for U.S International Family Planning Assistance" n.d. circa 2009, 5, http://www.jhsph.edu/sebin/u/d/MakingtheCase.pdf; Kaiser Family Foundation, "The U.S. Government and International Family Planning & Reproductive Health Efforts," June 2016, 3, http://files.kff.org/attachment/fact-sheet-the-u-s-government-and-international-family-planning-and-reproductive-health.

23   Speidel et al., "Making the Case."

24   United Nations, Department of Economic and Social Affairs, Population Division, *Population Facts: The End of High Fertility Is Near*, October 2017, https://population.un.org/wpp/Publications/Files/PopFacts_2017-3_The-end-of-high-fertility.pdf.

25   Paddock & Paddock, *Famine 1975!* 65; Haining Liu, "Xi Has Not Undone the Sorrows of China's One-Child Policy," *Financial Times*, November 2, 2015, 8.

26   Vicki Haddock, "The Bush Dynasty and Roe vs. Wade: Rubbery Politics Runs in the Family," *San Francisco Gate*, November 20, 2005, http://www.sfgate.com/politics/article/The-Bush-dynasty-and-Roe-vs-Wade-Rubbery-2593871.php.

27   George H. Bush in Phyllis Piotrow, *World Population Crisis: The United States Response* (New York: Praeger, 1973), vii.

28   Sara Fritz, "'92 Republican Convention: Rigid Anti-Abortion Platform Plank OKd Policy," *Los Angeles Times*, August 18, 1992, http://articles.latimes.com/1992-08-18/news/mn-5874_1_abortion-rights-advocates.

29   Judith Brown, *It's a Lifetime's Work, This Movement* (Gainesville, FL: Gainesville Women's Liberation, 1987). Brown is not related to the author.

30   Joan Robins, *Handbook of Women's Liberation* (North Hollywood, CA: NOW Library Press, 1970), 118.

31   Boston Women's Health Collective, *Women and Their Bodies: A Course* (Boston: Boston Women's Health Collective, 1970), 90–91.

32   Boston Women's Health Collective, *Women and Their Bodies*, 91.

33   Simone de Beauvoir, *The Second Sex* (1949) trans. Constance Borde and Sheila Malovany-Chevallier (New York: Vintage, 2011), 66. She is referring to the USSR legalizing abortion in 1920 and outlawing it again in 1936. Repopulation was needed because as many as 12 million died in the civil war and related famines following the 1917 Russian Revolution. The United States, France, Britain, Japan, and other capitalist powers lengthened the war by invading and fighting against the Bolsheviks.

34   Beauvoir, *Second Sex*, 524.

35   Beauvoir, 65.

36   Ti-Grace Atkinson, *Amazon Odyssey* (New York: Links Books, 1974), 195. Her claim about unemployment is examined in chapter 9, Cheap Labor.

37   Kathie Sarachild, "Myth of Abortion Law Repeal," *Woman's World* 1, no. 1 (April 15, 1971): 10. Redstockings Women's Liberation Archives for Action, http://www.redstockings.org/index.php/adp-catalog/woman-s-world-1-5.

38   Marlene Gerber Fried, "The Hyde Amendment: 30 Years of Violating Women's Rights," Center for American Progress, October 6, 2006, https://www.americanprogress.org/issues/women/news/2006/10/06/2243/the-hyde-amendment-30-years-of-violating-womens-rights/.

39   Stanley K. Henshaw et al., *Restrictions on Medicaid Funding for Abortions: A Literature Review* (New York: Guttmacher Institute, 2009), http://www.guttmacher.org/pubs/MedicaidLitReview.pdf.

40   July 12, 1977 President's News Conference, http://www.presidency.ucsb.edu/ws/index.php?pid=7786.

41   Maher v. Roe, 432 U.S. 464 (1977). Justice Lewis Powell's majority opinion and footnote 11, https://www.law.cornell.edu/supremecourt/text/432/464#ZO-432_US_464n11.

CHAPTER 6: LONGEVITY: CRISIS OR BLESSING?

1   Robert Pear, "Driven by Campaign Populism, Democrats Unite on Social Security Plan," *New York Times*, June 19, 2016, A14; Paul Ryan's website: http://paulryan.house.gov/issues/issue/?IssueID=12227.

2   Nancy Altman and Eric Kingson, *Social Security Works! Why Social Security Isn't Going Broke and How Expanding It Will Help Us All* (New York: The New Press, 2015), xvi.

3   Doug Henwood, "Pension Fund Socialism: The Illusion that Just Won't Die," talk at New School University, September 11, 2004, http://www.leftbusinessobserver.com/NSPensions.html.

4   Betty Friedan, "NOW's Statement of Purpose," 1966, http://now.org/about/history/statement-of-purpose.

5   Social Security also provides support for disabled workers, another situation in which parents used to have to rely on their children, if they had any, or other family members.

6   Robert Stein, "Tax Reform to Strengthen the Economy and Lighten the Burdens Families Bear," in *Room to Grow: Conservative Reforms for a Limited Government and a Thriving Middle Class*, YG [Young Guns] Network, 2014, 33–38.

7   Hartmann, *Reproductive Rights and Wrongs*, 9.

8   Benefits to spouses were instituted after Califano v. Goldfarb, 1977. See D.M. Douglas, "Social Security: Sex Discrimination and Equal Protection" *Baylor Law Review* 30 (1978): 199. For shortening the required duration of marriage, see Christopher R. Tamborini and Kevin Whitman, "Women, Marriage, and Social Security Benefits Revisited," *Social Security Bulletin* 67, no. 4 (2007), https://www.ssa.gov/policy/docs/ssb/v67n4/67n4p1.html#mt6.

9   Justin Elliot, "Santorum Blames Abortion for Social Security Woes," *Salon*, March 29, 2011, http://www.salon.com/2011/03/29/santorum_abortion_social_security/.

10   Jill Stanek, "Abort Pro-Choice Retirees from Social Security Program," *WorldNetDaily*, October 27, 2004, http://www.wnd.com/2004/10/27233/.

11   George W. Bush, "Fact Sheet: Strengthening the Social Security System for Future Generations," January 11, 2005, http://georgewbush-whitehouse.archives.gov/news/releases/2005/01/text/20050111-12.html.

12   Jonathan Last, *What to Expect When No One's Expecting: America's Coming Demographic Disaster* (New York: Encounter, 2014), 109.

13   Michelle Goldberg, *The Means of Reproduction: Sex, Power, and the Future of the World* (New York: Penguin, 2009), 205.

14   Doug Henwood, "Antisocial Insecurity." *Left Business Observer*, no. 87 (December 1998), http://www.leftbusinessobserver.com/AntisocInsec.html; Doug Henwood, "Social Security Revisited," *Left Business Observer* 110 (March 2005), http://www.leftbusinessobserver.com/SocialSecurityRevisited.html.

15   Paul Krugman, "Many Unhappy Returns," *New York Times*, February 1, 2005, http://www.nytimes.com/2005/02/01/opinion/many-unhappy-returns.html. Krugman does not credit Henwood.

16   Dean Baker, "Statement on the 2016 Social Security Trustees Report," Center for Economic and Policy Research, June 22, 2016, http://cepr.net/press-center/press-releases/dean-baker-s-statement-on-the-2016-social-security-trustees-report.

17   Martin Wolf, "America's Labor Market Is Not Working," *Financial Times*, November 4, 2015, 9.

18   Dean Baker, "Germany," November 29, 2004, Center for Economic and Policy Research, http://www.cepr.net/err/2004_11_29.htm.

19   Henwood, "Antisocial Insecurity."

20   Doug Henwood, "Social Security's Crisis, and Ours," *Left Business Observer* 129 (October 2010).

21   Simone de Beauvoir, *The Coming of Age*, trans. André Deutsch (New York: G.P. Putnam's Sons, 1970), 3.

22   There is no doubt that one incentive for this plan is that bankers and brokers will get rich from fees—but that's not the main reason for the establishment attack on Social Security.

23   Steven Gillon, *The Pact: Bill Clinton, Newt Gingrich, and the Rivalry That Defined a Generation* (Oxford: Oxford University Press, 2008), xvii.

24   The National Commission on Fiscal Responsibility and Reform, (Bowles-Simpson), "The Moment of Truth," (Washington, DC: White House) December 1, 2010.

25   "I see Obama is talking social security reform. Good. When the system started, life expectancy and benefit eligibility were in sync. Now we're entitled to an actuarial 20 year paid vacation. We shouldn't expect that and our descendants can't afford it." Comment at *New York Times*, February 23, 2009, http://thecaucus.blogs.nytimes.com/2009/02/22/governors-on-the-stimulus/comment-page-2/#comment-1167869. "Retirement cannot be a state-subsidized 20 year vacation in the sun if we are to progress as a society," comment at *Economist*, April 7, 2011, http://www.economist.com/node/18529505.

26   Charles Blahous and Jason J. Fichtner, "Social Security Reform and Economic Growth" in George W. Bush Institute, *The 4% Solution: Unleashing the Economic Growth America Needs*, ed. Brendan Miniter (New York: Crown Business, 2012), 208. The Obama administration in 2016 nominated Blahous to serve a second five-year term as a Social Security trustee, over the objections of Senators Elizabeth Warren, Chuck Schumer, and others. Robert Pear, "Driven by Campaign Populism, Democrats Unite on Social Security Plan," *New York Times*, June 19, 2016, A14.

27   Eighty-three percent of men and 85 percent of women took Social Security before their full retirement age, according to Laurence Kotlikoff et al., *Get What's Yours: The Secrets to Maxing Out Your Social Security* (New York: Simon & Schuster, 2015), 14, 17.

28   Blahous and Fichtner, "Social Security Reform," 211.

29   Steve Lohr, "The Late, Great Golden Years," *New York Times*, March 6, 2005, https://www.nytimes.com/2005/03/06/weekinreview/the-late-great-golden-years.html.

30   Lawrence Mishel, Elise Gould, and Josh Bivens, "Wage Stagnation in Nine Charts," Economic Policy Institute, January 6, 2015, fig. 8, http://www.epi.org/publication/charting-wage-stagnation/.

31   Called "maximum taxable earnings," the figure is for 2018 but rises with cost of living adjustments.

32   Cap figure is for 2018. Ron Baiman, Heather Boushey, and Dawn Saunders, eds., *Political Economy and Contemporary Capitalism* (New York: Routledge, 2015), 323.

33   Labor Party, "A Call for Economic Justice," 1996, http://www.thelaborparty.org/d_program.htm.

34   Beauvoir, *Coming of Age*, 6.

35   Sam Fleming, Demetri Sevastopulo, and David Crow, "Death Rate Surges among Middle-Aged U.S. Whites," *Financial Times*, November 4, 2015, 5. Black people's life expectancy remained lower than that of whites, but saw no such drops.

36   "This increase for whites was largely accounted for by increasing death rates from drug and alcohol poisonings, suicide, and chronic liver diseases and cirrhosis," wrote Anne Case and Angus Deaton in "Rising Morbidity and Mortality in Midlife among White Non-Hispanic Americans in the 21st Century," *Proceedings of the National Academy of Sciences of the United States*, September 17, 2015, http://www.pnas.org/content/early/2015/10/29/1518393112.full.pdf.

37   Barbara Ehrenreich, "Longevity Crisis? Kill Grandma," June 6, 2005, *Los Angeles Times*, http://articles.latimes.com/2005/jun/06/opinion/oe-ehrenreich6. Betty Friedan compares nursing homes to concentration camps in *The Fountain of Age* (New York: Simon & Schuster, 1993), 40–41, 51–52.

CHAPTER 7: IMMIGRATION: "INSTANT ADULTS"

1   The United States has by no means the largest immigrant population among comparable countries. Germany, Canada, Australia, New Zealand, and Sweden have more immigrants as a percentage of the population.

2   Michael Greenstone and Adam Looney, "What Immigration Means for U.S. Employment and Wages," The Brookings Institution, May 4, 2012, https://www.brookings.edu/blog/jobs/2012/05/04/what-immigration-means-for-u-s-employment-and-wages/; Center for American Progress, "Facts on Immigration Today," October 2014, 1, https://cdn.americanprogress.org/wp-content/uploads/2013/04/ImmigrationFacts-brief-10.23.pdf.

3   Robert Kaplan, "A Conversation with Robert Kaplan," interview by Tom Keene (Bloomberg News), Council on Foreign Relations, May 31, 2017, https://www.cfr.org/event/conversation-robert-kaplan.

4   Burgess Everett, "Koch Network Launches Ads to Revive Dreamers Talks," Politico, April 17, 2018, https://www.politico.com/story/2018/04/17/kochs-dreamers-talks-529687.

5   Sending countries face other harms, too, as towns empty of working-age adults to supply U.S. employers. See David Bacon, *The Right to Stay Home: How U.S. Policy Drives Mexican Immigration* (Boston: Beacon, 2013).

6   Ben Wattenberg, "The Easy Solution to the Social Security Crisis," *New York Times Magazine*, June 22, 1997, 30–31.

7   Jeb Bush and Clint Bolick, *Immigration Wars: Forging an American Solution* (New York: Threshold Editions, 2013). Bolick is a libertarian lawyer who founded a Koch-funded institute dedicated to overturning the New Deal, according to

Nancy MacLean, *Democracy in Chains: The Deep History of the Radical Right's Stealth Plan for America* (New York: Viking, 2017), 244.

8   Patrick Buchanan, *State of Emergency: The Third World Invasion and Conquest of America* (New York: Thomas Dunne, 2006), 18.

9   John Gibson, "The Big Story," Fox News, May 11, 2006; Ben Armbruster, "Gibson: 'Make More Babies' Because in 'Twenty-five Years…the Majority of the Population is Hispanic,'" Media Matters Action Network, May 12, 2006, https://www.mediamatters.org/research/2006/05/12/gibson-make-more-babies-because-in-twenty-five/135674.

10   Gibson, "The Big Story."

11   *Wall Street Journal* editorial board meeting, May 22, 2007, broadcast at http://online.wsj.com/public/page/8_0006.html?bcpid=86195573&bclid=212338097&bctid=92988510.

12   Bush and Bolick, *Immigration Wars*, 20–21.

13   Daniel Henninger, "Amnesty for the Market," (interview with Ed Crane), *Wall Street Journal*, May 31, 2007.

14   Nina Bernstein, "100 Years in the Back Door, Out the Front," *New York Times*, May 21, 2006, WK4.

15   Baker, Dean. *The Conservative Nanny State* (Washington, DC: Center for Economic and Policy Research, 2006), 32.

16   Don Gonyea, "How the Labor Movement did a 180 on Immigration," *All Things Considered*, National Public Radio, February 5, 2013.

17   AFL-CIO Executive Council, February 2000, http://www.aflcio.org/aboutus/thisistheaflcio/ecouncil/ec0216200b.cfm.

18   Jeffrey Sparshot, "Does Immigration Suppress Wages? It's Not So Simple," *Wall Street Journal*, June 1, 2015, https://blogs.wsj.com/economics/2015/06/01/does-immigration-suppress-wages-its-not-so-simple/.

19   David Card, "Comment: The Elusive Search for Negative Wage Impacts of Immigration," National Bureau of Economic Research, 2012, 215, http://davidcard.berkeley.edu/papers/jeea2012.pdf.

20   Gianmarco Ottaviano and Giovanni Peri, "Rethinking the Effects of Immigration on Wages," National Bureau of Economic Research Working Paper 12497, August 2006.

21   George Borjas, "The Labor Demand Curve Is Downward Sloping: Reexamining the Impact of Immigration on the Labor Market," *Quarterly Journal of Economics* 118 (2003): 1335–74.

22   Card, "Comment," 215.

23   Sarah Bohn and Eric Schiff, "Immigrants and the Labor Market," Public Policy Institute of California, March 2011, http://www.ppic.org/main/publication_show.asp?i=823.

24   Patricia Cohen, "In Rural Iowa, a Future Rests on Immigrants," *New York Times*, May 29, 2017, A1.

25   Human Rights Watch, *Blood, Sweat and Fear: Workers' Rights in U.S. Meat and Poultry Plants* (New York: Human Rights Watch, 2011).

26   David Bacon, "Common Ground on the Killing Floor," *Labor Notes*, April 12, 2012, http://labornotes.org/blogs/2012/04/common-ground-kill-floor-organizing-smithfield.

27   John O'Sullivan, "Nice Going, Karl. This Immigration Battle Is a Fine Mess," *National Review Online*, April 5, 2006, http://www.nationalreview.com/jos/osullivan200604051335.asp.

28   Bush and Bolick, *Immigration Wars*, 85.

29   Bush and Bolick, 94–95.

30   Jonathan V. Last, "America's Baby Bust," *Wall Street Journal*, February 12, 2013, http://www.wsj.com/articles/SB10001424127887323375204578270053387770718.

31   Greg Ip, "Population Implosion: How Demographics Rule the Global Economy," *Wall Street Journal*, November 22, 2015, https://www.wsj.com/articles/how-demographics-rule-the-global-economy-1448203724. Ip cites the International Monetary Fund for the "eightfold" figure.

CHAPTER 8: REPRODUCTION AND RACE

1   Betsy Hartmann, *Reproductive Rights and Wrongs: The Global Politics of Population Control* (Boston: South End Press, 1995), 255.

2   Dick Gregory, "My Answer to Genocide," *Ebony* 26, no. 12 (October 1971): 66–72, quoted in Dorothy Roberts, *Killing the Black Body* (New York: Pantheon, 1997), 98.

3   Black Feminist Working Group, "What Sistas Want, What Sistas Believe," August 30, 2011, https://blackfeministworkinggroup.wordpress.com/2011/08/30/what-sistas-want-what-sistas-believe-black-feminist-twelve-point-plan/.

4   Roberts, *Killing the Black Body*, 23.

5   Ned and Constance Sublette, *American Slave Coast: A History of the Slave-Breeding Industry* (Chicago: Chicago Review Press, 2015).

6   "The 'Breeder Woman,'" quoted in *Black Women in White America: A Documentary History*, ed. Gerda Lerner (Vintage: New York, 1972), 48.

7   Those days may be over, but we can hear their echoes in the Medicaid program which pays for prenatal care and birth for many women who aren't otherwise eligible for the program (up to 133 percent of the poverty level), but then denies care to the parents after the birth process is complete. J.J. Frost, A. Sonfield, and R.B. Gold, "Estimating the Impact of Expanding Medicaid Eligibility for Family Planning Services," Occasional Report, no. 28 (New York: Alan Guttmacher Institute, 2006).

8   Roberts, *Killing the Black Body*, 47.

9   Sublette and Sublette, *American Slave Coast*, 26.

10   Roberts, *Killing the Black Body*, 47.

11   Gerald Horne, *Confronting Black Jacobins: The U.S., the Haitian Revolution, and the Origins of the Dominican Republic* (New York: Monthly Review Press, 2015), 7.

12   Horne, *Confronting Black Jacobins*, 16.

13   Civil Rights Congress, *We Charge Genocide: The Historic Petition to the United Nations for Relief from a Crime of the United States Government against the Negro People* (New York: Civil Rights Congress, 1951), 22.

14   Nicholas Lemann, *The Promised Land: The Great Black Migration and How It Changed America* (New York: Vintage, 1992), 6.

15   Jacob Lawrence, *Migration Series*, Museum of Modern Art, New York City, 1941.

16   *Macon Telegraph*, September 15, 1916, 4, quoted in Wilkerson, *The Warmth of Other Suns: The Epic Story of America's Great Migration* (New York: Vintage, 2011), 162.

17   Wilkerson, *Warmth of Other Suns*, 163.

18   Wilkerson, 162.

19   Civil Rights Congress, *We Charge Genocide*, xi–xii.

20   Civil Rights Congress, 23–24.

21   Betty Goldstein [Friedan], *UE Fights for Women Workers*, United Electrical, Radio and Machine Workers of America Publication, no. 232, June 1952.

22   "America's Women and the Wage Gap," Fact Sheet from National Partnership for Women and Families, September 2018, http://www.nationalpartnership. org/research-library/workplace-fairness/fair-pay/americas-women-and-the-wage-gap.pdf. I was unable to find an estimate of the extra profits gained from racial discrimination.

23   Ted Allen makes this point in *Can White Radicals Be Radicalized?* (New York: NYC Revolutionary Youth Movement, 1969), 15.

24   Randall Hansen and Desmond King, *Sterilized by the State* (Cambridge: Cambridge University Press, 2013), 10–11.

25   Lemann, *Promised Land*, 49–50.

26   Student Nonviolent Coordinating Committee, *Genocide in Mississippi*, n.d. (ca. March 1964), Redstockings Women's Liberation Archives for Action.

27   Rebecca Kluchin, *Fit to Be Tied: Sterilization and Reproductive Rights in America, 1950-1980* (New Brunswick, NJ: Rutgers University Press, 2009), 177.

28   Relf v. Weinberger, 1974, 372 F. Supp. 1196, http://law.scu.edu/wp-content/ uploads/socialjustice/Relf%20v_%20Weinberger.pdf.

29   Roberts, *Killing the Black Body*, 93. See also *No Más Bebés* (film), dir. Renee Tajima-Peña, 2015.

30   Reported by NBC News, April 14, 1971. The clip is used in the film *No Más Bebés*, dir. Renee Tajima-Peña, 2015.

31   Hansen and King, *Sterilized by the State*, 257.

32   Adrienne Rich, *Of Woman Born: Motherhood as Experience and Institution* (New York: W.W. Norton, 1995), xix, 29.

33   Kluchin, *Fit to Be Tied*, 22.

34   Susan Brownmiller, "Everywoman's Abortions: 'The Oppressor Is Man,'" *Village Voice*, March 27, 1969. Audio of the whole speakout is available from the Redstockings Women's Liberation Archives: https://archive.org/details/Redsto ckingsAbortionSpeakoutNewYork1969March21.

35   See for example Diane Schulder and Florynce Kennedy, *Abortion Rap* (New York: McGraw Hill, 1971).

36   One example is Jennifer Nelson, *Women of Color and the Reproductive Rights Movement* (New York: NYU Press, 2003).

37   Gainesville Women's Liberation, "International Women's Day March 8," flier (Gainesville, FL: Gainesville Women's Liberation, 1970).

38   Gloria Molina, Comisión Femenil in *No Más Bebés* (film), dir. Renee Tajima-Peña, 2015, 34:55, http://www.pbs.org/independentlens/videos/no-mas-bebes/. See also Jael Silliman et al., eds., *Undivided Rights, Women of Color Organize for Reproductive Justice* (Boston: South End, 2004), 12.

39   New York Wages for Housework Committee, "Wages for Housework" (flier), Brooklyn, NY, ca. 1975, archives of Silvia Federici. Reprinted in Silvia Federici and Arlen Austin, eds., *The New York Wages for Housework Committee 1972-1977: History, Theory, Documents* (Brooklyn: Autonomedia, 2018), 56–57.

40   Sonya Borrero et al., "Medicaid Policy on Sterilization—Anachronistic or Still Relevant?" *New England Journal of Medicine* 370, no. 2 (January 9, 2014): 102–4.

41 Heather Boonstra, "Insurance Coverage of Abortion: Beyond the Exceptions for Life Endangerment, Rape and Incest," *Guttmacher Policy Review* 16, no. 3 (September 13, 2013), http://www.guttmacher.org/pubs/gpr/16/3/gpr160302.html. According to the 2010 Census, 55 percent of African Americans live in the South.

42 Figures are from before the Affordable Care Act. Kaiser Family Foundation, "Medicaid Enrollment by Race/Ethnicity FY 2011," http://kff.org/medicaid/state-indicator/medicaid-enrollment-by-raceethnicity/.

43 James Dao, "Black Women Enlisting at Higher Rates in U.S. Military," *New York Times*, December 22, 2011, http://www.nytimes.com/2011/12/23/us/black-women-enlist-at-higher-rates-in-us-military.html.

44 Boonstra, "Insurance Coverage of Abortion."

45 Shannon Brewer, director of the Jackson (Mississippi) Women's Health Organization, and Maisie Crow, speaking to Leonard Lopate, "Abortion Access Collides with Pro-Life Activists in the Deep South," WNYC, June 10, 2016.

46 As of 2016, they are Arizona, Arkansas, Connecticut, Delaware, Florida, Georgia, Indiana, Massachusetts, Mississippi, New Jersey, North Carolina, North Dakota, South Carolina, Tennessee, and Virginia. At the height of the craze in 2003, twenty-two states enforced them. Teresa Wiltz, "Growing Number of States Repeal Family Welfare Caps," PBS Newshour, July 13, 2016, https://www.pbs.org/newshour/nation/growing-number-states-repeal-family-welfare-caps.

47 Jodie Levin-Epstein, "Lifting the Lid off Family Caps," Center for Law and Social Policy, December 2003, http://www.clasp.org/resources-and-publications/files/0166.pdf.

48 Roberts, *Killing the Black Body*, 144–45; "Black Box Warning Added Concerning Long-Term Use of Depo-Provera Contraceptive Injection," Food and Drug Administration, November 17, 2005, https://web.archive.org/web/20051221195621/http://www.fda.gov/bbs/topics/ANSWERS/2004/ANS01325.html.

49 INCITE! Women of Color Against Violence, "Stop C.R.A.C.K.," undated poster, circa 2006.

50 Amie Newman, "Paying Drug-Addicted Women to Get Sterilized: Choice or Coercion?" *Rewire*, November 3, 2010, https://rewire.news/article/2010/11/03/paying-drugaddicted-women-sterilized/.

51 Loretta Ross, "Understanding Reproductive Justice," SisterSong Women of Color Reproductive Justice Collective, November 2006 (updated March 2011), http://www.trustblackwomen.org/our-work/what-is-reproductive-justice/9-what-is-reproductive-justice.

52 Jason Salzman, "Family Planning Initiative Rejected by Colorado GOP Has New Life," *Rewire*, August 31, 2015, https://rewire.news/article/2015/08/31/family-planning-initiative-rejected-colorado-gop-new-life/.

53 Ross, "Understanding Reproductive Justice."

54 Roberts, *Killing the Black Body*, 102.

55 Ross and others coined the term in 1994 and formed a group called Women of African Descent for Reproductive Justice in response to the exclusion of reproductive rights from the Clinton health care reform proposal. Loretta Ross and Rickie Solinger, *Reproductive Justice: A Primer* (Berkeley: University of California Press, 2017).

56 Ross, "Understanding Reproductive Justice."

CHAPTER 9: CHEAP LABOR

1   Adam Smith, *The Wealth of Nations* (1776; repr. London: MacMillan, 1869), 83–84.

2   Smith, *Wealth of Nations*, 83–84.

3   Karl Marx, *Capital: A Critique of Political Economy, Vol. 1* (London: Penguin, 1976), 790.

4   Marx, *Capital*, 790.

5   Lawrence Mishel, Elise Gould, and Josh Bivens, "Wage Stagnation in Nine Charts," Economic Policy Institute, January 6, 2015, fig. 4, http://www.epi.org/publication/charting-wage-stagnation/

6   Alan Budd in 1992 in *The Observer*, quoted in Michael Parenti, *Against Empire* (San Francisco: City Lights, 1995), 170–71.

7   Paul Krugman, "Secular Stagnation, Coalmines, Bubbles, and Larry Summers," *New York Times*, November 16, 2013, http://krugman.blogs.nytimes.com/2013/11/16/secular-stagnation-coalmines-bubbles-and-larry-summers/.

8   Since most people think of inflation as a rise in the price of goods, it might seem like a good thing for the Fed to curb inflation—until you realize it's your raise they're curbing.

9   Helen York, "Do Children Harvest Your Food?" *The Atlantic*, March 26, 2012, http://www.theatlantic.com/health/archive/2012/03/do-children-harvest-your-food/254853/.

10   Kim Moody and Charles Post, "The Politics of U.S. Labor: Paralysis and Possibilities," in *Socialist Register: Transforming Classes*, eds. Leo Panitch and Greg Albo (London: Merlin Press, 2014), 295–317.

11   See Jeremy Rifkin, *The End of Work: The Decline of the Global Labor Force and the Dawn of the Post-Market Era* (New York: Putnam, 1995). Or see Derek Thompson, "A World Without Work," *The Atlantic*, July/August 2015, http://www.theatlantic.com/magazine/archive/2015/07/world-without-work/395294/.

12   Thomas J. Sugrue, *The Origins of the Urban Crisis: Race and Inequality in Postwar Detroit* (Princeton, NJ: Princeton University Press, 1995), 125–40.

13   John Thornhill and Ralph Atkins, "Universal Basic Income: Money for Nothing," *Financial Times*, May 26, 2016, http://www.ft.com/cms/s/0/7c7ba87e-229f-11e6-9d4d-c11776a5124d.html#axzz4KRXRVmBH. The Southern Female Rights Union demanded an "adequate guaranteed annual income for every *individual* (not family)" in 1970 while that same year the National Organization for Women supported the principle of a guaranteed annual income. Kathie Sarachild, Jenny Brown, and Amy Coenen, eds., *Women's Liberation and National Health Care: Confronting the Myth of America* (New York: Redstockings, 2001), 24.

14   Jill Quadagno, *The Color of Welfare: How Racism Undermined the War on Poverty* (Oxford: Oxford University Press, 1996), 128.

15   Quadagno, *The Color of Welfare*, 128–33.

16   For example, Walmart has supported many American Legislative Exchange Council initiatives such as opposing the expansion of Medicaid. ALEC, "Resolution on the Tax and Fiscal Effects of Medicaid Expansion," July 24, 2015, https://www.alec.org/model-policy/resolution-on-the-tax-and-fiscal-effects-of-medicaid-expansion/.

17   Will Durant and Ariel Durant, *The Age of Napoleon* (New York: Simon & Schuster, 1975), 401.

18   Robert Heilbroner, *The Worldly Philosophers*, 7th, ed. (New York: Simon & Schuster, 1999), 104, 128.

19   William L. Langer, "The Origins of the Birth Control Movement in England in the Early Nineteenth Century," *Journal of Interdisciplinary History* 5, no. 4 (1975): 669–86, http://doi.org/10.2307/202864.

20   Francis Place, *Illustrations and Proofs of Population* (1822; Boston: Houghton Mifflin, 1930), 176.

21   Langer, "Origins of the Birth Control Movement," 682, quoting Graham Wallas, *The Life of Francis Place 1771–1854* (London: Longmans, Green and Co., 1898), 169–70.

22   It's a widely repeated error that Rosa Luxemburg supported a birth strike. This was promulgated by David Kennedy in *Birth Control in America* (1970), and repeated by Alice Rossi (*The Feminist Papers*, 1973), and Angela Davis (*Women, Race and Class*, 1981). We repeated the error in a Redstockings book I coauthored in 2001 (Sarachild, Brown, and Coenen, *Women's Liberation and National Health Care*). The 1913 issue of *Masses* that Kennedy cites for his claim says the opposite: "The two most prominent women members of the German Party, Rosa Luxemburg and Clara Zetkin, both oppose the birth-strike." William English Walling, "The Birth Strike," *The Masses* 5, no. 1 (October 1913): 20.

23   Joseph W. Bryce, "Socialists May Adopt Birth Strike in Berlin, Germany," *Square Deal* 13 (October 1913): 273.

24   Margaret Sanger, *Pivot of Civilization* (New York: Brentano's, 1922), chap. 7.

25   Marc Linder, *Dilemmas of Laissez-Faire Population Policy* (Westport, CT: Greenwood Press, 1997), 179.

26   Linder, *Dilemmas*, 179.

27   Margaret Sanger, *Margaret Sanger: An Autobiography* (New York: Norton, 1938), 274–75; Sanger, *Pivot of Civilization*, chap. 7.

28   V.I. Lenin, "The Working Class and Neo-Malthusianism," *Pravda*, no. 137, June 16, 1913. In *Lenin Collected Works*, vol. 19 (Moscow: Progress Publishers, 1977), 235–37.

29   Linder, *Dilemmas*, 172.

30   *Dilemmas*, 174. See also Robert Jütte, *Contraception: A History*, trans. Vicky Russell (Cambridge, MA: Polity Press, 2008), 170.

31   Catherine Rampell, "Want to Fight Poverty? Expand Access to Contraception," *Washington Post*, September 24, 2015, https://www.washingtonpost.com/opinions/a-powerful-tool-in-the-fight-against-poverty/2015/09/24/832c05fe-62f3-11e5-b38e-06883aacba64_story.html.

32   Dean Baker, "Education Is Not the Answer," *Jacobin*, April 14, 2014, https://www.jacobinmag.com/2014/04/unremedial-education/.

33   Lawrence Mishel, Elise Gould, and Josh Bivens, "Wage Stagnation in Nine Charts," Economic Policy Institute, January 6, 2015, fig. 5, http://www.epi.org/publication/charting-wage-stagnation/.

34   Cadena, Micaela, Raquel Z. Rivera, Tannia Esparza, and Denicia Cadena, *Dismantling Teen Pregnancy Prevention* (Albuquerque, NM: Young Women United, 2016), 8, 12.

35   Donald Kimelman, "Poverty and Norplant: Can Contraception Reduce the Underclass?" *Philadelphia Inquirer*, December 30, 1990, A18. Cited in Roberts, *Killing the Black Body*, 106.

36   Roberts, *Killing the Black Body*, 106–7.

37   Roberts, 102.

38   Sanger, *An Autobiography*, 274-75.

39   The United States ranked worst among 23 OECD countries in poverty defined as "share of individuals living in households with income below half of household-size-adjusted median income," after taxes and transfers. Elise Gould and Hilary Wething, "U.S. Poverty Rates Higher, Safety Net Weaker than in Peer Countries," Economic Policy Institute report, July 24, 2012, http://www.epi.org/publication/ib339-us-poverty-higher-safety-net-weaker/.

CHAPTER 10: CANNON FODDER

1   Jonathan V. Last, "America's Baby Bust," *Wall Street Journal*, February 12, 2013, http://www.wsj.com/articles/SB10001424127887323375204578270053387770718.

2   Leta Hollingworth, "Social Devices for Impelling Women to Bear Children" (1916) in *Pronatalism: The Myth of Mom and Apple Pie*, eds. Ellen Peck and Judith Senderowitz (New York: Thomas Y. Crowell, 1974), 21, 24.

3   Theodore Roosevelt, "Birth Control—From the Positive Side," *Metropolitan* 46, no. 5 (October 1917), http://www.theodore-roosevelt.com/images/research/treditorials/m13.pdf.

4   Roosevelt, "Birth Control," 69.

5   Susan B. Anthony, "Susan B. Anthony's Reply to President Roosevelt's Race Suicide Theory," *Socialist Woman* 2, no. 16 (September 1908): 6, https://books.google.com/books/reader?id=OvM4AQAAMAAJ.

6   Quoted in Linda Gordon, *The Moral Property of Women: A History of Birth Control Politics in America* (Champaign: University of Illinois Press, 2002), 93. Gordon believes the quote is from World War I. Gilman died in 1935.

7   Margaret Sanger, "Women and War," *Birth Control Review* 1, no. 4 (June 1917): 5.

8   Speech given to protest the centennial of France's Civil Code, October 29, 1904, published in *La Fronde*, November 1, 1904. Karen M. Offen, *European Feminisms, 1700–1950* (Stanford: Stanford University Press, 2000), 241.

9   Victor Serge, *What Everyone Should Know about Repression*, chap. 4, Marxists Internet Archive, https://www.marxists.org/archive/serge/1926/repression/ch4.htm

10   Martha Ruben-Wolf, *Abtreibung oder Verhütüng?* [Abortion or Contraception?] (Berlin: Internationaler Arbeiter-Verlag, 1929). Quote translated by Michael Pollak. Ruben-Wolf is quoted by Allan Carlson in *The Swedish Experiment in Family Politics* (New Brunswick, NJ: Transaction, 1990), 21.

11   Mark McLelland, *Love, Sex and Democracy in Japan during the American Occupation* (New York: St. Martin's, 2012), 42.

12   McLelland, *Love, Sex and Democracy*, 42, quoting Ike Nobutaka, "Birth Control in Japan," *Far Eastern Survey* 17, no. 23 (1948): 271-74.

13   Lawrence Lader, *Abortion* (New York: Bobbs-Merrill, 1966), 133.

14   McLelland, *Love, Sex and Democracy*, 42, quoting Nobutaka, "Birth Control," 272.

15   Linda Gordon, *Woman's Body, Woman's Right: A Social History of Birth Control in America* (New York: Grossman, 1976); Gordon, *Moral Property of Women*, 90, 93.

16   Barbara Segal, "Today Bucharest, Tomorrow the World," *Off Our Backs* 5, no. 1 (January 1975): 11. Quoted in Adrienne Rich, *Of Woman Born: Motherhood as Experience and Institution* (New York: W.W. Norton, 1995), 74-75.

17   Kathie Sarachild, "The Myth of Abortion Law Repeal," *Woman's World* 1, no. 1 (April 15, 1971): 10, Redstockings Women's Liberation Archives, redstockings. org.

18   Col. Robert D. Heinl, Jr., "The Collapse of the Armed Forces," *Armed Forces Journal*, June 7, 1971, https://msuweb.montclair.edu/~furrg/Vietnam/heinl.html.

19   Conscription expired in 1947 but was renewed in 1948.

20   Jennifer Mittelstadt, *The Rise of the Military Welfare State* (Cambridge, MA: Harvard University Press), 2015.

21   Phillip Longman, *The Empty Cradle: How Falling Birthrates Threaten World Prosperity and What to Do about It* (New York: Basic Books, 2004), 20.

22   "Half a Billion Americans?" *Economist* (special report), August 22, 2002, http://www.economist.com/node/1291056.

23   Peter G. Peterson, "Riding for a Fall," *Foreign Affairs* 83, no. 5 (September/October 2004): 111–25.

24   The seven countries, in order, are China, Saudi Arabia, Russia, the United Kingdom, India, France, and Japan. Stockholm International Peace Research Institute, "SIPRI Yearbook 2017: Armaments, Disarmament and International Security" (Oxford: Oxford University Press, 2017), https://www.sipri.org/sites/default/files/2017-09/yb17-summary-eng.pdf. National Priorities Project, "U.S. Military Spending vs. the World," (2015), https://www.nationalpriorities.org/campaigns/us-military-spending-vs-world/.

25   "American Troop Strength," *NOW*, PBS television program, February 11, 2005, http://www.pbs.org/now/politics/troopsforiraq.html.

26   The ten deployments the Army counts as significant are Korea, Vietnam, Watts, Dominican Republic, Detroit, Chicago, Sinai, Lebanon, Grenada, and Panama. Department of the Army, "Army Vision 2010," http://webapp1.dlib.indiana.edu/virtual_disk_library/index.cgi/4240529/FID378/pdfdocs/2010/varmy.pdf.

27   David Vine, "American Military Extends Its Reach Worldwide," Investigative Reporting Workshop, American University, August 25, 2015, http://investigativereportingworkshop.org/investigations/lily-pads/story/lily-pads/.

28   David Vine, "The United States Probably Has More Foreign Military Bases Than Any Other People, Nation, or Empire in History," *The Nation*, September 17, 2015, https://www.thenation.com/article/the-united-states-probably-has-more-foreign-military-bases-than-any-other-people-nation-or-empire-in-history/.

29   Barton Gellman, "Keeping the U.S. First, Pentagon Would Preclude a Rival Superpower," *Washington Post*, March 11, 1992, 1A. "Defense Planning Guidance" is the official name of the memo.

30   Noam Chomsky has developed the most exhaustive reviews of this data. But see Michael Parenti, *Against Empire* (San Francisco: City Lights Books, 1995) for an overview.

31   Stephen Peter Rosen, "The Future of War and the American Military," *Harvard Magazine*, May–June 2002, http://harvardmagazine.com/2002/05/the-future-of-war-and-th.html.

32   Army, "Army Vision 2010." Of course, here we could say the army is trying to promote its institutional growth against the other military branches. But it's not just the army, as we'll see.

33   Project for a New American Century, "Letter to Congress on Increasing U.S. Ground Forces," January 28, 2005.

34   Rosen, "The Future of War," 2002.

35 Barack Obama, "Remarks to the Chicago Council on Global Affairs," April 23, 2007, http://www.presidency.ucsb.edu/ws/?pid=77043.

36 Hillary Clinton's speech to the Veterans of Foreign Wars Convention, August 20, 2007, Kansas City, Missouri.

37 Mattea Cramer, "Sequestration's Impact on Military Spending, 2013–2014," National Priorities Project, March 4, 2014, https://www.nationalpriorities.org/analysis/2014/sequestration-impact-on-military-spending-2013-2014/.

38 Louis Jacobson and Amy Sherman, "PolitiFact Sheet: Military Spending under Obama," *Politifact*, December 14, 2015, http://www.politifact.com/truth-o-meter/article/2015/dec/14/politifact-sheet-our-guide-to-military-spending-/.

39 The figure is for 2015 and doesn't count Social Security and Medicare, which receive designated revenue streams from payroll taxes. National Priorities Project, "Military Spending in the United States," https://www.nationalpriorities.org/campaigns/military-spending-united-states/.

40 David S. Cloud, "U.S. Is Extending Tours of Army," *New York Times*, April 12, 2007, http://www.nytimes.com/2007/04/12/world/middleeast/12military.html.

41 See, for example, "'One Weekend a Month, My Ass!!' sign posted on an Army Reserve vehicle in Iraq," Wikipedia, https://en.wikipedia.org/wiki/One_weekend_a_month,_two_weeks_a_year#/media/File:USAR.OneWeekendMyAss.jpg.

42 Gregg Zoroya, "Army to Expand Citizen Soldiers' Training Periods," *USA Today*, July 30, 2012, http://usatoday30.usatoday.com/news/military/story/2012-07-30/army-guard-reserve-training/56595948/1.

43 Mark Benjamin, "Out of Jail, into the Army," *Salon*, February 2, 2006, https://www.salon.com/2006/02/02/waivers/; Lizette Alvarez, "Army Giving More Waivers in Recruiting," *New York Times*, February 14, 2007, A1.

44 Mark Thompson, "Why Are Army Recruiters Killing Themselves?" *Time*, April 2, 2009, http://content.time.com/time/magazine/article/0,9171,1889152,00.html.

45 Jamie McIntyre, "Army to Order One-Day Break from Recruiting," CNN, May 11, 2005, http://www.cnn.com/2005/US/05/11/army.recruiting/.

46 At this writing, the policy seems to have survived President Trump's stated desire to reverse it.

47 Michael S. Schmidt, "2 Generals Say Women Should Register for Draft," *New York Times*, February 2, 2016, http://www.nytimes.com/2016/02/03/us/politics/2-generals-say-women-should-register-for-draft.html.

48 Figures are from 2010. An additional 850,000 fill the ranks of the National Guard and the Reserves.

49 Michael Ignatieff, "American Empire (Get Used to It)," *New York Times Magazine*, January 5, 2003.

CHAPTER 11: CONTROLLING THE MEANS OF REPRODUCTION

1 Judith Brown, *It's a Lifetime's Work, This Movement* (Gainesville, FL.: Gainesville Women's Liberation, 1987), 6.

2 "Demography and the West; Half a Billion Americans?" *Economist*, August 22, 2002, http://www.economist.com/displaystory.cfm?story_id=1291056.

3 Sheryl Ubelacker, "Two-Child Families Becoming the Norm in Canada," *Canadian Press*, February 8, 2012, http://www.theglobeandmail.com/news/national/two-child-families-becoming-the-norm-in-canada/article544511/.

4 Eberstadt, Nicholas, "America the Fertile," *Washington Post*, May 6, 2007, B07; Robert J. Samuelson, "Behind The Birth Dearth," *Washington Post*, May 24, 2006,

A23, http://www.washingtonpost.com/wp-dyn/content/article/2006/05/23/AR2006052301529.html.

5   Sheryl Ubelacker, "Falling Birth Rate Follows Ebbing 'Religiosity,'" *Toronto Star*, March 13, 2007, http://www.thestar.com/news/2007/03/13/falling_birth_rate_follows_ebbing_religiosity.html.

6   Not counting miscarriages. Pregnancies are unintended if the woman didn't want to become pregnant until later or wanted no more children ever. "Unintended Pregnancy in the United States," Alan Guttmacher Institute, May 2016, https://www.guttmacher.org/fact-sheet/unintended-pregnancy-united-states.

7   Stanley K. Henshaw, "Unintended Pregnancy in the United States," *Family Planning Perspectives* 30, no. 1 (January/February 1998): 24–46.

8   "Sharing Responsibility: Women, Society and Abortion Worldwide," (report) New York: Alan Guttmacher Institute, 1999, https://www.guttmacher.org/sites/default/files/pdfs/pubs/sharing.pdf.

9   The Centers for Disease Control and Prevention estimates that 37 percent of U.S. births are unintended, but do not attempt an international comparison. W.D. Mosher et al. "Intended and Unintended Births in the United States: 1982–2010." National Health Statistics Reports, no. 55 (Hyattsville, MD: National Center for Health Statistics, 2012).

10   Jacqueline Darroch, Jennifer J. Frost, and Susheela Singh, "Teenage Sexual and Reproductive Behavior in Developed Countries: Can More Progress Be Made?" Occasional Report, no. 3 (New York: Alan Guttmacher Institute, 2001). It could be argued that religiosity reduces contraceptive use because those who believe it's sinful to have sex may also regard the premeditation required to use birth control as sinful.

11   Stanley K. Henshaw and Rachel K. Jones, "Unmet Need for Abortion in the United States," Alan Guttmacher Institute, September 20, 2007, http://paa2008.princeton.edu/papers/80673.

12   Joerg Dreweke, "New Clarity for the U.S. Abortion Debate: A Steep Drop in Unintended Pregnancy Is Driving Recent Abortion Declines," *Guttmacher Policy Review* 19, no. 1 (March 18, 2016), https://www.guttmacher.org/gpr/2016/03/new-clarity-us-abortion-debate-steep-drop-unintended-pregnancy-driving-recent-abortion.

13   Kathie Sarachild, "Consciousness-Raising: A Radical Weapon," in *Feminist Revolution*, eds. Redstockings (New York: Random House: 1978), 144–50.

14   Carol Hanisch, "The Personal Is Political," March 1969, in Redstockings, *Feminist Revolution*, (New York: Random House, 1978), 204. See Hanisch's history of the article at http://www.carolhanisch.org/CHwritings/PIP.html.

15 - Hanisch, "Personal Is Political," 204.

16   Sheryl Sandberg, *Lean In: Women, Work, and the Will to Lead* (New York: Knopf, 2013), 9. Gloria Steinem represents an earlier version of this type of feminism. See *Revolution from Within: A Book of Self-Esteem* (New York: Little, Brown, 1992). For a critique of the Sandberg book, see Susan Faludi, "Facebook Feminism, Like It or Not," *Baffler*, August 2013, https://thebaffler.com/salvos/facebook-feminism-like-it-or-not.

17   See Kathie Sarachild, Jenny Brown, and Amy Coenen, eds. *Women's Liberation and National Health Care: Confronting the Myth of America* (New York: Redstockings, 2001), http://www.redstockings.org/index.php/main/redstockings-confronts-the-myth-of-america; Michael Moore's movies *SiCKO*

(2007) and *Where to Invade Next* (2016) use international comparisons to break through the myth.

18   Women's Liberation Taskforce for National Health Care and Redstockings Allies and Veterans Social Wage Committee, "What Every Woman in America Should Know," *National NOW Times*, Fall 2004, 14.

19   Jennifer Ludden, "On Your Mark, Give Birth, Go Back to Work," *All Things Considered*, National Public Radio, October 4, 2016, https://www.npr.org/2016/10/04/495839747/on-your-mark-give-birth-go-back-to-work.

20   Stephen Stromberg, "Why Hillary Clinton Is More Progressive than Bernie Sanders, in One Sentence," *Washington Post*, October 6, 2015, https://www.washingtonpost.com/blogs/post-partisan/wp/2015/10/06/why-hillary-clinton-is-more-progressive-than-bernie-sanders-in-one-sentence.

21   The late and legendary Dr. Quentin Young of Physicians for a National Health Program raised this chant when he traveled the country rallying people for national health insurance.

22   "Our most personal health care decision" is from an email from Wendy Davis on behalf of NARAL Pro-Choice America, March 1, 2016.

23   Canadian law allows abortions at any stage of pregnancy, but in the United States cutoff times and rules about how later abortions may be performed are being used to stop women from exercising their rights.

24   Doctors use mifepristone in combination with misoprostol for medical abortions in pregnancies under ten weeks.

25   Mifeprex REMS Study Group, "Sixteen Years of Overregulation: Time to Unburden Mifeprex," *New England Journal of Medicine* 376, no. 8 (February 23, 2017): 790–94.

26   In October 2017, the American Civil Liberties Union sued the U.S. government agencies responsible for the restrictions, https://www.aclu.org/legal-document/chelius-v-wright-complaint.

27   "Medication Abortion" (report) Alan Guttmacher Institute, March 1, 2018, https://www.guttmacher.org/state-policy/explore/medication-abortion.

28   The main use is to protect patients from stomach damage due to long-term use of nonsteroidal anti-inflammatory drugs (like ibuprofen) for chronic conditions like arthritis pain.

29   Erika Hellerstein, "The Rise of the DIY Abortion in Texas," *The Atlantic*, June 27, 2014, https://www.theatlantic.com/health/archive/2014/06/the-rise-of-the-diy-abortion-in-texas/373240/.

30   Phoebe Zerwick, "The Rise of the DIY Abortion," *Glamour*, July 2016, http://www.glamour.com/story/the-rise-of-the-diy-abortion.

31   Emily Bazelon, "A Mother in Jail for Helping Her Daughter Have an Abortion," *New York Times Magazine*, September 22, 2014, https://www.nytimes.com/2014/09/22/magazine/a-mother-in-jail-for-helping-her-daughter-have-an-abortion.html.

32   National Women's Health Network, "Abortion with Pills vs. Miscarriage: Demystifying the Experience," https://www.nwhn.org/abortion-pills-vs-miscarriage-demystifying-experience/.

33   Emily Bazelon, "The Dawn of the Post-Clinic Abortion," *New York Times Magazine*, August 28, 2014, https://www.nytimes.com/2014/08/31/magazine/the-dawn-of-the-post-clinic-abortion.html.

34 Zerwick, "DIY Abortion." It has also been suggested that Women on Web has to weigh the chance that United States prosecutors may threaten legal action.

35 Emily Shugerman, "U.S. Abortion Pill Website, Aid Access, Under Investigation by the FDA," *Daily Beast*, October 22, 2018, https://www.thedailybeast.com/us-abortion-pill-website-aid-access-under-investigation-by-the-fda.

36 NARAL Pro-Choice America, "Who Decides? The Status of Reproductive Rights in the United States," January 2017, https://www.prochoiceamerica.org/report/2017-decides-status-womens-reproductive-rights-united-states/.

37 Lucinda Cisler, "Abortion Law Repeal (Sort Of): A Warning to Women," in *Notes from the Second Year: Women's Liberation*, eds. Shulamith Firestone and Anne Koedt, 89–93 (New York: Radical Feminism, 1970). Redstockings Women's Liberation Archives.

38 Joanna Rothkopf, "Sheryl Sandberg on Being a Single Mother: 'I Did Not Really Get How Hard It Is,'" *Jezebel*, May 9, 2016, https://jezebel.com/sheryl-sandberg-on-being-a-single-mother-i-did-not-rea-1775499426.

39 Institute on Taxation and Economic Policy, "Fact Sheet: Facebook and Tax Avoidance," November 5, 2017, https://itep.org/fact-sheet-facebook-and-tax-avoidance/; Kartikay Mehrotra, "Facebook Tax Bill Over Ireland Move Could Cost $5 Billion," *Bloomberg*, July 28, 2016, http://www.bloomberg.com/news/articles/2016-07-28/facebook-gets-3-5-billion-irs-tax-notice-over-ireland-move.

40 ITEP, "Fact Sheet: Facebook"; Richard Phillips et al., "Offshore Shell Games 2017: The Use of Offshore Tax Havens by Fortune 500 Companies," Institute on Taxation and Economic Policy, October 2017, https://itep.org/wp-content/uploads/offshoreshellgames2017.pdf; Mehrotra, "Facebook Tax Bill Over Ireland Move."

41 Alexandra Bradbury et al., *How to Jump-Start Your Union: Lessons from the Chicago Teachers* (Detroit: Labor Notes, 2012).

42 Katha Pollitt, "Village Idiot," *The Nation*, February 5, 1996, 9.

43 Figure from the Bureau of Labor Statistics, May 2015, http://www.bls.gov/oes/current/oes399011.htm.

44 Hillary Clinton, *What Happened* (New York: Simon and Schuster, 2017), 238. Quoted in Doug Henwood, "Doug Henwood Dispatches Hillary and Her New Book to Remainder Bin of History," *Washington Babylon*, September 25, 2017.

45 Clinton, *What Happened*, 227, 238.

46 Redstockings, "Dues-Paying Feminist" (button), http://www.redstockings.org/index.php/main/buttons.

47 Emily McNeill and Crystal Hall, *The National Union of the Homeless: A Brief History* (New York: Poverty Scholars Program, 2011), 7.

48 INCITE! Women of Color Against Violence, *The Revolution Will Not Be Funded: Beyond the Non-Profit Industrial Complex* (Durham, NC: Duke University Press, 2017).

49 Ian Angus and Simon Butler, *Too Many People?* (Chicago: Haymarket Books, 2011), 180–83.

APPENDIX: CONSCIOUSNESS-RAISING QUESTIONS

1 Kathie Sarachild, "Consciousness-Raising: A Radical Weapon," in *Feminist Revolution*, eds. Redstockings (New York: Random House: 1978), 144–50.

BIBLIOGRAPHY

Addati, Laura, Naomi Cassirer, and Katherine Gilchrist. *Maternity and Paternity at Work: Law and Practice across the World.* Geneva: International Labour Organization, 2014.

Allen, Ted. *Can White Radicals Be Radicalized?* New York: NYC Revolutionary Youth Movement, 1969.

Altman, Nancy, and Eric Kingson. *Social Security Works! Why Social Security Isn't Going Broke and How Expanding It Will Help Us All.* New York: New Press, 2015.

Angus, Ian, and Simon Butler. *Too Many People?* Chicago: Haymarket Books, 2011.

Anthony, Susan B. "Susan B. Anthony's Reply to President Roosevelt's Race Suicide Theory." *Socialist Woman* (Girard, Kansas) 2, no. 16 (September 1908): 6.

Asbell, Bernard. *The Pill: A Biography of a Drug That Changed the World.* New York: Random House, 1995.

Atkinson, Ti-Grace. *Amazon Odyssey.* New York: Links Books, 1974.

Bacon, David. "Common Ground on the Killing Floor." *Labor Notes,* April 12, 2012. http://labornotes.org/blogs/2012/04/common-ground-kill-floor-organizing-smithfield.

———. *The Right to Stay Home: How U.S. Policy Drives Mexican Immigration.* Boston: Beacon, 2013.

Baiman, Ron, Heather Boushey, and Dawn Saunders, eds. *Political Economy and Contemporary Capitalism.* New York: Routledge, 2015.

Baker, Dean. *The Conservative Nanny State.* Washington, DC: Center for Economic and Policy Research, 2006.

———. "Education Is Not the Answer." *Jacobin,* April 14, 2014. https://www.jacobinmag.com/2014/04/unremedial-education/.

———. "Statement on the 2016 Social Security Trustees Report." Center for Economic and Policy Research, June 22, 2016. http://cepr.net/press-center/press-releases/dean-baker-s-statement-on-the-2016-social-security-trustees-report.

Bassett, Laura. "Jeb Bush in 1995: Unwed Mothers Should Be Publicly Shamed." *Huffington Post,* June 9, 2015. http://www.huffingtonpost.com/2015/06/09/jeb-bush-1995-book_n_7542964.html.

Bazelon, Emily. "The Dawn of the Post-Clinic Abortion." *New York Times Magazine*, August 28, 2014, https://www.nytimes.com/2014/08/31/magazine/the-dawn-of-the-post-clinic-abortion.html.

Beal, Frances. "Double Jeopardy: To Be Black and Female." New York: Redstockings Women's Liberation Archives for Action, 1969.

Beauvoir, Simone de. *The Coming of Age.* Translated by André Deutsch. New York: G.P. Putnam's Sons, 1970.

———. *The Second Sex.* Translated by Constance Borde and Sheila Malovany-Chevallier. New York: Vintage, 2011. First published 1949.

Beisel, Nicola Kay. *Imperiled Innocents: Anthony Comstock and Family Reproduction in Victorian America.* Princeton, NJ: Princeton University Press, 1998.

Berlatsky, Noah. "Why Are Liberals Obsessed with Using Contraception to Fight Poverty?" *New Republic*, October 2, 2015. http://www.newrepublic.com/article/122992/why-are-liberals-obsessed-using-contraception-fight-poverty.

Bird, Caroline. *Born Female: The High Cost of Keeping Women Down.* New York: David MacKay, 1968; New York: Simon & Schuster, 1969.

Black Feminist Working Group. "What Sistas Want, What Sistas Believe." August 30, 2011. https://blackfeministworkinggroup.wordpress.com/2011/08/30/what-sistas-want-what-sistas-believe-black-feminist-twelve-point-plan/.

Blahous, Charles, and Jason J. Fichtner. "Social Security Reform and Economic Growth." In *The 4% Solution: Unleashing the Economic Growth America Needs*, George W. Bush Institute, edited by Brendan Miniter, 204–25. New York: Crown Business, 2012.

Bohn, Sarah, and Eric Schiff. "Immigrants and the Labor Market." Public Policy Institute of California, March 2011. http://www.ppic.org/main/publication_show.asp?i=823.

Bok, Sissela. *Alva Myrdal: A Daughter's Memoir.* Reading, MA: Addison-Wesley, 1991.

Boonstra, Heather. "Emergency Contraception: Steps Being Taken to Improve Access." *Guttmacher Policy Review* 5, no. 5 (December 1, 2002): 10–13.

———. "Insurance Coverage of Abortion: Beyond the Exceptions for Life Endangerment, Rape and Incest." *Guttmacher Policy Review* 16, no. 3 (September 13, 2013). http://www.guttmacher.org/pubs/gpr/16/3/gpr160302.html.

Borjas, George. "The Labor Demand Curve Is Downward Sloping: Reexamining the Impact of Immigration on the Labor Market." *Quarterly Journal of Economics* 118, no. 4 (November 2003): 1335–74.

Borrero, Sonya, et al. "Medicaid Policy on Sterilization—Anachronistic or Still Relevant?" *New England Journal of Medicine* 370, no. 2 (January 9, 2014): 102–4.

Boston Women's Health Collective. *Women and Their Bodies: A Course.* Boston: Boston Women's Health Collective and New England Free Press, 1970. https://www.ourbodiesourselves.org/cms/assets/uploads/2014/04/Women-and-Their-Bodies-1970.pdf.

Bradbury, Alexandra, et al. *How to Jump-Start Your Union: Lessons from the Chicago Teachers.* Detroit: Labor Notes, 2012.

Braudel, Fernand. *The Structures of Everyday Life.* New York: Harper & Row, 1979.

Brewer, Shannon. "Abortion Access Collides with Pro-Life Activists in the Deep South." Interview by Leonard Lopate, WNYC, June 10, 2016.

Brown, Jenny, and Stephanie Seguin, National Women's Liberation. "How We Won the Fight on the Morning-After Pill." *Huffington Post*, June 22, 2013. http://www.

huffingtonpost.com/jenny-f-brown/how-we-won-the-fight-on-t_b_3134796.html.

Brown, Judith. *It's a Lifetime's Work, This Movement*. Gainesville, FL: Gainesville Women's Liberation, 1987.

Brownmiller, Susan. "Everywoman's Abortions: 'The Oppressor Is Man.'" *Village Voice*, March 27, 1969. Redstockings Women's Liberation Archives. http://www.redstockings.org/images/stories/redstockings/ReplacementImages/ReplacementPDFs/AbortionSpeakoutArchivesforAction19691989Redstockings.pdf.

Bruenig, Elizabeth. "Marco Rubio and Mike Lee Want You to Have Kids—Unless You're Poor." *New Republic*, March 4, 2015. https://newrepublic.com/article/121216/rubio-lee-tax-plan-features-penalties-poor-families.

Bruenig, Matt. "Promoting Marriage Has Failed and Is Unnecessary to Cut Poverty." *Demos*, December 4, 2015. http://www.demos.org/blog/12/4/15/promoting-marriage-has-failed-and-unnecessary-cut-poverty.

Bruenig, Matt, and Elizabeth Bruenig. "Republicans and Democrats Both Claim to Be Pro-Family. Here's How They Can Prove It." *New Republic*, April 20, 2014. https://newrepublic.com/article/117453/monthly-child-allowance-best-way-support-strong-families.

Bryce, Joseph W. "Socialists May Adopt Birth Strike in Berlin, Germany." *Square Deal* 13 (October 1913): 273.

Buchanan, Patrick. *The Death of the West: How Dying Populations and Immigrant Invasions Imperil Our Country and Civilization*. New York: St. Martin's Griffin, 2002.

———. *State of Emergency: The Third World Invasion and Conquest of America*. New York: Thomas Dunne, 2006.

Burkett, Elinor. *The Baby Boon: How Family-Friendly America Cheats the Childless*. New York: Free Press, 2000.

Bush, George W. "Fact Sheet: Strengthening the Social Security System for Future Generations," January 11, 2005. http://georgewbush-whitehouse.archives.gov/news/releases/2005/01/text/20050111-12.html.

Bush, Jeb, and Clint Bolick, *Immigration Wars: Forging an American Solution*, New York: Threshold Editions, 2013.

Cadena, Micaela, Raquel Z. Rivera, Tannia Esparza, and Denicia Cadena. *Dismantling Teen Pregnancy Prevention*. Albuquerque: Young Women United, 2016.

Caldwell, John, and Thomas Schindlmayr. "Explanations of the Fertility Crisis in Modern Societies: A Search for Commonalities." In *Population and Society* (2nd ed.), edited by Frank Trovato, 197–214. Oxford: Oxford University, 2012.

Card, David. "Comment: The Elusive Search for Negative Wage Impacts of Immigration." National Bureau of Economic Research, 2012. http://davidcard.berkeley.edu/papers/jeea2012.pdf.

Carlson, Allan. *The Swedish Experiment in Family Politics*. New Brunswick, NJ: Transaction, 1990.

Case, Anne, and Angus Deaton, "Rising Morbidity and Mortality in Midlife among White Non-Hispanic Americans in the 21st Century." Proceedings of the National Academy of Sciences of the United States, September 17, 2015. http://www.pnas.org/content/early/2015/10/29/1518393112.full.pdf.

Center for American Progress, "Facts on Immigration Today," October 2014. https://cdn.americanprogress.org/wp-content/uploads/2013/04/ImmigrationFacts-brief-10.23.pdf.

Cisler, Lucinda. "Abortion Law Repeal (Sort Of): A Warning to Women." In *Notes from the Second Year: Women's Liberation,* edited by Shulamith Firestone and Anne Koedt, 89–93. New York: Radical Feminism, 1970. Redstockings Women's Liberation Archives.

———. "Unfinished Business: Birth Control and Women's Liberation." In *Sisterhood Is Powerful,* edited by Robin Morgan, 245–89. New York: Vintage, 1970.

Civil Rights Congress. *We Charge Genocide: The Historic Petition to the United Nations for Relief from a Crime of the United States Government against the Negro People.* New York: n.p., 1951.

Clark, Fiona. "Russia Ponders Restrictions on Abortion Rights," *Deutsche Welle,* June 14, 2015. http://www.dw.com/en/russia-ponders-restrictions-on-abortion-rights/a-18509939.

Clark, Victor S., et al., *Porto Rico and Its Problems.* Washington, DC: *Brookings Institution,* 1930. http://quod.lib.umich.edu/p/philamer/agd9090.0001.001.

Clinton, Hillary Rodham. *It Takes a Village.* New York: Simon & Schuster, 1996.

———. *Living History.* New York: Simon & Schuster, 2004.

———. *What Happened.* New York: Simon & Schuster, 2017.

Communist Party of the Soviet Union. *History of the Communist Party of the Soviet Union (Bolsheviks) Short Course.* New York: International Publishers, 1939.

Conniff, Ruth. "Rick Santorum's America." *Progressive,* October 2005. http://progressive.org/mag_conniff1005.

Covert, Bryce. "Why America Gave Up on the Fight for a Family-Friendly Workplace, and Why It's Starting Again." *ThinkProgress,* July 31, 2014. https://thinkprogress.org/why-america-gave-up-on-the-fight-for-a-family-friendly-workplace-and-why-its-starting-again-54f536b27572/.

Cramer, Mattea. "Sequestration's Impact on Military Spending, 2013–2014." National Priorities Project, March 4, 2014. https://www.nationalpriorities.org/analysis/2014/sequestration-impact-on-military-spending-2013-2014/.

Critchlow, Donald. *Intended Consequences: Birth Control, Abortion, and the Federal Government in Modern America.* Oxford: Oxford University, 2001.

Darroch, Jacqueline, Jennifer J. Frost, and Susheela Singh. "Teenage Sexual and Reproductive Behavior in Developed Countries: Can More Progress Be Made?" New York: Alan Guttmacher Institute, November 2001.

Davis, Angela Y. *Women, Race and Class.* New York: Random House, 1981.

Denis, Nelson. *War Against All Puerto Ricans: Revolution and Terror in America's Colony.* New York: Nation Books, 2015.

Dennett, Mary Ware. *Birth Control Laws: Shall We Keep Them, Change Them, or Abolish Them?* New York: Frederick H. Hitchcock, the Grafton, 1926.

DeSarno, Judith M., and Marilyn J. Keefe. "Weathering the Storm: Federal Legislative and Regulatory Action on Reproductive Health in 2005." National Family Planning and Reproductive Health Association, January 13, 2006.

Dixon, Marlene. *The Future of Women.* San Francisco: Synthesis, 1980.

Douglas, D.M. "Social Security: Sex Discrimination and Equal Protection." *Baylor Law Review* 30 (1978): 199–205.

Douthat, Ross. "Author: GOP Needs to Refocus on the Working Class." Interview by Robert Siegel, *All Things Considered*, National Public Radio, November 18, 2005. https://www.npr.org/templates/story/story.php?storyId=5019085.

Douthat, Ross, and Reihan Salam. "The Party of Sam's Club," *Weekly Standard*, November 14, 2005. http://www.weeklystandard.com/the-party-of-sams-club/article/7501.

Dreweke, Joerg. "New Clarity for the U.S. Abortion Debate: A Steep Drop in Unintended Pregnancy Is Driving Recent Abortion Declines." *Guttmacher Policy Review* 19 (March 18, 2016). https://www.guttmacher.org/news-release/2016/steep-drop-unintended-pregnancy-behind-2008-2011-us-abortion-decline.

Du Bois, W.E.B. *Darkwater: Voices from Within the Veil*. New York: Harcourt Brace, 1920; Mineola, NY: Dover, 1999.

Durant, Will, and Ariel Durant. *The Age of Napoleon*. New York: Simon & Schuster, 1975.

Eastman, Crystal. "Birth Control in the Feminist Program." *Birth Control Review* 2, no. 1 (January 1918): 3.

Elliot, Justin. "Santorum Blames Abortion for Social Security Woes," *Salon*, March 29, 2011. http://www.salon.com/2011/03/29/santorum_abortion_social_security/.

Erickson, Megan. "The Privatization of Childhood." *Jacobin*, September 3, 2015. https://www.jacobinmag.com/2015/09/children-testing-schools-education-reform-inequality/.

Faludi, Susan. "Facebook Feminism, Like It or Not." *Baffler*, August 2013. https://thebaffler.com/salvos/facebook-feminism-like-it-or-not.

Federici, Silvia, and Arlen Austin, eds. *The New York Wages for Housework Committee 1972–1977: History, Theory, Documents*. Brooklyn: Autonomedia, 2018.

Firestone, Shulamith. *The Dialectic of Sex: The Case for Feminist Revolution*. New York: Farrar, Straus & Giroux, 1970.

Folbre, Nancy. *Valuing Children: Rethinking the Economics of the Family*. Cambridge, MA: Harvard University, 2008.

———. *Who Pays for the Kids? Gender and the Structures of Constraint*. New York: Routledge, 1994.

Forster, Margaret. *Significant Sisters: Grassroots of Active Feminism*. New York: Knopf, 1985.

Frank, Thomas. *What's the Matter with Kansas? How Conservatives Won the Heart of America*. New York: Henry Holt, 2004.

Fried, Marlene Gerber. "The Hyde Amendment: 30 Years of Violating Women's Rights." Center for American Progress, October 6, 2006. https://www.americanprogress.org/issues/women/news/2006/10/06/2243/the-hyde-amendment-30-years-of-violating-womens-rights/.

Friedan, Betty. *The Feminine Mystique*. New York: Dell, 1963.

———. *The Fountain of Age*. New York: Simon & Schuster, 1993.

———. "NOW's Statement of Purpose." National Organization for Women, 1966. http://now.org/about/history/statement-of-purpose/.

Friedan, Betty [Goldstein]. *UE Fights for Women Workers*. United Electrical, Radio and Machine Workers of America Publication, no. 232, June 1952.

Friedman, Uri. "Sweden: The New Laboratory for a Six-Hour Work Day." *The Atlantic*, April 9, 2014. http://www.theatlantic.com/international/archive/2014/04/sweden-the-new-laboratory-for-a-six-hour-work-day/360402/.

Frost, J.J., A. Sonfield, and R.B. Gold. "Estimating the Impact of Expanding Medicaid Eligibility for Family Planning Services." Occasional Report no. 28. New York: Alan Guttmacher Institute, 2006.

Gainesville Women's Liberation, "International Women's Day March 8," (flier) Gainesville, FL: Gainesville Women's Liberation, 1970.

Gal, Susan, and Gail Kligman, eds. *Reproducing Gender: Politics, Publics, and Everyday Life after Socialism.* Princeton, NJ: Princeton University Press, 2000.

Geiger, H. Kent. *The Family in Soviet Russia.* Cambridge, MA: Harvard University, 1968.

Giardina, Carol. *Freedom for Women: Forging the Women's Liberation Movement, 1953–1970.* Gainesville: University Press of Florida, 2010.

Gillon, Steven. *The Pact: Bill Clinton, Newt Gingrich, and the Rivalry That Defined a Generation.* Oxford: Oxford University, 2008.

Goldberg, Michelle. *The Means of Reproduction: Sex, Power, and the Future of the World.* New York: Penguin, 2009.

———. "Texas Is Hell-Bent on Ending Reproductive Health Care Access for Poor Women." *Slate*, October 19, 2015. https://slate.com/human-interest/2015/10/texas-cuts-planned-parenthood-out-of-medicaid.html

Goldman, Emma. Letter to Margaret Sanger, May 26, 1914. Berkeley: University of California, The Emma Goldman Papers. http://emmagoldmanpapers.tumblr.com/post/115237727585/the-birth-strike.

Gordon, Linda. *The Moral Property of Women: A History of Birth Control Politics in America.* Champaign: University of Illinois Press, 2002.

———. *Woman's Body, Woman's Right: A Social History of Birth Control in America.* New York: Grossman, 1976.

Greenstone, Michael, and Adam Looney. "What Immigration Means for U.S. Employment and Wages." The Brookings Institution, May 4, 2012. https://www.brookings.edu/blog/jobs/2012/05/04/what-immigration-means-for-u-s-employment-and-wages/.

Griswold, L.D., Toland Jones, and Henry West. "Additional Report from the Select Committee to Whom was Referred S.B. No. 285." (Ohio Senate committee). *Journal of the Senate of the General Assembly of Ohio* 63, 1867, 235.

Grossman, Daniel, et al. "Knowledge, Opinion and Experience Related to Abortion Self-Induction in Texas." Texas Policy Evaluation Project, November 17, 2015. https://utexas.edu/cola/txpep.

Guttmacher Institute. "Abortion in Context: United States and Worldwide," *Issues in Brief 1999 Series*, no. 1.

Hale, Edwin M. *The Great Crime of the Nineteenth Century.* Chicago: C.S. Halsey, 1867.

Hamilton, Brady E., et al. *Births: Provisional data for 2016. Vital statistics rapid release*; no 2. Hyattsville, MD: National Center for Health Statistics. June 2017. https://www.cdc.gov/nchs/data/vsrr/report002.pdf.

Hanisch, Carol. "The Personal Is Political (March 1969)." In *Feminist Revolution*, edited by Redstockings, 204. New York: Random House, 1978.

Hansen, Randall, and Desmond King. *Sterilized by the State.* Cambridge: Cambridge University, 2013.

Hartmann, Betsy. *Reproductive Rights and Wrongs: The Global Politics of Population Control.* Boston: South End, 1995.

Heilbroner, Robert. *The Worldly Philosophers*, 7th ed. New York: Simon & Schuster, 1999.

Heinl, Col. Robert D., Jr. "The Collapse of the Armed Forces," *Armed Forces Journal*, June 7, 1971. https://msuweb.montclair.edu/~furrg/Vietnam/heinl.html.

Hellerstein, Erika. "The Rise of the DIY Abortion in Texas." *The Atlantic*, June 27, 2014. https://www.theatlantic.com/health/archive/2014/06/the-rise-of-the-diy-abortion-in-texas/373240/.

Henshaw, Stanley K. "Unintended Pregnancy in the United States." *Family Planning Perspectives* 30, no. 1 (January/February 1998): 24–46.

Henshaw, Stanley K., and Rachel K. Jones. "Unmet Need for Abortion in the United States," Alan Guttmacher Institute, September 20, 2007. http://paa2008.princeton.edu/papers/80673.

Henwood, Doug. "Antisocial Insecurity." *Left Business Observer*, no. 87 (December 1998), http://www.leftbusinessobserver.com/AntisocInsec.html.

———. "Pension Fund Socialism: The Illusion That Just Won't Die." Talk at New School University, New York, September 11, 2004. http://www.leftbusinessobserver.com/NSPensions.html.

———. "Social Security Revisited." *Left Business Observer*, no. 110 (March 2005): 3–7.

———. "Social Security's Crisis, and Ours," *Left Business Observer*, no. 129 (October 2010), http://www.leftbusinessobserver.com/SocialSecurityAndUs.html.

Hesketh, Therese, Li Lu, and Zhu Wei Xing. "The Effect of China's One-Child Family Policy after 25 Years." *New England Journal of Medicine* 353, no. 11 (September 15, 2005): 1171–76.

Holley, Anna. "Margaret Sanger and the African American Community," *Trust Black Women*, July 2010. https://www.trustblackwomen.org/2011-05-10-03-28-12/publications-a-articles/african-americans-and-abortion-articles/26-margaret-sanger-and-the-african-american-community-.

Hollingworth, Leta. "Social Devices for Impelling Women to Bear Children (1916)." In *Pronatalism: The Myth of Mom and Apple Pie*, edited by Ellen Peck and Judith Senderowitz, 19–28. New York: Thomas Y. Crowell, 1974.

Holt, Marilyn Irvin. *The Orphan Trains: Placing Out in America*. Lincoln: University of Nebraska Press, 1992.

Horne, Gerald. *Confronting Black Jacobins: The U.S., the Haitian Revolution, and the Origins of the Dominican Republic*. New York: Monthly Review, 2015.

Hull, N.E.H., and Peter Charles Hoffer. *Roe v. Wade: The Abortion Rights Controversy in American History*. Lawrence: University Press of Kansas, 2001.

Human Rights Watch. *Blood, Sweat and Fear: Workers' Rights in U.S. Meat and Poultry Plants*. New York: 2011.

Ignatieff, Michael. "American Empire (Get Used to It)," *New York Times Magazine*, January 5, 2003.

INCITE! Women of Color Against Violence. *The Revolution Will Not Be Funded: Beyond the Non-Profit Industrial Complex*. Durham, NC: Duke University Press, 2017.

Jing-Bao, Nie. *Behind the Silence: Chinese Voices on Abortion*. Lanham, MD: Rowman and Littlefield, 2005.

Jütte, Robert. *Contraception: A History*. Translated by Vicky Russell. Cambridge: Polity, 2008.

Kennedy, David. *Birth Control in America*. New Haven, CT: Yale University Press, 1970.

Klein, Herbert S. *A Population History of the United States*. Cambridge: Cambridge University Press, 2012.

Kluchin, Rebecca. *Fit to Be Tied: Sterilization and Reproductive Rights in America, 1950–1980*. New Brunswick, NJ: Rutgers University Press, 2009.

Kotlikoff, Laurence, et al. *Get What's Yours: The Secrets to Maxing Out Your Social Security*. New York: Simon & Schuster, 2015.

Kramer, Steven Philip. *The Other Population Crisis: What Governments Can Do about Falling Birth Rates*. Washington, DC: Woodrow Wilson Center, 2014.

Labor Party, "A Call for Economic Justice," Washington, DC: Labor Party, 1996. http://www.thelaborparty.org/d_program.htm.

Lader, Lawrence. *Abortion*. New York: Bobbs-Merrill, 1966.

Langer, William L., "The Origins of the Birth Control Movement in England in the Early Nineteenth Century." *Journal of Interdisciplinary History* 5, no. 4 (1975): 669–86. http://doi.org/10.2307/202864.

Last, Jonathan. *What to Expect When No-One's Expecting: America's Coming Demographic Disaster*. New York: Encounter, 2014.

Lemann, Nicholas. *The Promised Land: The Great Black Migration and How It Changed America*. New York: Vintage, 1992.

Lenin, V.I. "The Working Class and Neo-Malthusianism," *Pravda*, no. 137, June 16, 1913. In *Lenin Collected Works* vol. 19, 235–37. Moscow: Progress Publishers, 1977.

Lerner, Gerda, ed. *Black Women in White America: A Documentary History*. Vintage, New York, 1972.

Levin-Epstein, Jodie. "Lifting the Lid off Family Caps." Center for Law and Social Policy, December 2003. http://www.clasp.org/resources-and-publications/files/0166.pdf.

Linder, Marc. *Dilemmas of Laissez-Faire Population Policy*. Westport, CT: Greenwood Press, 1997.

Longman, Phillip. *The Empty Cradle: How Falling Birthrates Threaten World Prosperity and What to Do About It*. New York: Basic Books, 2004.

Lundqvist, Asa. *Family Policy Paradoxes: Gender Equality and Labour Market Regulation in Sweden, 1930–2010*. Bristol: Policy Press, 2011.

MacLean, Nancy. *Democracy in Chains: The Deep History of the Radical Right's Stealth Plan for America*. New York: Viking, 2017.

Mandel, William M. *Soviet Women*. New York: Doubleday, 1975.

Martin, Rachel. "Germany Frets about Women in Shrinking Workforce." National Public Radio, May 24, 2006.

Marx, Karl. *Capital: A Critique of Political Economy, Vol. 1* (1867). London: Penguin, 1976.

McLelland, Mark. *Love, Sex and Democracy in Japan during the American Occupation*. New York: St. Martin's, 2012.

McNeill, Emily, and Crystal Hall. *The National Union of the Homeless: A Brief History*. New York: Poverty Scholars Program, 2011. https://homelessunion.wdfiles.com/local--files/curriculum/BriefHistoryPamphlet.pdf.

Mencimer, Stephanie. "The Baby Boycott." *Washington Monthly*, June 2001. http://www.washingtonmonthly.com/features/2001/0106.mencimer.html.

———. "Rick Santorum's School Scandal: How the Public-School-Loathing GOP Candidate Used Pennsylvania's Taxpayer Dollars to School His Kids in Virginia." *Mother Jones*, January 4, 2012. http://www.motherjones.com/politics/2012/01/rick-santorums-school-scandal.

Mifeprex REMS Study Group. "Sixteen Years of Overregulation: Time to Unburden Mifeprex." *New England Journal of Medicine* 376, no. 8 (February 23, 2017): 790–94.

Mishel, Lawrence, Elise Gould, and Josh Bivens. "Wage Stagnation in Nine Charts." Economic Policy Institute, January 6, 2015. http://www.epi.org/publication/charting-wage-stagnation/.

Mitchell, Michele. *Righteous Propagation: African Americans and the Politics of Racial Destiny after Reconstruction.* Chapel Hill: University of North Carolina Press, 2005.

Mittelstadt, Jennifer. *The Rise of the Military Welfare State.* Cambridge, MA: Harvard University Press, 2015.

Mohr, James C. *Abortion in America: The Origins and Evolution of National Policy.* Oxford: Oxford University Press, 1978.

Moody, Kim, and Charles Post. "The Politics of U.S. Labor: Paralysis and Possibilities." In *Socialist Register: Transforming Classes,* edited by Leo Panitch and Greg Albo, 295–317. London: Merlin, 2014.

Mosher, W.D., and J. Jones. "Use of Contraception in the United States: 1982–2008." National Center for Health Statistics, *Vital Health Statistics* 23, no. 29 (2010): 1–44.

Mosher, W.D., et al. *Intended and Unintended Births in the United States: 1982–2010.* National Health Statistics Reports, no. 55. Hyattsville, MD: National Center for Health Statistics, 2012.

NARAL Pro-Choice America, "Who Decides? The Status of Reproductive Rights in the United States." January 2016. http://www.prochoiceamerica.org/assets/download-files/2016-wd-report.pdf?akid=1731.2407362.7Cv__x&rd=1&t=5.

Nelson, Claudia. *Little Strangers: Portrayals of Adoption and Foster Care in America, 1850–1929.* Bloomington: Indiana University Press, 2003.

Nelson, Jennifer. *Women of Color and the Reproductive Rights Movement.* New York: NYU Press, 2003.

Newman, Amie. "Paying Drug-Addicted Women to Get Sterilized: Choice or Coercion?" *Rewire,* November 3, 2010. https://rewire.news/article/2010/11/03/paying-drugaddicted-women-sterilized/.

New York Wages for Housework Committee. "Wages for Housework" (flier, n.d., ca. 1975). Archives of Silvia Federici, Brooklyn.

Offen, Karen M. *European Feminisms, 1700–1950.* Stanford: Stanford University Press, 2000.

O'Sullivan, John. "Nice Going, Karl: This Immigration Battle is a Fine Mess." *National Review Online,* April 5, 2006. https://www.nationalreview.com/2006/04/nice-going-karl/.

Ottaviano, Gianmarco and Giovanni Peri. "Rethinking the Effects of Immigration on Wages," National Bureau of Economic Research Working Paper no. 12497, August 2006.

Paddock, William, and Paul Paddock. *Famine, 1975! America's Decision: Who Will Survive?* Boston: Little, Brown, 1967.

Parenti, Michael. *Against Empire.* San Francisco: City Lights Books, 1995.

Perry, Jeffrey B., ed. *Hubert Harrison Reader.* Middletown, CT: Wesleyan University Press, 2001.

Peterson, Pete G. "Riding for a Fall." *Foreign Affairs* 83, no. 5 (September/October 2004): 111–25.

Place, Francis. *Illustrations and Proofs of Population.* Boston: Houghton Mifflin, 1930. First published 1822.

Pollitt, Katha. *Pro: Reclaiming Abortion Rights.* New York: Picador, 2014.

———. "Village Idiot." *The Nation,* February 5, 1996, 9.

Quadagno, Jill. *The Color of Welfare: How Racism Undermined the War on Poverty.* Oxford: Oxford University Press, 1996.

Ramírez de Arellano, Annette B., and Conrad Seipp. *Colonialism, Catholicism, and Contraception: A History of Birth Control in Puerto Rico.* Chapel Hill: University of North Carolina Press, 1983.

Redstockings Allies and Veterans Social Wage Committee and Women's Liberation Taskforce for National Health Care. "What Every Woman in America Should Know" (signature ad). *National NOW Times,* Fall 2004, 14.

Redstockings. *The Redstockings Manifesto.* New York: July 7, 1969. Redstockings Women's Liberation Archives for Action. http://redstockings.org/index.php/42-uncategorised/76-rs-manifesto.

———. The *Redstockings' Organizational Collection: Women's Liberation Archives for Action, 1940s–1991* (Microfilm, 89 reels). Boston: Cengage, 2011.

Rich, Adrienne. *Of Woman Born: Motherhood as Experience and Institution.* New York: W.W. Norton, 1995.

Richards, Cecile. "They're Even Anti-Contraception." Letter from Planned Parenthood, October 19, 2006.

Rifkin, Jeremy. *The End of Work: The Decline of the Global Labor Force and the Dawn of the Post-Market Era.* New York: Putnam, 1995.

Roberts, Dorothy. *Killing the Black Body: Race, Reproduction, and the Meaning of Liberty.* New York: Pantheon, 1997.

———. *Shattered Bonds: The Color of Child Welfare.* New York: Civitas Books, 2009.

Robins, Joan. *Handbook of Women's Liberation.* North Hollywood: NOW Library Press, 1970.

Rodrique, Jesse M. "The Black Community and the Birth-Control Movement." In *Unequal Sisters: A Multicultural Reader in U.S. Women's History,* edited by Ellen Carol DuBois and Vicki Ruíz, 333–44. New York: Routledge, 1990.

Roosevelt, Theodore. "Birth Control—From the Positive Side." *Metropolitan* 46, no. 5 (October 1917). http://www.theodore-roosevelt.com/images/research/treditorials/m13.pdf.

———. "On American Motherhood." Address to the National Congress of Mothers, Washington, DC, March 13, 1905. http://www.bartleby.com/268/10/29.html.

Rosen, Stephen Peter. "The Future of War and the American Military." *Harvard Magazine,* May–June 2002. http://harvardmagazine.com/2002/05/the-future-of-war-and-th.html.

Ross, Loretta. "Understanding Reproductive Justice." Atlanta: SisterSong Women of Color Reproductive Justice Collective, November 2006 (updated March 2011). http://www.trustblackwomen.org/our-work/what-is-reproductive-justice/9-what-is-reproductive-justice.

Ross, Loretta, and Rickie Solinger. *Reproductive Justice: A Primer.* Berkeley: University of California Press, 2017.

Rossi, Alice, ed. *The Feminist Papers: From Adams to de Beauvoir.* New York: Columbia University Press, 1973.

Rowan, Andrea. "Prosecuting Women for Self-Inducing Abortion: Counterproductive and Lacking Compassion," *Guttmacher Policy Review* 18, no. 3 (2015): 70–76 .

Ruben-Wolf, Martha. *Abtreibung oder Verhütung?* [Abortion or Contraception?]. Berlin: Internationaler Arbeiter-Verlag, 1929.

Salzman, Jason. "Family Planning Initiative Rejected by Colorado GOP Has New Life." *Rewire,* August 31, 2015. https://rewire.news/article/2015/08/31/family-planning-initiative-rejected-colorado-gop-new-life/.

Sandberg, Sheryl. *Lean In: Women, Work, and the Will to Lead.* New York: Knopf, 2013.

Sanger, Margaret. *Margaret Sanger: An Autobiography.* New York: Norton, 1938.

———. "Pivot of Civilization." New York: Brentano's, 1922. https://www.marxists.org/subject/women/authors/sanger/pivot.htm#a4.

———. "Why Not Birth Control Clinics in America?" *American Medicine* 25 (March 1919): 164–67.

———. "Women and War." *Birth Control Review* 1, no. 4 (June 1917): 5.

Sanger, Margaret, Frederick A. Blossom, and Elizabeth Stuyvesant. "To the Men and Women of the United States." *Birth Control Review* 1, no. 1 (February 1917): 3.

Santorum, Rick. *It Takes a Family: Conservatism and the Common Good.* New York: Open Road Media, 2014.

Sarachild, Kathie. "Beyond the Family Wage: A Women's Liberation View of the Social Wage." In *Women's Liberation and National Health Care: Confronting the Myth of America,* edited by Kathie Sarachild, Jenny Brown, and Amy Coenen, 21–29. New York: Redstockings, 2001. http://www.redstockings.org/index.php/main/redstockings-confronts-the-myth-of-america.

———. "Consciousness-Raising: A Radical Weapon." (March 1973) In *Feminist Revolution,* edited by Redstockings, 144–50. New York: Random House, 1978.

———. "The Myth of Abortion Law Repeal." *Woman's World* 1, no. 1 (April 15, 1971): 10. Redstockings Women's Liberation Archives, redstockings.org.

———. "A Program for Feminist Consciousness-Raising" (November 1968). In Redstockings, *Feminist Revolution,* edited by Redstockings, 202–3. New York: Random House, 1978.

Schlesinger, Rudolf, ed. "Decree on the Legalization of Abortions of November 18, 1920." In *The Family in the USSR: Documents and Readings.* London: Routledge, 1949.

Schulder, Diane, and Florynce Kennedy. *Abortion Rap.* New York: McGraw Hill, 1971.

Segal, Barbara. "Today Bucharest, Tomorrow the World." *Off Our Backs* 5, no. 1 (January 1975): 11.

Sen, Amartya. *Poverty and Famines: An Essay on Entitlement and Deprivation.* Oxford: Oxford University, 1982.

Silliman, Jael, et al., eds. *Undivided Rights, Women of Color Organize for Reproductive Justice.* Boston: South End, 2004.

Smith, Adam. *The Wealth of Nations.* London: Macmillan, 1869. First published 1776.

Sorensen, Elaine, et al. "Assessing Child Support Arrears in Nine Large States and the Nation." Urban Institute, July 11, 2007. http://www.urban.org/research/publication/assessing-child-support-arrears-nine-large-states-and-nation/view/full_report.

Stan, Adele M. "Anatomy of the War on Women: How the Koch Brothers Are Funding the Anti-Choice Agenda." *RH Reality Check,* November 5, 2013. (*RH Reality Check* is now called *Rewire.*)

Stanek, Jill. "Abort Pro-Choice Retirees from Social Security Program." *WorldNetDaily,* October 27, 2004. http://www.wnd.com/2004/10/27233/.

Stein, Robert. "Tax Reform to Strengthen the Economy and Lighten the Burdens Families Bear." In *Room to Grow: Conservative Reforms for a Limited Government and a Thriving Middle Class,* YG [Young Guns] Network, 2014, 33–38.

Steinem, Gloria. *Revolution from Within: A Book of Self-Esteem.* New York: Little, Brown, 1992.

Stevenson, Amanda J., et al. "Effect of Removal of Planned Parenthood from the Texas Women's Health Program." *New England Journal of Medicine* 374, no. 9 (March 3, 2016): 853–60.

Stites, Richard. *The Women's Liberation Movement in Russia: Feminism, Nihilism and Bolshevism, 1960–1930.* Princeton, NJ: Princeton University Press, 1978.

Stockholm International Peace Research Institute. "SIPRI Yearbook 2017: Armaments, Disarmament and International Security." Oxford: Oxford University Press, 2017. https://www.sipri.org/sites/default/files/2017-09/yb17-summary-eng.pdf.

Storer, Horatio R. *Why Not? A Book for Every Woman.* Boston: Lee and Shepherd, 1866.

Student Nonviolent Coordinating Committee. "Genocide in Mississippi." (N.d., ca. March 1964). New York: Redstockings Women's Liberation Archives for Action.

Sublette, Ned and Constance Sublette. *American Slave Coast: A History of the Slave-Breeding Industry.* Chicago: Chicago Review Press, 2015.

Sugrue, Thomas J. *The Origins of the Urban Crisis: Race and Inequality in Postwar Detroit.* Princeton, NJ: Princeton University Press, 1995.

Tamborini, Christopher R., and Kevin Whitman. "Women, Marriage, and Social Security Benefits Revisited." *Social Security Bulletin* 67, no. 4 (2007). https://www.ssa.gov/policy/docs/ssb/v67n4/67n4p1.html.

Thompson, Derek. "A World Without Work." *The Atlantic,* July–August 2015. http://www.theatlantic.com/magazine/archive/2015/07/world-without-work/395294/.

Thompson, Mark. "Why Are Army Recruiters Killing Themselves?" *Time,* April 2, 2009. http://content.time.com/time/magazine/article/0,9171,1889152,00.html.

Vine, David. "American Military Extends Its Reach Worldwide." Washington, DC: American University Investigative Reporting Workshop, August 25, 2015. http://investigativereportingworkshop.org/investigations/lily-pads/story/lily-pads/.

———. "The United States Probably Has More Foreign Military Bases Than Any Other People, Nation, or Empire in History." *The Nation,* September 17, 2015.

Wallas, Graham. *The Life of Francis Place 1771-1854.* London: Longmans, Green and Co., 1898.

Walling, William English. "The Birth Strike." *The Masses* 5, no. 1, October 1913, 20.

Wattenberg, Ben. "The Easy Solution to the Social Security Crisis." *New York Times Magazine,* June 22, 1997, 30–31.

———. *Fewer: How the New Demography of Depopulation Will Shape Our Future.* Chicago: Ivan R. Dee, 2004.

Wexler, Alice. *Emma Goldman in America.* Boston: Beacon, 1984.

York, Helen. "Do Children Harvest Your Food?" *The Atlantic,* March 26, 2012. http://www.theatlantic.com/health/archive/2012/03/do-children-harvest-your-food/254853/.

Zerwick, Phoebe. "The Rise of the DIY Abortion." *Glamour,* May 2016. http://www.glamour.com/story/the-rise-of-the-diy-abortion.

INDEX

ABOUT THE AUTHOR

Jenny Brown first studied the radical history of the women's liberation movement with Gainesville (Florida) Women's Liberation and then with Redstockings, where she developed materials for the Redstockings Women's Liberation Archives for Action. She was a leader in the grassroots campaign to win over-the-counter morning-after pill contraception in the United States and was a plaintiff in the winning lawsuit. For ten years she co-chaired the Alachua County Labor Party, organizing for national health insurance, the right to a job at a living wage, free higher education and a working person's political party under the Labor Party slogan, "The corporations have two parties, we need one of our own." More recently she worked as a staff writer and editor for *Labor Notes* magazine, covering labor struggles in hotels, restaurants, retail, farmwork, airlines, telecommunications, and the building trades, and coauthored, with other *Labor Notes* staff, *How to Jump-Start Your Union: Lessons from the Chicago Teachers* (2014). She writes, teaches, and organizes with the dues-funded feminist group National Women's Liberation (womensliberation.org).

ABOUT PM PRESS

PM Press was founded at the end of 2007 by a small
collection of folks with decades of publishing, media, and
organizing experience. PM Press co-conspirators have
published and distributed hundreds of books, pamphlets,
CDs, and DVDs. Members of PM have founded enduring
book fairs, spearheaded victorious tenant organizing campaigns, and worked
closely with bookstores, academic conferences, and even rock bands to deliver
political and challenging ideas to all walks of life. We're old enough to know what
we're doing and young enough to know what's at stake.

We seek to create radical and stimulating fiction and nonfiction books, pamphlets,
T-shirts, visual and audio materials to entertain, educate, and inspire you. We
aim to distribute these through every available channel with every available
technology—whether that means you are seeing anarchist classics at our bookfair
stalls, reading our latest vegan cookbook at the café, downloading geeky fiction
e-books, or digging new music and timely videos from our website.

PM Press is always on the lookout for talented and skilled volunteers, artists,
activists, and writers to work with. If you have a great idea for a project or can
contribute in some way, please get in touch.

PM Press
PO Box 23912
Oakland, CA 94623
www.pmpress.org

PM Press in Europe
europe@pmpress.org
www.pmpress.org.uk

FRIENDS OF PM PRESS

These are indisputably momentous times—the financial system is melting down globally and the Empire is stumbling. Now more than ever there is a vital need for radical ideas.

In the years since its founding—and on a mere shoestring—PM Press has risen to the formidable challenge of publishing and distributing knowledge and entertainment for the struggles ahead. With over 300 releases to date, we have published an impressive and stimulating array of literature, art, music, politics, and culture. Using every available medium, we've succeeded in connecting those hungry for ideas and information to those putting them into practice.

Friends of PM allows you to directly help impact, amplify, and revitalize the discourse and actions of radical writers, filmmakers, and artists. It provides us with a stable foundation from which we can build upon our early successes and provides a much-needed subsidy for the materials that can't necessarily pay their own way. You can help make that happen—and receive every new title automatically delivered to your door once a month—by joining as a Friend of PM Press. And, we'll throw in a free T-shirt when you sign up.

Here are your options:

- **$30 a month** Get all books and pamphlets plus 50% discount on all webstore purchases

- **$40 a month** Get all PM Press releases (including CDs and DVDs) plus 50% discount on all webstore purchases

- **$100 a month** Superstar—Everything plus PM merchandise, free downloads, and 50% discount on all webstore purchases

For those who can't afford $30 or more a month, we have **Sustainer Rates** at $15, $10 and $5. Sustainers get a free PM Press T-shirt and a 50% discount on all purchases from our website.

Your Visa or Mastercard will be billed once a month, until you tell us to stop. Or until our efforts succeed in bringing the revolution around. Or the financial meltdown of Capital makes plastic redundant. Whichever comes first.

Revolution at Point Zero: Housework, Reproduction, and Feminist Struggle

Silvia Federici

ISBN: 978-1-60486-333-8
$15.95   208 pages

Written between 1974 and 2012, *Revolution at Point Zero* collects forty years of research and theorizing on the nature of housework, social reproduction, and women's struggles on this terrain—to escape it, to better its conditions, to reconstruct it in ways that provide an alternative to capitalist relations.

Indeed, as Federici reveals, behind the capitalist organization of work and the contradictions inherent in "alienated labor" is an explosive ground zero for revolutionary practice upon which are decided the daily realities of our collective reproduction.

Beginning with Federici's organizational work in the Wages for Housework movement, the essays collected here unravel the power and politics of wide but related issues including the international restructuring of reproductive work and its effects on the sexual division of labor, the globalization of care work and sex work, the crisis of elder care, the development of affective labor, and the politics of the commons.

"Finally we have a volume that collects the many essays that over a period of four decades Silvia Federici has written on the question of social reproduction and women's struggles on this terrain. While providing a powerful history of the changes in the organization of reproductive labor, Revolution at Point Zero *documents the development of Federici's thought on some of the most important questions of our time: globalization, gender relations, the construction of new commons."*
—Mariarosa Dalla Costa, coauthor of *The Power of Women and the Subversion of the Community* and *Our Mother Ocean*

"As the academy colonizes and tames women's studies, Silvia Federici speaks the experience of a generation of women for whom politics was raw, passionately lived, often in the shadow of an uncritical Marxism. She spells out the subtle violence of housework and sexual servicing, the futility of equating waged work with emancipation, and the ongoing invisibility of women's reproductive labors. Under neoliberal globalization women's exploitation intensifies—in land enclosures, in forced migration, in the crisis of elder care. With ecofeminist thinkers and activists, Federici argues that protecting the means of subsistence now becomes the key terrain of struggle, and she calls on women North and South to join hands in building new commons."
—Ariel Salleh, author of *Ecofeminism as Politics: Nature, Marx, and the Postmodern*

Anarchy and the Sex Question: Essays on Women and Emancipation, 1896–1926

Emma Goldman
Edited by Shawn P. Wilbur

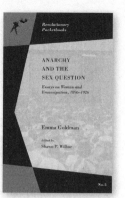

ISBN: 978-1-62963-144-8
$14.95   160 pages

For Emma Goldman, the "High Priestess of Anarchy," anarchism was "a living force in the affairs of our life, constantly creating new conditions," but "the most elemental force in human life" was something still more basic and vital: sex.

"The Sex Question" emerged for Goldman in multiple contexts, and we find her addressing it in writing on subjects as varied as women's suffrage, "free love," birth control, the "New Woman," homosexuality, marriage, love, and literature. It was at once a political question, an economic question, a question of morality, and a question of social relations.

But her analysis of that most elemental force remained fragmentary, scattered across numerous published (and unpublished) works and conditioned by numerous contexts. *Anarchy and the Sex Question* draws together the most important of those scattered sources, uniting both familiar essays and archival material, in an attempt to recreate the great work on sex that Emma Goldman might have given us. In the process, it sheds light on Goldman's place in the history of feminism.

"Emma Goldman left a profound legacy of wisdom, insight, and passionate commitment to life. Shawn Wilbur has carefully selected her best writings on that most profound, pleasurable, and challenging of topics: sex. This collection is a great service to anarchist, feminist, and queer communities around the world."
—Jamie Heckert, coeditor of *Anarchism & Sexuality: Ethics, Relationships and Power*

"Shawn Wilbur has done a great job assembling and introducing Emma Goldman's writings on women, feminism, and sexuality. As he notes, Goldman's essays continue to provoke and inspire. The collection artfully documents the evolution of Goldman's views on freedom, sex, and human liberation."
—Robert Graham, editor of *Anarchism: A Documentary History of Libertarian Ideas*